Dr. Reeder's zeal for the gospel of the Lord Jesus Christ is beautifully honored in *A Pastor's Heart*, celebrating God's kindness in calling and raising up this courageous shepherd and leader of God's people. Rekindle the embers of your heart for the Lord and His church as you read through and reflect on these lovingly and thoughtfully gathered pages from faithful ministers and the Reeder family.

CHRIS LARSON
President & CEO, Ligonier Ministries
Sanford, Florida

Harry Reeder was unlike anyone I've ever known. He was a magnetic figure, vibrant and engaging among all kinds of people. He was a consummate communicator, full of fresh ways of explaining timeless biblical truth. He loved learning new things, but he was really about one big thing — making disciples for his Savior, Jesus Christ. That is why this book of essays is so worthwhile. The chapters contained in this book encompass so many of the things that Harry Reeder stood for, a love for people, an ability to teach, a love of ideas — all of it in service to Christ and to His church.

JONATHAN L. MASTER
President, Greenville Presbyterian Theological Seminary
Greenville, South Carolina

Harry Reeder was a genuine man of God, in the Pauline sense: a preacher, leader, evangelist, and shepherd of souls. Through his Spirit-filled, Scripture-shaped life and ministry he equipped scores of pastors and the churches they serve for the mission, the message, and the ministries Jesus has entrusted to them. This volume not only honors God for the gift he gave us in Harry it also provides deep insights into his character, convictions, and competencies as a pastor which a new generation should aspire to imitate.

JOHN CURRIE
Professor and Dean of Pastoral Theology, Westminster Theological Seminary
Philadelphia, Pennsylvania

The legacy of the Rev. Dr. Harry Reeder is written not just in words in this volume or in the books that he wrote or in his sermons and commentary that have been captured in multiple media. Rather, his legacy is written in countless lives who have been shaped by his teaching, his example, his counsel, his passionate wisdom, and his remarkable loving leadership for and deep commitment to the truths of Jesus Christ, his Lord and Savior.

I am grateful for these articles that have been written to highlight his ministry contributions and the theological distinctives of his long and fruitful ministry. I pray that they will be used by the Lord to continue his vision to see the Church of Christ "on message and in ministry" for the things that matter forever, namely, the sovereign grace of God revealed in the gospel of Jesus Christ as revealed in the infallible Scriptures. Our brother Harry Reeder is missed, but his legacy is cherished and will yield fruit for generations to come.

PETER A. LILLBACK
President, Westminster Theological Seminary
Philadelphia, Pennsylvania

God warns us that these last days will be full of difficulty, soft doctrine, muddled mission, dechurching membership, and godlessness. Even so, against that very real backdrop, Harry Reeder's life, ministry, and legacy still thunders in God's hands. These chapters are such a fitting tribute at such a tender time for the Church. May pastors, ministry leaders, and believers of all stripes be refreshed, reinvigorated, and renewed in this shared glorious vision of Christ, his Church, and his Great Commission.

DAVID GENTINO
Senior Pastor, Columbia Presbyterian Church
Columbia, South Carolina

Ephesians 4 says God has given to the church pastors and teachers to equip the saints for the work of ministry. God used and is using Pastor Harry Reeder's ministry to impact many pastors, teachers and leaders in the church around the world. Pastor Reeder was a true pastor of pastors. This book, written with his legacy in mind, is an outstanding tribute to that work and will be helpful for pastors for generations to come.

ALTON HARDY
Senior Pastor, Urban Hope Community Church
Fairfield, Alabama

The call to be a Pastor/Teacher is the highest of the high calls upon a man's life. James 3:1 makes this calling upon a man's life very clear: "Let not many of you become teachers, my brethren, knowing that as such we will incur a stricter judgment." Harry always referred to himself as a Pastor/Teacher. This title, position, and call is one that is unique and very specific in the eyes of God. Each chapter in the *festschrift* speaks to the responsibilities, the necessities, and the obligations of this high call on the Pastor/Teacher. This *festschrift* is a must have, a must read and a must hide-in-your-heart work for every young man and equally for someone like me who was called to ministry later in life. This *festschrift* is a "how to" from the life and heart of a true Pastor/Teacher.

THAD JAMES
Director of the Prison Initiative and International Programs
Birmingham Theological Seminary
Birmingham, Alabama

I met Harry Reeder in the fall of 1990. At that time, he, James Baird, and Terry Gyger (of course, I had no idea at the time who they were; I just saw them as a good bunch of guys) were encouraging me to become a part of the Presbyterian Church in America. Although they were very persuasive, it was only when I heard Harry preach at a Wednesday night fellowship dinner that I opened my heart to the PCA. I had never heard anyone in a local church expound the word of God with such humility, clarity, love, power, and impact as he did. I said to the Lord, "I would like to be used like that!" Shortly after that, I became the first African American to come under care for the gospel ministry in the Mississippi Valley Presbytery. In the spring of 1993, I preached my first sermon in the PCA at the same Wednesday night fellowship dinner where I had heard Harry preach, in the exact same spot. It was at the church we now know as Redeemer Church in Jackson, Mississippi. In all the years that I personally encountered Harry Reeder, he was always loving, kind, encouraging, and humorous. The year before he died, he introduced me to his staff, who gave me great counsel in my desire to reach every historic black college and university (HBCU) in America. Harry believed, taught, and lived the things quoted from and written about him in this book. He had a laser focus on the gospel. In my opinion, this *festschrift* in his memory to the glory of God is very appropriate. I will never forget his last message sent to me, "James, I can not be there today but Ike is coming. I have given you my best. I have given you my son!" Harry Reeder truly had a pastor's heart!

JAMES WILLIAMS
Founder and President of The Center for Urban Renewal and Evangelism
(C.U.R.E.) Gospel Movement
Montgomery, Alabama

A Pastor's Heart

Essays in Memory of
HARRY L. REEDER III

ed. Derrick E. Brite

MENTOR

Unless otherwise notes, Scripture quotations are from *The Holy Bible, English Standard Version*, copyright © 2001 by Crossway Bibles, a publishing ministry of Good News Publishers. Used by permission. All rights reserved. ESV Text Edition: 2011.

Copyright © InPerspective Ministries, 2024

paperback ISBN 978-1-5271-1141-7
ebook ISBN 978-1-5271-1184-4

10 9 8 7 6 5 4 3 2 1

Published in 2024
in the
Mentor Imprint
by
Christian Focus Publications Ltd,
Geanies House, Fearn, Ross-shire,
IV20 1TW, Scotland.

www.christianfocus.com

Cover design by Daniel Van Straaten

Printed and bound by Bell & Bain, Glasgow

All rights reserved. No part of this publication may be reproduced, stored in a retrieval system, or transmitted, in any form, by any means, electronic, mechanical, photocopying, recording or otherwise without the prior permission of the publisher or a licence permitting restricted copying. In the U.K. such licences are issued by the Copyright Licensing Agency, 4 Battlebridge Lane, London, SE1 2HX. www.cla.co.uk

Contents

Editor's Note
Derrick E. Brite 9

Introduction
Ike Reeder 11

Harry & Cindy Reeder: A Biographical Sketch
Ike Reeder 17

1. On Mission, On Message, In Ministry
The Reeder Vision
George Grant 25

2. Preaching that Moves Men to God:
The Preaching Legacy of Dr. Harry L. Reeder
Neil C. Stewart 45

3. The Primacy of Lord's Day Worship
John E. Haines 69

4. The Pastor's Passion for Evangelism:
Lessons in Sharing Christ from Dr. Harry L. Reeder
Derrick E. Brite 81

5. The Mission and Missions of the Church
Brian H. Cosby 93

6. A True Soldier of Christ:
The Call of Christian Discipleship
Jon D. Payne 105

7. The Pastor as Shepherd
Jason Helopoulos 117

8. Harry Reeder, The Consummate Biblical Counselor
Howard A. Eyrich 131

9. Life, Love, and Leadership
Kevin DeYoung 149

10. Leading a Ministry Team
David Strain 161

11. The Church at Work:
Church Governance
Fred Greco 175

12. Christian Education:
The Leadership and Legacy of Harry Reeder
Niel Nielson 187

13. Cultural Engagement as Spiritual Warfare:
Lessons from Harry Reeder
Rob Pacienza 209

14. The Pastor's Personal Life
Sandy Willson 225

15. The Pastor's Heart for His Family
Jennifer Toomer-Hay & Bruce Stallings 235

Contributors 251
Resources by Harry L. Reeder III 255

Editor's Note [1]

Derrick E. Brite

On May 18, 2023, after spending a lifetime devoted to serving Christ and His church, Dr. Harry Reeder was called to receive his eternal reward. The impact of his sudden home-going is still being felt all across the evangelical landscape. Harry was a uniquely gifted man who poured his whole self into everything that he did. He was a man who, following after the example set by the Apostle Paul, worked harder than everyone, yet did so by the grace of God working in him (1 Cor. 15:10).

Though he was a sought-after conference speaker, Harry cared most about serving his local congregation, Briarwood Presbyterian Church. For over twenty years, Lord's Day after Lord's Day, he modeled faithful Bible expositions and passionate calls for discipleship. His preaching was memorable, and the love and passion that he had for biblical and theological truth was contagious. His ability to alliterate or turn a phrase was legendary, coining many "Harry-isms" that would become mantras to many. In fact, I believe I have quoted "on mission, on message, and in ministry" a few dozen times myself since his passing.

Perhaps the only rival gift to his preaching was his natural ability at being a disciple-maker. Harry spent countless hours investing in men at every stage of their ministry career, pouring

---

1. This originally appeared in the Birmingham Theological Journal. See Derrick Brite, "In Memoriam for Dr. Harry Reeder" in *The Birmingham Theological Journal* 1, no. 1 (Dec. 2023): 3.

out every ounce of wisdom he had. I was fortunate enough to experience this first-hand, as I sat in his office on the edge of my seat, while he seamlessly transitioned from alliterated point to alliterated point, answering all the questions I had, and some I did not have.

More than being an effective minister, Harry was a kind and gracious Christian man. I remember the first time I met him, and I addressed him as "Dr. Reeder." He quickly corrected me, saying, "Please don't call me doctor. I'm not even good enough to be a nurse!" But he *was* a doctor—a doctor of souls—skillfully working on the men and women that the great heavenly Physician had placed in his care, from his own sheep at Briarwood, to students, men and women in the denomination, and even men incarcerated at Bibb County Correctional Facility.

It is in light of this that we present *A Pastor's Heart: Essays in Memory of Harry L. Reeder III*. Within the pages of this *festschrift*, you will find articles written by men and women who were shaped by his ministry in one way or another. This includes professors, pastors, counselors, and his children. Much like Harry, *A Pastor's Heart* is devoted to the glory of God and to help Christ's church be "on mission, on message, and in ministry."

Introduction

Ike Reeder

For those who knew my father, Pastor/Teacher Harry L. Reeder III, it will come as no surprise to hear that he was a fan of history. Next to his love of God's word, he had no deeper passion than to study history—great men and women of faith and how they responded and reacted to the events that surrounded them according to their faith. Whether it was the early church, the Reformation, the first hundred years of American history, or just military history in general, he was captivated by the historian's task of trying to figure out—trying to get inside the minds— the *why* of people's actions and decisions and to try to learn from them in a way that informed his own actions and decisions in his own life and ministry.

And yet, at the same time, my father also consistently cautioned himself and others from holding up the great men and women of faith in history to the level of lionization—ensuring that while they might be "heroes" of the faith who went before, we did not elevate them to a level of worship. He consistently cautioned against the danger of elevating these individuals, canonizing them at the expense of the direction of a biblical-centered, Gospel-driven Christian world and life view.

In light of that caution, it is appropriate here, at the beginning of this collection of essays, to say clearly that my father would have no interest in this book—whether written in his honor or not—unless it pointed its readers beyond the life of Harry Reeder and instead to the Word of God. When the idea of a *festschrift* was first proposed to me by my good friend, William Mackenzie, my father was still alive, still the Senior Pastor of Briarwood Presbyterian Church, still a board member of Westminster Theological Seminary and Birmingham Theological Seminary, still a professor at both schools, still a member of the Gospel Reformation Network Executive Council, still the primary speaker and convener of the Lampstand Conference, still a husband, still a father, still a brother, still a grandfather, and still an uncle.

The original idea at the time was that this work would be done in his honor, and more specifically in honor of his work as a mentor for so many young pastors in the PCA (Presbyterian Church in America) and in denominations beyond. Just as anyone who knew Harry Reeder knew of his love for history, so too did anyone who knew Harry Reeder know of his passion for leadership—and, more specifically, leadership for the church.

This, in part, was because, throughout his life as a pastor/teacher, my father actively sought out mentors for himself. He talked often of how, as a young pastor, some of the giants of the reformed faith—Dr. Frank Barker, Dr. Jim Baird, Dr. Jim Boice, Dr. R.C. Sproul, Dr. D. James Kennedy, and Dr. Sinclair Ferguson, among others—mentored him often and closely, some with great regularity and some with less frequency. And yet, because my father always saw himself as a learner, he never sought mentoring relationships with younger pastors but responded to them when they came to him to ask for advice and counsel. He was often amazed that younger pastors would ask him for advice and counsel! He mostly saw himself as a lower-middle-class kid from East Charlotte whose mom worked at Sears and his dad worked in baseball. Outside of his mentoring group of young men on staff at Briarwood Presbyterian Church, Dad primarily focused on teaching leadership through his book, *3D Leadership*,[1] and the teaching opportunities afforded him at Christ Covenant Church

---

1. Harry L. Reeder III, *3D Leadership: Defining, Developing and Deploying Christian Leaders Who Can Change The World* (Fearn, Ross-shire: Christian Focus Publications, 2018).

INTRODUCTION

and Briarwood Presbyterian Church, as well as the seminaries with whom he partnered.

These ideas about mentoring and leadership training, then, help us to frame the purpose of this book.

First, my father would have no qualms about being used as an example of ministry but would be horrified if this collection was simply about him. He desired nothing more than the prayer of John the Baptist: "He must increase, but I must decrease" (John 3:30).

Second, my father recognized the value of history and studied the life and ministry of those who have walked the journey before us. He saw the clear biblical precedent for this and recognized how few biographical sketches in scripture are actually of those that finished well.

Third, my father had a passion for seeing young men and even older men called to ministry and fully to commit and dedicate themselves to the "high calling" of ministry. He wanted those who "aspire to be an overseer" to truly recognize the nature of that work as a "noble task" or a "good work" (1 Tim. 3:1, ESV and LSV respectively) and thus to receive training for that work from experienced pastors, learning from their work and life experiences.

Fourth, this collection of essays on the multi-faceted and different elements of pastoral ministry are each written by men who readily acknowledge my father's influence on their ministry—either in a direct and sustained mentored relationship or even from just watching and learning from outside that circle of intimacy.

Finally, this collection recognizes one of my father's primary beliefs about ministry: while the pastor must be deeply committed to the mission of the church (Matt. 28:16-20), the message of the church (1 Cor. 2:2), and the ministry of the church (Acts 2:42-47), the pastor must also have a full-orbed and deep biblical formulation of all *aspects* of the complexity of that ministry.

In this collection, you will find essays on preaching, missions, and evangelism, on discipleship, shepherding, and Christian education. You will find essays on mission and vision, on leadership and staff leadership, and on the pastor and cultural engagement. You will also find essays on the pastor's personal spiritual life and the pastor's family life, among even more ministerial endeavors. If my father offered us one possible lesson—even if one were to disagree with many of the lessons that are brought out in the essays—it would be that pastors in particular must be deeply thoughtful about every aspect of their lives. He genuinely believed there was no sphere or area of life or ministry in which the pastor must not have a deeply and richly developed biblical perspective from a rich and deep biblical worldview. These are not arenas for thoughtless experimentation, but rather the outworkings of the "noble task."

    I will conclude this introduction with a few thoughts. First, this book is designed to the hopeful benefit of young pastors as a guide to beginning their journey to biblical spiritual formation in their ministry calling. I pray it is used as such for many generations to come. As the President of a seminary and as my father's son, I too am deeply committed to training the next generation, even this generation, of pastors committed to biblically faithful ministry. May this work not be the work of a cultural moment, but rather stand timeless in biblical fidelity. May we never follow one man blindly but test his teaching and actions against the Word of God.

    Second, contraposing the first thought, is that it is good and right to learn from men and women who have run the race before us. Even more to the point, it is good and right to learn from men and women who have run the race before us and have, in fact, finished their race with faithfulness. As was quoted at my father's funeral: "For I am already being poured out as a drink offering, and the time of my departure has come. I have fought the good fight, I have finished the race, I have kept the faith" (2 Tim. 4:6-7). My father died coming home from leading a prayer breakfast with lawmakers in Montgomery in which he challenged them to be leaders that adhere to God's Word and not to man's wishes. Dad said many times from the pulpit, in teaching, and even in our private family conversations that he desired to be poured out as a drink offering. He wanted to serve in such a way that when the Lord called him home there would be nothing left in the cup. May we all have such a commitment to our Savior.

Third, even when it went out of fashion both academically and culturally, my father never faltered in his deep conviction in the necessity of a holistic biblical world and life view. In fact, that theme is one of the first books we are working on publishing posthumously. My father believed deeply in the Reformation doctrine of *Sola Scriptura*. He believed the Scriptures alone were the only rule of faith and practice and sufficient for the cares and concerns of the day. While he certainly believed in natural and general revelation and the common grace and common sense of interpretation, he believed that only the scriptures give us the true foundation upon which our ideas and our actions can be judged rightly before the rightly divided Word of Truth. A Christian worldview is first built on the Scriptures, infused with the Scriptures, and mapped by the Scriptures. Only then can it be a useful tool in interpreting the natural and general revelation around us. Scripture is not "integrated" into work and our life; it alone "illuminates" our work and life. Only then can we, by the illumination of Scripture, truly integrate our faith and our work. This was as true for him as a minister of God's Word as it would be for a brick mason or an accountant, a teacher or a lawn care specialist. This will be born out in the essays that follow.

Finally, it is appropriate to include slightly more than a brief biography of my parents' life to provide some context for these essays. There is a film version of my father's testimony and ministry life available on YouTube for your use called "For the Good: The Life and Ministry of Harry Reeder." Hopefully, it will give you some insight into my father's life and ministry story.

I'd like to personally thank my good friend, Derrick Brite, for his tireless and diligent work in editing these essays. When asked to participate, he jumped in without hesitation. It's been a pleasure to work with him. I'd like to thank all of the authors, my friends and family, for their willingness to participate in this project. Your contributions, I hope and pray, will be of benefit to the church for years to come. From all the authors, from

Derrick Brite and myself, from the publishing team at Christian Focus Publications and William Mackenzie and family, and finally from the Reeder family—we pray this book will be a mighty tool in the hands of a mighty God to raise up mighty men of faith that they might lead the Church triumphant to the promised time of the coming of our Lord Jesus Christ. For we are ordinary people in ordinary circumstances experienced by thousands who have gone before us and that will be experienced by thousands that come after. But our mighty God is mighty in both His deliverance of His people and in the execution of His plan of redemption and reconciliation. So may we each and all stand in the might of the Holy Spirit, more than we were, less than we are to become, and yet united in bonds of family and spirit—all for the glory of God.

Harry & Cindy Reeder

A Biographical Sketch

Ike Reeder

Harry and Cindy Reeder were both born in 1948 in Charlotte, North Carolina. Harry (or "Ike" as he was known until his early 20s), was born Harry Lloyd Reeder III to Harry L. Reeder, Jr. and Evelyn Sheehan Reeder, born in Augusta, Georgia, and Charlotte, North Carolina, respectively. Cindy Reeder was born to Carl and Clara Miller, from Pennsylvania and South Dakota, respectively. Harry's father was in baseball, so by 7th grade, Harry, had lived in ten different states from North Carolina to Texas. Cindy grew up in the same house on Olinda Ln. from 1st grade until college.

Ike's parents were both Christians and had given their lives to Jesus at a Billy Graham rally when they were nineteen years old, walking down the aisle together, carrying their first-born son, Ike. Harry Jr. had dropped out of high school to join the Marines in 1945 at the tail end of World War Two and his girlfriend Evelyn had also dropped out to follow him to Paris Island. After his discharge, he returned to Charlotte with a wife who was soon to be a mother and played football for his final year at Harding High School. They were members of a local Christian Missionary Alliance Church and faithful attendees, taking their son, Ike, and his sister Vicky, four years his junior, to church consistently.

Despite that faithfulness, Harry, Jr. traveled increasingly for work in minor league baseball and Ike began to drift away from Christ's teaching, abandoning it entirely by the time he was a student at East Mecklenburg High School. From there, he went on to East Carolina University in Greenville, South Carolina, to play baseball and golf. After two fruitless and unproductive years, he was asked to leave the school for poor academic performance, lack of attendance, and disciplinary problems. Ike returned home to Charlotte working several different jobs that summer.

Cindy grew up in a Baptist home: her mother hailed from the Mennonites in Bridgewater, South Dakota and her father from the Lutherans in Allentown, Pennsylvania. Carl had been a baseball sensation growing up and, in 1941, was drafted into the major leagues by the Washington Senators. However, within a few short months, he was drafted into service for World War Two and would spend the entire war stationed in Alaska with other prop players, such as Ted Williams. Upon being released in 1945, he traveled back to Washington D.C. to try to pick up his baseball career and instead found a wife—Clara Hofer. His career in the majors finished, and he and Clara moved to Charlotte, North Carolina in 1947 so Carl could begin a career playing in what was known as the "Textile Leagues"—one of the many regional minor leagues up and down the East Coast. Carl played with any number of teams, while Clara stayed in Charlotte, eventually working for Douglas Aircraft first and then the Selective Service. Carl eventually retired from baseball and went to work for the tax office, and they raised their two daughters—Cindy and Linda. Like Harry, Cindy graduated from high school in 1966. Cindy graduated from Garinger High School and left Charlotte to go to Mars Hill College (now University) for her freshman year and sophomore year in the mountains of northwest North Carolina. In her senior year of high school, Cindy got a job working at Sears, Co. to help defray the cost of a private college.

Unbeknownst to Cindy, in the summer of 1967, she was moved from working in records to ladies' sportswear, where her new boss happened to be a woman by the name of Evelyn Reeder.

Evelyn had, at that time, worked for Sears for over a decade. In the summer of 1968, Evelyn's favorite past time was asking her son, Ike, to come pick her up from work and then identifying young women who worked for her also in need of a ride home, trying to get her son to "settle down" and give up his partying ways. This would backfire one night in the middle of the summer when she asked him to take one young lady home but found out another young lady had caught Ike's eye—it was Cindy. So, Harry and Cindy met and shortly thereafter he asked her out. She said yes, and they began dating in the summer of 1968.

Because Cindy was from a Christian home and profoundly serious about her faith, Ike prevaricated about his relationship with Christ. He was able to say with some degree of honesty that he had gone forward to give his life to Jesus because in the Christian Missionary Alliance church he had done that multiple times. Having grown up in a Christian home, he knew what needed to be said to convince her he was a Christian. In the Fall of 1968, Ike remained in Charlotte and worked with Kinney Shoes, while Cindy went to Chapel Hill. That would only last for one semester, as when Cindy came home for Thanksgiving, Ike proposed, and they were married on January 26, 1969, in Charlotte.

After their wedding, Cindy came back to Charlotte from UNC-Chapel Hill to finish her college studies at the University of North Carolina in Charlotte, and live as a married woman. Ike's agreement with Carl and Clara was that he could marry their daughter, but only if he promised to work and pay to put her through college. Ike continued to work, while Cindy studied at UNCC in the spring of 1969. However, once married, Ike's façade of faith began to wash away. By the late summer, Ike and Cindy were not doing well. Ike was back to his old ways and out with friends engaging in activities that were characteristic of the embedded sin that had plagued his teenage years—drinking, smoking, and gambling. Finally, at their wits' end, with their marriage on the rocks, Ike decided to return to church with Cindy. But he did not want to go to his family church or her family church, so they found a small Presbyterian church—Faith Presbyterian—and decided to visit. On their first visit, a man overheard Ike say his name, "Ike Reeder." "You're not Ike Reeder," he said. "I played high school football with Ike Reeder." The man was Harold Jones, and he was an elder at Faith Presbyterian. Eventually, Harold figured out that Ike as a baby had been at the Shrine Bowl, when Harold and Harry, Jr. had both played together at Harding High School. At that moment, Harold decided he would be God's hound of heaven and pursue Ike with the good news of Jesus Christ.

Over the Fall of 1969, Ike and Cindy also became friends with the Elliot family: Jim and Imogene and their four daughters. For some reason, the four girls had taken a shine to Ike and Cindy. So it was with great sorrow that, on Christmas Day, 1969, Ike got a phone call from Harold Jones telling them that Imogene Elliot had collapsed at the family Christmas table and died that evening of a medical condition. The Elliot girls had asked if Ike and Cindy could come over and take care of them. Over the next few days, Ike and Cindy were around the family helping with the girls constantly. Finally, the funeral service was held, and Ike went back to the Elliot home with close family friends (Cindy being sick with the flu). From there, one by one people left and only family and a few very close friends remained.

Before leaving, Ike went to speak with Jim, Imogene's husband. After asking him if he could help in any way, Mr. Elliot pulled Ike aside and told him: "Ike, I appreciate the offer. I'm going to miss my wife. We've been together since we were fourteen years old. But I know she's in heaven. I know that all things aren't good, but I believe that God promises us that all things work together for the good of those who are in Jesus and for His glory. If Imogene was standing here right now, she'd only want to ask you one question: do you know Jesus personally and trust Him for your salvation?" Ike couldn't comprehend this, and so he walked over to a side room to try to process it. Harold Jones found him there and explained what the assurance of salvation meant and how to be right with God. It was in that small side room that Ike knelt and gave his life to Christ. As he was walking out of the room, he turned back in and prayed again: "God, if you've got anything specific you want me to do, just let me know and I'll do it for you." Little did he know how God would answer that prayer!

After his conversion, Ike became the youth director of the church. Then, through a series of events, after Cindy graduated from UNCC and their first daughter, Jennifer, was born in 1971, Ike found himself studying at Covenant College in Chattanooga, Tennessee, having felt called to ministry in the early Fall of 1970 in the middle of a tobacco field in Greenville, North Carolina. Dick Tevebaugh, the pastor of Faith Presbyterian, and Dr. Robert Rayburn, the President of Covenant Theological Seminary and Covenant College, convinced Ike that transferring to Covenant would be the next step in his journey to becoming a pastor. After completing his studies at Covenant College in 1974, a bible study Ike had been leading in Lookout Valley, Tennessee, grew to become a church plant, and eventually a church with a membership of around three hundred.

Convinced of the doctrines of the Reformed faith and drawn to the young Presbyterian Church in America denomination, Ike and Cindy left Chattanooga for Miami, Florida so he (now called "Harry") could become an intern at Pinelands Presbyterian Church and attend an extension of Westminster Theological Seminary, Philadelphia, the Florida Institute for Theological Training (FITT) with their three children—Jennifer (1971), Harry IV "Ikie" (1975), and Abigail (1976). Unbeknownst to Harry and Cindy, the senior pastor of Pinelands was stepping down and a former pastor declared that "the mark of Satan" was on the doors of Pinelands Presbyterian Church. Harry went from being an "intern" to being an "interim" student supply pastor almost overnight. Over the next three years (1980–1983), Harry completed his studies at Westminster Theological Seminary (MDiv), was ordained in the Presbyterian Church in America, and oversaw God's work at Pinelands, seeing it grow from a handful of people to a vibrant, Gospel-centered, multi-ethnic church of around three hundred members.

It was at this time that Dr. Frank Barker and Rev. Terry Gyger, senior pastor of Briarwood Presbyterian Church, Birmingham,

Alabama, and the Director of Mission to North America, respectively, contacted Harry to see if he would be willing to plant a church or replant a church that had made an effort to plant but had not succeeded: Alexander Road Presbyterian Church. After much prayer and consideration, Harry and Cindy decided God was calling them both back to their hometown of Charlotte.

Christ Covenant Church, the replant of Alexander Road Presbyterian Church, welcomed its new pastor in February of 1983. Early during this period, the church had advertised that Harry would be sharing his testimony. At the time, the church had thirty-six members and met in a double-wide trailer. The trailer had three large weight-bearing pillars in the middle of the room used for worship. As Harry shared his story to a packed house, he noticed that one young woman was almost hiding behind one of the pillars and avoiding his eye contact, especially as Harry told the story of Imogene's death and his conversation with Mr. Elliot. After the service was over, she got up and headed straight for the door. As Harry hurried to catch her before she left, she turned around to see him coming towards her and Harry saw that tears were streaming from her eyes. Harry asked her if she was OK and she said: "You don't recognize me, do you? I'm one of the four little girls! One of the Elliot girls that you and Cindy used to babysit! I heard you were here and sharing your testimony, so I had to come and hear you. I haven't been to a church in over a decade. I've been so angry at God for taking my Momma away from me and over and over again I've told him—'God, if you can show me just one good thing that's come from my mother's death, I'll come back to you.' But I haven't seen anything until now. I want to come back to Jesus!" The woman was Jane Elliot, one of the four sisters. Eventually, God used the ministry of Christ Covenant to bring all four sisters back to a right relationship with God.

In the meantime, Harry's father, Harry, Jr., had completely walked away from the Lord and his remaining three children, Harry's siblings—Vicki, Amy, and Beth—and his wife, Evelyn, through divorce. Through the continued ministry of Christ Covenant, Harry, Jr. came back to a right relationship with the

Lord and even remarried Eveyln, with a service conducted by their own son, Harry III.

Eventually, God worked through Harry's ministry at Christ Covenant to grow the church from thirty-six core members in 1983 to over three thousand individuals in regular attendance and over two thousand five hundred members by 1999. It was during these years that Harry launched the Embers to a Flame Conference on Church Revitalization. In 1999, Harry and Cindy were issued a call from Briarwood Presbyterian Church to follow Dr. Frank Barker, one of the Founding Fathers of the PCA. Briarwood had been the church that called Harry to go and plant Christ Covenant and they were now calling for him to come succeed Dr. Barker. Discerning this as God's leading, Harry and Cindy moved to Briarwood Presbyterian. Their eldest daughter Jennifer was then living in Alaska; Ike (Harry IV) was living in Vienna, Austria; and Abigail had just finished college at Appalachian State University in Boone, North Carolina.

Harry became the Senior Pastor of Briarwood Presbyterian Church in 1999, bringing with him the Embers to a Flame Ministry. Shortly after that, he completed his Doctor of Ministry degree from RTS Charlotte. In following Dr. Barker, Harry made a conscious decision to learn how to follow great men in ministry. Dr. Barker remained as Senior Pastor Emeritus of Briarwood and the chairman of the Birmingham Theological Seminary board and the Barker family remained at Briarwood for the entirety of Dr. Barker's retiring ministry and all of Harry's ministry—a testimony to the respect and relationship between the two men.

Over those twenty-three years, Briarwood maintained its emphasis on global missions, evangelism, and church planting, and added church revitalization and leadership training to its essential ministries list. Briarwood helped plant multiple churches in Birmingham, in America, and around the world, and provided coaches for countless church revitalization projects. Ministry themes over the years included "Lifestyle Stewardship," "Everyone Evangelizing Everywhere," "For Coming Generations," and "Revival!" among many others. Harry helped lead Briarwood through an economic recession and a global pandemic, turning each into an opportunity for Christians to think about "For what purpose has God called me to this time and for this season?" Over those years he launched a podcast ("Today in Perspective"), a daily audio devotional guide ("Fresh Bread"), a conversational podcast series that lasted for over a decade ("Conversations with Harry"), an irregular blog with thoughts and musings, and two books (*Embers to a Flame*[1] and *3D Leadership*). In addition, he worked with the Gospel Reformation Network in the PCA, the Alliance of Confessing Evangelicals, and Ligonier Ministries as a writer and speaker. He was on the board of Westminster Theological Seminary and Birmingham Theological Seminary, teaching for both schools and teaching occasionally for Reformed Theological Seminary.

Dr. Reeder passed away on May 18, 2023 from a car accident, likely caused by a heart attack while driving. He left behind on this mortal plain his wife, Cindy Reeder; his three children, Jennifer (Philip) Toomer-Hay, Ike (Angie) Reeder, and Abigail (Ryan) Leib; his sister, Beth (Robert) Thomas; and a host of grandchildren and nephews and nieces. He also left behind thousands upon thousands of spiritual brothers and sisters and spiritual children whom he fathered in ministry with a shepherd's heart, a king's vision, a priest's intercession, and a prophet's passion for the truth.

---

1. Harry L. Reeder III, *From Embers to a Flame: How God Can Revitalize Your Church* (Phillipsburg: P&R Publishing, 2008).

1.

On Mission, On Message, In Ministry

The Reeder Vision

George Grant

> *The 'first things' of the church are actually the lifelines of the church: Christ-centered, Gospel-driven ministry, personal spiritual formation, the ministry of prayer, the ministry of the Word, Biblical mission and vision, leadership multiplication and mobilization, small group disciple-making and a great commitment to the Great Commission and the Great Commandment.*[1]
>
> Harry Reeder

It has been said of Isaac Watts, the hymn writer and successor to John Owen at London's Mark Lane Chapel, that his native tongue was iambic pentameter. From earliest childhood to aged maturity, he naturally spoke in rhymes and verse. It may

---

1. Harry Reeder, "Interview with Dr. Harry Reeder (Part 2)," Westminster Theological Seminary, April 13, 2013, YouTube Video, https://www.youtube.com/watch?v=-uFNXgcpdJ4&list=UUquovPPE8bMQsdI6RZXiDYg&index=415.

likewise be said of Harry Reeder that his native tongue was the alliterative adage. Memorable maxims, engaging epigrams, and apt aphorisms peppered his discourses effortlessly. He naturally spoke in witticisms, saws, and apothegms.

A host of his iconic sayings remain indelibly etched in the hearts and minds of the tens of thousands who benefited from his ministry over the years:

> Never take counsel from your fears.
>
> Salvation is free but discipleship costs.
>
> The Promise Maker gets it done through His Son, the Promise Keeper.
>
> The world is not your measuring stick, it's your mission field.
>
> If I didn't cause it, can't cure it, or can't control it, I ought to stop worrying about it.
>
> Occasionally, the best action is no action.
>
> Satan's three schemes are Infiltration, Imitation, and Intimidation.
>
> Leadership revolves around Character, Competency, and then Content.
>
> Under the radar is a beautiful place to be.
>
> We are called to be the light of the world, not the light of the church.
>
> The Gospel is the Foundation, the Formation, and the Motivation of the Christian life.
>
> We want a Great Commission church with a Great Commandment culture.
>
> Motivation and mission eventually determine the message.
>
> The Gospel must be the priority, the parameter, and the preeminent point of our ministry.
>
> The Gospel of salvation by grace is the foundation, formation, and motivation for a first love church.

These were not merely clever oratorical quips; they were the embodiment of Reeder's indefatigable vision for pastoral care and communication; they were anchors for his theological convictions; they were arrows to send his exhortations straight and true to hearts and minds. As well as anyone since perhaps the time of Charles Simeon, Thomas Chalmers, and C.H. Spurgeon, he was powerfully able to match rhetorical means with ministerial ends.

But of all his maxims, there was one that he reiterated time and again, one that succinctly captured his life purpose, one that summarized his expansive vision for a prayer-drenched, Gospel-focused, love-marked, Christ-centered, evangelistically-engaged calling: *On Mission, On Message, In Ministry*.[2]

In a very real sense, this epigrammatic declaration defined Harry Reeder and—he would argue—it ought to define every believer, every family, and every church. All the abiding principles that he taught—Biblical preaching, church vitality, shepherding the flock, replicating leaders, and personal and family spiritual formation—emanated from this idea.

On Mission

"Our mission," Reeder asserted, "is very narrow: we are to make disciples."[3] And again, "The Great Commission is our great calling."[4] God is sovereign over all. As David puts it, "The earth is the Lord's and everything in it, the world and all who live in it" (Ps. 24:1). Despite the disruption of the Fall, the Lord's authority remains unabated, uninterrupted, and unimpeded. There is "nothing outside His sovereign control" (Heb. 2:8). He rules and reigns from His "throne on high" (Ps. 11:4) for His is "an everlasting dominion" (Dan. 4:3).

---

2. For just one example, see: "Conversations with Harry Reeder and Bruce Stallings, Part Twenty Seven," Briarwood Presbyterian Church, September 27, 2020, https://briarwood.org/wp-content/uploads/2020/09/157960_9-27_20_pm.pdf.

3. Harry Reeder, "Reflecting on 50 Years in the PCA," Gospel Reformation Network, May 16, 2023, https://www.youtube.com/watch?v=SZyJngy2nnE.

4. Ibid.

Simultaneously, though, the Lord graciously mobilizes and deputizes His people to affirm His purposes at all times in all places. He commissions us to exercise careful stewardship over His creation. We are to be more than just salt, preserving; we are to be light, reclaiming (Matt. 5:13-16). Justice, mercy, and humility, grace, courage, and kindness, faith, hope, and love: these are among the many virtues we are called to joyfully manifest before a lost and dying world.

This is the crux of the Biblical worldview. It is what Christ dramatically underscored in His final instructions to His disciples in the Great Commission. He said,

> All authority in heaven and on earth has been given to me. Therefore, go and make disciples of all nations, baptizing them in the Name of the Father and of the Son and of the Holy Spirit, and teaching them to obey everything I have commanded you. And surely, I will be with you always, to the very end of the age (Matt. 28:18-20).

All authority in heaven is His, of course. The heights and the depths, the angels and the principalities, are under His providential rule. But all authority on earth is His as well. Man and creature, as well as every invention and institution, are under His sovereign prerogative. There are no neutral areas in the cosmos that escape the authority of the Lord Jesus Christ (Col. 1:17).

On this basis then, the Great Commission calls upon believers to do the work of extending Christ's Kingdom, making disciples in all nations by going, baptizing, and teaching. This mandate is the essence of the New Covenant which is but an extension of the Old Covenant: go and begin the process of restoring every broken thing in heaven and on earth for His Name's sake (Gen. 1:28). We are called to be a part of that which will, in the fullness of time, "bring all things in heaven and on earth together under one Head, even Christ" (Eph. 1:10).

This is the thrust of the Great Commission. It is the spiritual, emotional, and cultural mandate to bring light into the darkness, to win a fallen world for Jesus. And though we know that only Christ Himself can fulfill that mandate in its entirety at the close of human history, our duty is but to trust and obey by the empowerment of the Holy Spirit. We are to "occupy until He comes" (Luke 19:13). Commenting on this comprehensive mission, Charles Haddon Spurgeon said:

> There are certain pious moderns who will not allow the preacher to speak upon anything but those doctrinal statements concerning the way of salvation which are known as 'the Gospel.' We do not stand in awe of such criticism, for we clearly perceive that our Lord Jesus Christ himself would very frequently have come under it. Read the Sermon on the Mount and judge whether certain among the pious would be content to hear the like of it preached to them. Indeed, they would condemn it as containing very little Gospel and too much good works. They would condemn it as containing all too much of the legal. But we must never let be forgotten Christ's emphasis: the law must be preached, for what the law demands of us, the Gospel produces in us, else ours is no Gospel at all.[5]

A biblical worldview, as Spurgeon asserts, embraces the comprehensive implications of the Great Commission. It applies Scripture to every area of life and godliness. The salvation of souls is the immediate aim of the Great Commission. But the more ultimate aim is the promotion of the glory of the Triune God (Rom. 16:25-27). We must have a passion for souls (2 Cor. 5:11). We must take every opportunity (Col. 4:5), expend every energy (2 Cor. 6:4-10), and risk every expense (Acts 4:29), beseeching men to be reconciled to God (2 Cor. 5:20). But individualistic redemption is not the do-all and end-all of the Great Commission. Our evangelism must include sociology as well as salvation; it must include a new social order as well as a new birth; it must include reform and redemption, culture and conversion, a reformation as well as a regeneration. Read the sermons of the great evangelists through the ages and you will immediately see that kind of balance—they invariably begin by addressing the

---

5. C. H. Spurgeon as quoted in, Harold Latternic, *Spurgeon and Society* (London: New Baptist Union, 1981), p. 33.

grave injustices of the day, proceed to tender examples of human need, and conclude with a vital appeal to reconcile with Christ.

This principle runs all through the Bible. God's redemptive work involves making "all things new" (2 Cor. 5:17). We are to "make disciples," not merely converts. As Francis Schaeffer once said:

> If Christ is indeed Lord, He must be Lord of all of life—in spiritual matters, of course, but just as much across the whole spectrum of life, including intellectual matters and the areas of culture, law, and government.[6]

And again:

> Evangelism is primary, but it is not the end of our work and indeed cannot be separated from the rest of the Christian life. We must acknowledge and then act upon the fact that if Christ is our Savior, He is also our Lord in all of life. He is our Lord not just in the religious things and not just in cultural things such as the arts and music, but in our intellectual lives, and in business, and in our relation to society, and in our attitude toward the moral breakdown of our culture.[7]

The Great Commission, therefore, necessarily means we must "go" into the world and not merely invite the world to "come." Harry Reeder explained,

> The Greek text literally reads, 'As you are going, make disciples.' The participial form of the verb 'go' assumes that believers will be going out into the world, and the point is that while we are going, we should be making disciples. ... The church should be going. We are not waiting for the seekers to come—we are going, like Jesus, 'to seek and save the lost.'[8]

But that presents something of a perplexing paradox. We know, for instance, that the world is only a temporary dwelling place. It is "passing away" (1 John 2:17) and we are here but for a little while as "aliens and sojourners" (Acts 7:6). Because we are a part "of God's household" (Eph. 2:19), our true "citizenship is in

---

6. Francis Schaeffer, *The Great Evangelical Disaster* (Wheaton: Crossway, 1984), p. 11.
7. Ibid., p. 39.
8. Harry Reeder, *From Embers*, p. 173.

heaven" (Phil. 3:20). Our affections are naturally "set on things above" (Col. 3:2).

In addition, the world is filled with "dangers, toils, and snares" (Jer. 18:22). In tandem with "the flesh and the devil," it "makes war" on the saints (John 15:18). "All that is in the world, the lust of the flesh, the lust of the eyes, and the pride of life are not of the Father" (1 John 2:16). The world "cannot receive the Spirit of Truth" because "the cares of this world choke the Word, and it becomes unfruitful" (Matt. 8:22).

Thankfully, Christ "overcame the world" (John 16:33) and then "chose us out of the world" (John 15:19). Thus, we are not to be "conformed to the world" (Rom. 12:2), neither are we to "love the world" (1 John 2:15) because "Christ gave Himself for us, that He might deliver us from this present evil world" (Gal. 1:4). Though we once "walked according to the course of the world" (Eph. 2:2), now we are to keep ourselves "unspotted by the world" (Jas. 1:27). Indeed, "friendship with the world is enmity with God" so that whoever is "a friend of the world is the enemy of God" (Jas. 4:4).

Not surprisingly then, warnings against worldliness, carnal mindedness, and earthly attachments dominate Biblical ethics. But, therein lies the paradox. We must continue to live in the world. We must be "in" it but we are not to be "of" it. And that is no easy feat. As John Calvin wrote, "Nothing is more difficult than to forsake all carnal thoughts, to subdue and renounce our false appetites, and to devote ourselves to God and our brethren, and to live the life of angels in a world of corruption."[9]

To make matters even more complex, we not only have to live in this dangerous fallen world, but we have to work in it (1 Thess. 4:11), serve in it (Luke 22:6), and minister in it (2 Tim. 4:5). We have been appointed ambassadors to it (2 Cor. 5:20), priests for it (1 Pet. 2:9), and witnesses in it (Matt. 24:14). We even have to go to "the uttermost parts" of it (Acts 1:8), offering "a good confession of the eternal life" to which we were called (1 Tim. 6:12).

---

9. John Calvin, *The Golden Booklet of the Christian Life*, trans. Henry Van Andel, (Grand Rapids, MI: Baker, 1952), p. 26.

The reason for this seemingly contradictory state of affairs—enmity with the world on the one hand, responsibility to it on the other—is simply that "God so loved the world that He gave His only begotten Son" (John 3:16). Though the world is "in the power of the evil one" (1 John 5:19) and "knows not God, neither the children of God" (1 Cor. 1:21), God is "in Christ reconciling the world unto Himself" (2 Cor. 5:19). Jesus is "the light of the world" (John 1:12). He is the "savior of the world" (John 4:14). He is the "lamb of God who takes away the sin of the world" (John 1:29). Indeed, He was made "the propitiation for our sins; and not for ours only, but also for the whole world" (1 John 2:2). Through Christ "all things are reconciled to the Father" (Col. 1:20) so that finally "the kingdoms of this world shall become the kingdoms of our God and of His Christ" (Rev. 11:15).

The Great Commission necessitates cognizance of both perspectives of the world—treating them with equal weight. We must be engaged in the world and with the worldly. We must be unengaged in their carnal worldliness. We must somehow correlate eternal spiritual concerns with temporal physical concerns. We must coalesce heavenly hope and earthly life. We must coordinate heart-felt faith and down-to-earth practice. By vitally connecting the head with the hand with the heart, by placing emphasis on hard-hitting issues, gentle human compassion, deep and abiding relationships, and unflinching holiness, and by establishing the priorities of cultural, interpersonal, and devotional integrity, the high ideals of a Biblical worldview are happily instituted by the grace of God.

That's what it means to be "On Mission." Thus, Harry Reeder declared, "No Bible passage should inform our mission and shape our vision, more than the Great Commission."[10]

On Message

According to Reeder, "The Gospel-framed-and-wrapped-ministry presents a sufficient Christ by means of a sufficient Word."[11]

---

10. Reeder, *From Embers*, p. 167.
11. Reeder, "Reflecting on 50 Years in the PCA."

He believed that a Great Commission vision would always necessarily be rooted in the deep and wondrous life-changing truths of Scripture systematically and substantively studied, proclaimed, taught, believed, and applied.

As Thomas Chalmers long ago asserted, "The Spirit guides us unto all truth and all truth is to be found in the Bible; the Spirit therefore guides us unto the Bible."[12] And again,

> We have to make the Bible our Vade Mecum: our book of reference, our book of trust. Let us be convinced more and more of the prodigious fertility of the Bible. How much lies hidden and unobserved, even after many perusals; and surely if it be true that a man may read it a hundred times and find something on his next reading which he missed on all his former ones, oftener recourse to this means of grace bids fair for multiplying our blessings. Therefore, let us be quick to be in the way of grace.[13]

Indeed, Chalmers goes on,

> He who truly accepts Christ as the alone foundation of his meritorious acceptance before God is stimulated by the circumstances of his new condition to breathe holy purposes and to abound in holy performances. He is created anew unto good works. He is made the workmanship of God in Christ Jesus. The Gospel is no mere system of inert and unproductive orthodoxy.... It is the office of the Holy Spirit to sanctify men,... He does so largely through the tangible intermedium of the Word.[14]

The Bible is the Word of God. It is His revelation of wisdom, knowledge, understanding, and truth. It is not simply a splendid collection of inspiring sayings and stories. It is God's message to man. It is God's instruction. It is God's direction. It is God's guideline, His plumbline, and His bottom line.

From Genesis to Revelation, the Bible is God's own Word. Nearly five thousand times throughout, the narrative is punctuated with phrases like "thus says the Lord," "thus the Lord commanded His people," or "thus came the Word of the Almighty."

---

12. Joseph John Gurney, *Chalmeriana: Colloquies with Dr. Chalmers* (Edinburgh: Oliver and Boyd, 1853), p, 43.
13. Ibid., p. 41.
14. Ibid., p. 46.

Jesus constantly upheld the validity of God's Word as a guide for living and an expression of the unchanging standards of His sovereign rule:

> Man shall not live on bread alone, but on every Word that proceeds out of the mouth of God (Matt. 4:4).

> It is easier for heaven and earth to pass away than for one stroke of a letter of the Law to fail (Luke 16:17).

> Whoever then annuls one of the least of these commandments, and so teaches others, shall be called least in the Kingdom of Heaven; but whoever keeps and teaches them, he shall be called great in the Kingdom of Heaven (Matt. 5:19).

Again and again He affirmed the truth that the Apostle Paul would later articulate that, "All Scripture is God-breathed" (2 Tim. 3:16), and that it "cannot be broken" (John 10:35). Jesus did not come to do away with the commands of God—to abolish or abrogate them. On the contrary, He came to fulfill them—to confirm and uphold them (Matt. 5:17). He reiterated the Old Testament dictums that every one of "His righteous ordinances is everlasting" (Ps. 119:160) and that "the Word of our God shall stand forever" (Isa. 40:8).

Jesus was affirming that, unlike human sages, moralists, philosophers, or lawmakers, God does not change His mind or alter His standards: "My covenant I will not violate, nor will I alter the utterance of my lips" (Ps. 89:34). When the Lord speaks, His Word stands firm forever. His assessments of right and wrong do not change from age to age: "All His precepts are trustworthy. They are established forever and ever, to be performed with faithfulness and uprightness" (Ps. 111:7-8).

Jesus appealed to God's eternal statutes to bolster His teaching (John 8:17). He used them to vindicate His behavior (Matt. 12:5). He used them to answer His questioners (Luke 10:26), to indict His opponents (John 7:19), to identify God's will (Matt. 19:17), to establish Kingdom citizenship (Matt. 7:24), to confront Satan (Matt. 4:1-11), and to confirm Christian love (John 14:21).

Clear proclamation of this "sufficient Word" was one of the most obvious hallmarks of Harry Reeder's public and private ministry. He was committed to the expository preaching of the whole counsel of God, from Genesis to Revelation—verse by verse, line by line, precept by precept. In his book, *From Embers to Flame*, Harry quoted John MacArthur's "paean of praise to the kind of preaching that proceeds directly from the Scriptures."[15]

> Expository preaching—expressing exactly the will of the glorious Sovereign—allows God to speak, not man. Expository preaching—retaining the thoughts of the Spirit—brings the preacher into direct and continual contact with the mind of the Holy Spirit who authored Scripture. Expository preaching frees the preacher to proclaim all the revelation of God, producing a ministry of wholeness and integrity. Expository preaching promotes Biblical literacy, yielding rich knowledge of redemptive truths. Expository preaching carries ultimate divine authority, rendering the very voice of God. Expository preaching transforms the preacher, leading to transformed congregations.[16]

Throughout the ages, men like Cain have used religion to get what they want (Gen. 4:3-8; Heb. 11:4; 1 John 3:12). Men like Balaam have used religion to control circumstances (Num. 31:16; 2 Pet. 2:15; Rev. 2:14). Men like Korah have used religion to enhance their position (Num. 16:1-3; 31-35). Cain, Balaam, and Korah all believed in the universal power of magic—either the magic of law or the magic of lawlessness. They believed that not only could they manipulate human society and natural elements with their peculiar approach to moral and ethical standards, but that God would also be forced to conform Himself to the desires and demands of men who act in terms of certain legal strictures: say certain things, do certain things, believe certain things, or act out certain things, and God will have to respond. In essence, they believed that man controlled his own destiny, using either the rituals and formulas of legalism or the license and autonomy

---

15. Reeder, *From Embers to Flame*, p. 102.
16. John MacArthur, *Rediscovering Expository Preaching*, (Dallas: Word Publishing, 1992), as quoted in Reeder, *From Embers to Flame*, pp. 102–03.

of lawlessness like magical talismans to save mankind, to shape history, to govern society, and even to manipulate God. It seems that men are forever rejecting the grace of God, "going the way of Cain, rushing headlong into the error of Balaam, and perishing in the rebellion of Korah" (Jude 11).

This is why the prophet Jeremiah urged the faithful to steadfastly pursue the "old paths" and the "good way." He declared, "Thus says the LORD: 'Stand by the roads, and look, and ask for the old paths, where the good way is, and walk in it, and find rest for your souls'" (Jer. 6:16).

Only the Word can give perfect and objective guidance into all truth (Ps. 119:160), for it is "a lamp to our feet and a light to our path" (Ps. 119:105). Only the Word can keep us within the confines of covenantal and confessional faithfulness (1 Cor. 4:6).

The discipling work of the Great Commission, our mission, can only be accomplished by clear and diligent proclamation of the Christ-centered, sufficient Word, our message. Lest we fall into the trap of attempting to do "what is right in our own eyes" (Judg. 21:25), we must rest and rely on the unchanging, inerrant, objective standard God has given us in the Bible:

> This Book of the Law shall not depart from your mouth, but you shall meditate in it day and night, that you may observe to do according to all that is written in it. For then you will make your way prosperous, and then you will have good success (Josh. 1:8).
>
> All Scripture is given by inspiration of God, and is profitable for doctrine, for reproof, for correction, for instruction in righteousness, that the man of God may be complete, thoroughly equipped for every good work (2 Tim. 3:16-17).
>
> We also have the prophetic Word made more sure, which you do well to heed as a light that shines in a dark place, until the day dawns and the morning star rises in your hearts; knowing this first, that no prophecy of Scripture is of any private interpretation, for prophecy never came by the will of man, but holy men of God spoke as they were moved by the Holy Spirit (2 Pet. 1:19-21).

> Every word of God is pure; He is a shield to those who put their trust in Him. Do not add to His Words, lest he reprove you, and you be found a liar (Prov. 30:5-6).
>
> The entrance of Your words gives light; it gives understanding to the simple (Ps. 119:130).

Thomas Chalmers sagely observed,

> You must not forget that though doubted, decried, and disowned, the Bible is the Word of God with power to recall a lost world from its state of exile and degeneracy and to dethrone sin from its ascendancy. So, let me be well instructed in the mysteries of the Kingdom, and let the Word of Christ dwell in me richly.[17]

Thus, Harry Reeder asserted,

> All truth is God's truth, but God's Word is all truth, so every assertion of truth must be based on the Word of God and tested by it. Only the inspired Word of God has the ability to change the hearts of people, and only the inspired Word of God is sufficient to meet all of their deepest needs.[18]

This is the means by which we are able to remain steadfastly on mission and on message.

In Ministry

According to Reeder, any church or people, "seeking to be faithful to the foundation of the church (which is the Word of God), the cornerstone of the church (which is Jesus Christ), and the purpose of the church (which is the Great Commission)," must simultaneously work toward a loving "culture of the church (which is the Great Commandment)."[19]

When the disciples came to Jesus asking, "Teacher, which is the great commandment in the Law?" He answered them saying,

> You shall love the Lord your God with all your heart and with all your soul and with all your mind. This is the great and first commandment. And a

---

17. Gurney, p. 81.
18. Reeder, p. 109.
19. "Conversations with Harry Reeder and Bruce Stallings, Part Twenty Seven"

second is like it: You shall love your neighbor as yourself. On these two commandments depend all the Law and the Prophets (Matt. 22:36-40).

God's people are to be marked by a selfless, servant-hearted love. Our calling in ministry is to pursue our mission and proclaim our message with graciousness, kindness, mercy, and care—both within the church and without.

In the Old Testament, the Hebrew word most often used for the service of believers is *sharath*. It literally means "to minister" or "to treat with affection." Similarly, in the New Testament, the Greek word *diakoneo* is most often used. It literally means "to care for" or to "offer relief." In both cases, the priestly connotations and the merciful intentions of ministry are quite evident. In both cases, the emphasis is on the interpersonal dimension rather than the institutional dimension, on merciful service rather than efficient management, on true righteousness rather than mere rightness. Biblical ministry is far more concerned about taking care of souls than about taking care of business.

This fastidious distinction between the ministry of service and the business of service is like the difference between faith in God and faith in faith. God is merciful and just. He works righteousness and justice for all (Ps. 33:5). Morning by morning, He dispenses His justice without fail (Zeph. 3:5) and without partiality (Job 32:21). All His ways are just (Deut. 32:4) so that injustice is an abomination to Him (Prov. 11:1).

Thus, He is adamant about ensuring the cause of the meek and the weak, the broken-hearted and the distressed, the marginalized and the oppressed (Ps. 103:6). People matter. From the least and the last to the first and the foremost, all people matter. They matter to God. Scripture persistently and adamantly stresses this important attribute of God:

> But the Lord abides forever; He has established His Throne for judgment, and He will judge the world in righteousness; He will execute judgment for the peoples with equity. The Lord also will be a Stronghold for the oppressed, a Stronghold in times of trouble (Ps. 9:7-9).

"Because of the devastation of the afflicted, because of the groaning of the needy, now I will arise," says the LORD; "I will set him in the safety for which he longs" (Ps. 12:5).

A father of the fatherless and a judge for the widows, is God in His holy habitation. God makes a Home for the lonely; He leads out the prisoners into prosperity, only the rebellious dwell in a parched land (Ps. 68:5-6).

The afflicted and needy are seeking water, but there is none, and their tongue is parched with thirst; I, the LORD, will answer them Myself, as the God of Israel I will not forsake them. I will open rivers on the bare heights, and springs in the midst of the valleys; I will make the wilderness a pool of water. I will put the cedar in the wilderness, the acacia, and the myrtle, and the olive tree; I will place the juniper in the desert, together with the box tree and the cypress, that they may see and recognize, and consider and gain insight as well, that the hand of the LORD has done this, and the Holy One of Israel has created it (Isa. 41:17-20).

God cares for the needy, the despised, the rejected, the confused, and the lost. And His people are to do likewise. God desires that we follow Him (Matt. 4:19). We are to emulate Him (1 Pet. 1:16). We are to do as He does. In effect, we are to do unto others as He has done unto us. That is the ethical principle that underlies the "Golden Rule" (Matt. 7:12; Luke 6:31).

If God has comforted us, then we are to comfort others (2 Cor. 1:4). If God has forgiven us, then we are to forgive others (Eph. 4:32). If God has loved us, then we are to love others (1 John 4:11). If He has taught us, then we are to teach others (Matt. 28:20). If He has borne witness to us, then we are to bear witness to others (John 15:26-27). If He has laid down His life for us, then we are to lay down our lives for one another (1 John 3:16).

Whenever God commanded the priestly nation of Israel to imitate Him in ensuring justice for the wandering homeless, the alien, and the sojourner, He reminded them that they were once despised, rejected, and homeless themselves (Exod. 22:21-27; 23:9; Lev. 19:33-34). It was only by the grace and mercy of God that they had been redeemed from that low estate (Deut. 24:17-22). Thus, they were to exercise compassion for the broken-hearted and the dispossessed. They were to serve.

Priestly privilege brings priestly responsibility. If Israel refused to take up that responsibility, then God would revoke their privilege (Isa. 1:11-17). If they refused to exercise reciprocal mercy then God would rise up in His anger to visit the land with His wrath and displeasure, expelling them into the howling wilderness once again (Exod. 22:24). On the other hand, if they fulfilled their calling to live lives of merciful service then they would ever be blessed (Ps. 41:1-2).

The principle still holds. Those of us who have received the compassion of the Lord on High are to demonstrate tenderness in kind to all those around us. This is the lesson Jesus was driving at in the parable of the unmerciful slave:

> For this reason the kingdom of heaven may be compared to a certain king who wished to settle accounts with his slaves. And when he had begun to settle them, there was brought to him one who owed him ten thousand talents. But since he did not have the means to repay, his lord commanded him to be sold, along with his wife and children and all that he had, and repayment to be made. The slave therefore falling down, prostrated himself before him, saying, "Have patience with me, and I will repay you everything." And the lord of that slave felt compassion and released him and forgave him the debt. But that slave went out and found one of his fellow slaves who owed him a hundred denarii; and he seized him and began to choke him, saying, "Pay back what you owe." So his fellow slave fell down and began to entreat him, saying, "Have patience with me and I will repay you." He was unwilling however, but went and threw him in prison until he should pay back what was owed. So when his fellow slaves saw what had happened, they were deeply grieved and came and reported to their lord all that had happened. Then summoning him, his lord said to him, "You wicked slave, I forgave you all that debt because you entreated me. Should you not also have had mercy on your fellow slave, even as I had mercy on you?" And his lord, moved with anger, handed him over to the torturers until he should repay all that was owed him. So shall My heavenly Father also do to you, if each of you does not forgive his brother from your heart (Matt. 18:23-35).

The moral of the parable is crystal clear. The needy around us are living symbols of our own former helplessness and privation. We are therefore to be living symbols of God's justice, mercy, compassion, and love. We are to do as He has done and love as He has loved (John 15:1-8), doing so in the power of the indwelling Spirit (John 14:15-26).

In other words, the Gospel calls us to live daily as if people really matter. It calls us to live lives of selfless concern. We are to pay attention to the needs of others—in both word and deed, in both thought and action, we are to weave ordinary kindness into the very fabric of our lives (Deut. 22:4).

This kind of ingrained mercy goes far beyond mere politeness. We are to demonstrate concern for the poor (Ps. 41:1). We are to show pity toward the weak (Ps. 72:13). We are to rescue the afflicted from violence (Ps. 72:14). We are to familiarize ourselves with the case of the helpless (Prov. 29:7), give of our wealth (Deut. 26:12-13), and share of our sustenance (Prov. 22:9). We are to "put on tender mercies, kindness, humbleness of mind, meekness, and long-suffering" (Col. 3:12). We are to become "a father to the poor," and to "search out the case of the stranger" (Job 29:16). We are to love our neighbors as ourselves (Mark 12:31) and "rescue the perishing" (Prov. 24:10-12), thus "fulfilling the law" (Rom. 13:10).

According to Scripture, this kind of comprehensive servanthood emphasis is, in fact, a primary indication of the authenticity of our faith: "This is pure and undefiled religion in the sight of our God and Father, to visit the orphans and widows in their distress and to keep oneself unstained by the world" (James 1:27).

We are called to "do justice" and to "love kindness" (Gen. 18:19). We are to be ministers of God's peace (Matt. 5:9), instruments of His love (John 13:35), and ambassadors of His Kingdom (2 Cor. 5:20). We are to care for the helpless, feed the hungry (Ezek. 18:7), clothe the naked (Luke 3:11), shelter the homeless (Isa. 16:3-4), visit the prisoner (Matt. 25:36), and protect the innocent (Ps. 82:4).

In writing to Titus, the young pastor of Crete's pioneer church, the Apostle Paul pressed home this vision of ministry. The task before Titus was not an easy one. The Cretan culture was terribly worldly. It was marked by deceit, ungodliness, sloth, and gluttony (Titus 1:12). Thus, Paul's instructions were strategically precise and right to the point. Titus was to preach the glories of grace, but he was also to make good deeds evident. Priestly mercy and selfless servanthood were to be central priorities in his new work:

> For the grace of God has appeared, bringing salvation to all men, instructing us to deny ungodliness and worldly desires, and to live sensibly, righteously and godly in the present age, looking for the blessed hope and the appearing of the glory of our great God and Savior, Christ Jesus; who gave Himself for us, that He might redeem us from every lawless deed and purify for Himself a people for His own possession, zealous for good deeds (Titus 2:11-14).

Paul tells Titus he should build his fledgling ministry around works of mercy: He was "to be an example of good deeds" (Titus 2:7). He was to teach the people "to be ready for every good deed" (Titus 3:1). The older women and the younger women were to be thus instructed, so "that the Word of God might not be dishonored" (Titus 2:5); and the bond servants, that "they might adorn the doctrine of God our Savior in every respect" (Titus 2:10). They were all to "learn to engage in good deeds to meet pressing needs, that they might not be unfruitful" (Titus 3:14). There were those within the Church who professed "to know God, but by their deeds they deny Him, being detestable and disobedient, and worthless for any good deed" (Titus 1:16). These, Titus was to "reprove severely that they might be sound in the faith" (Titus 1:13). He was to "speak confidently, so that those who had believed God might be careful to engage in good deeds" (Titus 3:8).

What was true for Titus then, is true for us all today, for "these things are good and profitable for all men" (Titus 3:8). According to the Westminster Confession of Faith:

> Good works, done in obedience to God's commandments, are the fruits and evidences of a true and lively faith: and by them believers manifest their

thankfulness, strengthen their assurance, edify their brethren, adorn the profession of the Gospel, stop the mouths of the adversaries, and glorify God whose workmanship they are, created in Christ Jesus thereunto; that, having their fruit unto holiness, they may have the end, eternal life.[20]

Wherever committed Christians have gone, throughout Europe, into the depths of Africa, to the outer reaches of China, along the edges of the American frontier, and beyond to the Australian outback, this kind of selfless care for the needy has been in evidence. In fact, most of the church's greatest heroes are those who willingly gave the best of their lives to the less fortunate. Service was their hallmark. Mercy was their emblem. "And so the Word of God spread rapidly" (Acts 6:7).

Harry Reeder has affirmed the fact that,

> A Gospel-Driven, Christ-Centered ministry will always emphasize personal and family formation, prioritize prayer and the ministry of the Word, worship in Spirit and in truth, pursue missions and world evangelism, multiply servant leadership, be committed to the Great Commission, connect to the past with an eye to the future, and all this in a culture of love.[21]

This is what it means to be *on mission, on message, and in ministry*. This is the Reeder vision for a faithful Gospel Calling.

---

20. Westminster Confession of Faith, 16.2
21. Harry Reeder, From Embers to Flame Conference, Briarwood Presbyterian Church, Birmingham, AL, 2017.

2

Preaching That Moves Men to God

The Preaching Legacy of Dr. Harry L. Reeder

Neil C. Stewart

In the summer of 2023, shortly after his homegoing, I took a stroll around the Briarwood campus to ponder the life and legacy of Dr. Harry L. Reeder. Standing outside, at the top of the steps leading up to the sanctuary, I looked up at those grand arches. By design, their towering majesty make us feel small; they ready us for worship. From another perspective, however, their height heralds the ministry of one of God's giants, a humble man who spoke with his hand on the Bible, his feet on the earth, and his head in the heavens. In my mind's eye, I see him pass through those august portals for the last time. Walking out to his car, Harry's going home. Soon, faith will become sight, and God's servant will attain his full stature—the measure of the stature that belongs to the fullness of Christ (Eph. 4:13). With his passing, American Presbyterianism has lost her elder statesman. We feel Harry's absence everywhere, but it is in the pulpit that we feel it most keenly of all.

Harry was one of a kind. In the pulpit, he was "logic on fire." Preaching as a man enthralled with God, his words came with heart-invading, mind-changing, affection-stirring, will-confronting, gates-of-hell-storming power. Because he had been so affected by his own message, we who heard him could not help but be affected as well. In a way far beyond my ability to express, a quote from Dr. Martyn Lloyd-Jones captures the distinctive power of Harry's ministry, "What is the chief end of preaching? I like to think that it is this. It is to give men and women a sense of God and of His presence."[1] When this is missing—and I fear it is missing in much of what passes for preaching today—nothing on earth can make up the want.

This sense of God has both heavenly and earthly roots. God must speak and be felt to speak in the sermon, but we must also speak as those uttering the oracles of God (1 Pet. 4:11). In a day when the word of the Lord is fast becoming rare (1 Sam. 3:1), Dr. Reeder leaves the church a faithful model in Christ of the kind of preaching we need—the kind that moves men to God. I write this essay to honor this legacy. What lessons must we learn if we are to follow his example?

Biblical Perspective

The first lesson is that the Word of God must be central in our preaching. Even with such a commanding personality and voice, the Bible took center stage when Harry preached, not him. Borrowing from Spurgeon, the central thrust of Harry's ministry was simple: "Preach the Bible, the whole Bible, and nothing but the Bible." The Bible alone is God-breathed, inerrant, and absolute. As Harry never tired of reminding us, "If God says it, that settles it." This dictum gives the preacher his message, his mission, and his mandate.

Is this the central thrust of your ministry and mine? So many factors conspire to distract preachers from this foundation, but two questions should always draw us back.

First, will I be faithful to my master? Our commission is clear—we are to proclaim God's word, not our opinion, cultural

---

1. Martyn Lloyd-Jones, *Preaching and Preachers* (Grand Rapids: Zondervan, 1976), p. 110.

commentary, or what we believe the church wants or needs to hear: "To the law and to the testimony! If they do not speak according to this word, it is because there is no light in them" (Isa. 8:20, NKJV). Let the pundits worry about staying on the right side of history. Our only concern should be to be found on the right side of eternity. As Stuart Olyott reminds us, "A herald is a traitor if he does not convey exactly what the King says."[2]

Second, will I be effective in my ministry? Preaching *sola Scriptura* is the secret of fruitful ministry. God's word alone has real power. He can do what we cannot. He speaks, and it is done. He commands, and it holds fast. Only His promises shape reality. Only His precepts give what they require. Only His word creates faith (Rom. 10:17), begets new life (James 1:18), restores the soul (Ps. 19:7), and bestows the wisdom that leads to salvation (2 Tim. 3:15). Only Christ preaching Scripture through us can call sinners home to God (Eph. 2:17).

To preach any other message than Scripture alone represents more than just a misstep; it is absolute folly—like a soldier trading bullets and bombs for paper planes and peas. If the sermon's power begins with the preacher's genius, the force of his personality, and the pathos of his rhetorical skills, he will inevitably end up with no power at all. There is a reason no one calls a doctor to tend the corpse at a funeral. The most a man can do is—well, the most a man can do.

In his letter to Titus, Paul explains his passion for preaching: "At the proper time, in the message preached, [God] made His word tangible" (Titus 1:3, translation mine). This intrigues me. Is Paul suggesting in a Barthian sense that, as we encounter Scripture in the sermon, it becomes the word of God? No, Paul's doctrine of Scripture is much too high for that (2 Tim. 3:16). Rather, I believe Paul underscores the unique power a sermon has to bring God's word home—as the word of God—into the hearts and minds of the hearer. In the sermon, we don't get a better Bible, but we do get the Bible better.

---

2. Stuart Olyott, *Preaching - Pure and Simple* (Bridgend: Bryntirion Press, 2005), p. 29.

This is what the Thessalonian Christians experienced when they heard Paul preach. It's what we all experienced when we heard Harry preach: "Our gospel came to you not simply with words but also with power, with the Holy Spirit and deep conviction; just as you know what manner of men we proved to be among you for your sake" (1 Thess. 1:4–5).

Preaching like this takes hard spade work and exegetical determination in the study. In the words of John Brown of Haddington, the preacher's fundamental job is "to bring the hearts of his hearers into direct contact with the mind of the Spirit in a given text."[3] We need to show the congregation how the text of Scripture drives the sermon. To do this, we should get into the habit of clearly stating the point we are trying to make, explicitly rooting it in the text, and explaining its significance from its immediate context.

Listen to Dr. Reeder preach; you will hear him do this constantly. Like the needle of a sewing machine, his sermons go up and down through the text of Scripture, stitching its message onto the souls of his hearers. Too many preachers treat their texts the way long-distance pilots treat "fly over country." They hardly ever refer to the text again once they read the passage and "take off" in the sermon. Good sermons don't do that.

Our aim should not be to impress people with how smart we are, how funny we are, or how likeable we are. Our role as preachers must be to impress the congregation with the truth, authority, sufficiency, and relevance of Scripture—to get out of the way and leave them seeing none but Jesus only. And, as one of the Worthies put it, "A crucified style best befits the preaching of a crucified Savior!"

Theological Nuance

Our people need a balanced diet from the pulpit that communicates not just the whole counsel of God but also a well-

---

3. I first heard this quote from a mentor of mine who attributed it to John Brown of Haddington, though I have as yet been unable to track down the specific source.

rounded systematic and biblical theology. As has been said so often and by so many, "It takes a whole Bible to make a whole Christian"—to which I would add, it takes a whole theology preached by a whole theologian. Half-a-doctrine is often the first step to heresy. As J.I. Packer noted, most theological missteps start as a half-truth told as a whole truth, which then quickly becomes a whole untruth.[4] Therefore, our sermons must reflect the full truth of the Bible and its doctrines, not just the parts we find most meaningful, challenging, or comforting.

As an example of such half-truth telling, consider the recent confusion surrounding the doctrine of sanctification. Some preachers, at the radical end of the Sonship movement, seem to know only how to preach texts like, "Where sin abounds, grace does much more abound" (Rom. 5:20). On the other side of the theological aisle, those of a more legal frame seem to prefer lashing the consciences of God's people with, "Remember Lot's wife," (Luke 17:32), or "Not everyone who says to me, 'Lord, Lord' shall enter the Kingdom of heaven" (Matt. 7:21), or "Without holiness, no one will see the Lord" (Heb. 12:14).

Of course, these texts are all in the Bible; our people need to hear them. But as preachers, we need to handle them thoughtfully and with nuance. The key to such nuance is to root both law and grace in the person of Jesus Christ and our union with Him.[5]

Without the warm personal touch of the Father's Son, the law becomes a cold, heartless, ruthless rule—one much better at cursing the child of God than blessing him, better at exposing his failure than empowering his obedience. But what a difference Jesus and our union with Him makes, transforming the law of sin and death into the law of the Spirit of life (Rom. 8:1-4).

The same can be said of grace: without Jesus Christ, the grace of God becomes impersonal, your fuzzy and flexible, soft and

---

4. J. I. Packer, *A Quest for Godliness: The Puritan Vision of the Christian Life* (Wheaton, IL: Crossway, 1990), p. 126.
5. I am indebted to Sinclair Ferguson and his work on the Marrow Controversy: Sinclair B. Ferguson, *The Whole Christ: Legalism, Antinomianism, and Gospel Assurance – Why the Marrow Controversy Still Matters* (Wheaton: Crossway, 2016), p. 83.

spongy friend—one better suited to leading the Christian to compromise his faith rather than confirming it through a life of earnest, grace-driven, principled obedience.

However, the difference is palpable once we connect grace to Christ, as Paul does in his letter to Titus (Titus 2:11-14). Grace came down in Bethlehem's rude stable—not just as an idea or a posture on God's part, but Grace as the Person of His beloved Son. Here is Grace with flesh and blood, grit and gumption; Grace with hands and feet; Grace with thoughtful verve and with holy violence; Grace urging us to say "No" to sin and "Yes" to godliness. Here is Grace with the power to liberate a man from the tyranny of momentary pleasures, problems, and priorities—grace that bids him look up and forward to the blessed hope and the appearing of the glory of our great God and Savior, Jesus Christ.

It was this gracious, glorious person who gave Himself for us. The same glorious Christ who will soon rend the heavens and bring fallen human history to an end is the same God who humbled Himself in Golgotha's bleak darkness. There, the Son did not merely surrender His human nature; He surrendered *Himself* in our nature—His Person—He offered *Himself* without hesitation, reserve, or limit. Here is an indicative to drive home every imperative we preach from the pulpit.

Such preaching requires wisdom and Gospel nuance. On the one hand, we should never tire of telling God's people that they can never sin their way out of God's love. No matter what we do, God will never de-son us. Yet, without denying that, our moments of faithlessness can and do grieve our Father's heart (Eph. 4:29ff.), and they should bitterly grieve us as well. On the other hand, the doctrine of justification should never leave the Christian feeling he can safely toy with sin. When preaching texts like, "For if you live according to the flesh you will die, but if by the Spirit you put to death the deeds of the body, you will live" (Rom. 8:13), our presentation of grace must in no way negate Paul's warning. John Murray's commentary on this verse bears quoting in full:

Here is an inevitable and invariable sequence, a sequence which God himself does not and cannot violate. To make life the issue of life after the flesh would be an inherent contradiction. God saves from the flesh but not in it. Paul is speaking here to believers and to them he says, "if ye live after the flesh, ye shall die." The death referred to must be understood in its broadest scope and does not stop short of death in its ultimate manifestation, eternal separation from God. The doctrine of the security of the believer does not obviate this sequence. The only way of avoiding the issue of death is to be delivered and desist from the life of the flesh.[6]

Even the Christian, by the Spirit, must be busy killing sin, or sin will be busy killing him. This is the way to make our calling and election sure. Could it be that the reason we fail to deal decisively with our sins is that we think so little of God and His grace? As John Owen said, "The generality of men make light work of sin; and yet in nothing doth it more appear what thoughts they have of God. He that hath slight thoughts of sin had never great thoughts of God."[7]

Artful Illustration

The key to effective preaching, just as with effective writing, is to go beyond simply telling our hearers what we are trying to say; we must show them with illustrations.

An informed critic once complained that I used too many illustrations in my sermons. Preferring the linear logic of Dr. Martyn Lloyd-Jones, he said, "Son, do you know how many sermons 'the Doctor' preached using illustrations?"

"None?" I replied—this is not true, but it was the answer he was expecting, so dutifully, I supplied it.

"Yes, that's right!" he said, "None," and, to drive his point home, he even spelled it out, "N—O—N—E!"

What to say? Well, I couldn't resist being a bit cheeky. "Sir, you might be right," I replied, "maybe I do use too many, but do you

---

6. John Murray, *The Epistle to the Romans*, The New International Commentary on the Old and New Testament (Grand Rapids: Eerdmans, 1968), 1:293–94.
7. John Owen, *The Works of John Owen*, ed. William H. Goold (Edinburgh: T&T Clark), 6:394.

know how many sermons the Lord Jesus preached *without* using illustrations?" He looked at me and scowled. Then, with a wink, I said, "Sir, as much as I love 'the Good Doctor,' if you don't mind, I think I'll side with Jesus on this one!"

In his book *Ministering Like the Master*, Stuart Olyott distills Jesus's teaching method into three steps—State. Illustrate. Apply.[8] If you watch what Olyott says, you will note that Jesus rarely deploys these elements alone. Instead, He is constantly stating and illustrating or illustrating and applying. Quite commonly, you will find Him doing all three at once.

Reflect on Christ's teaching ministry: He spoke of two gates—only two (Matt. 7:13-14). One is narrow—rip-the-buttons-off-your-waistcoat narrow; the other is wide—wide as a marathon's starting line, with all kinds of people herding down to destruction. He spoke of two trees: one laden with ripe, sweet peaches; the other bearing old, wrinkled fruit, as tasteless as an old turnip (Matt. 6:16-20). He described men building their lives on one of two very different foundations. The buildings look great, but on the horizon, a storm looms, ready to test the wisdom of each man's work (Matt. 7:24-27).

He described a man scattering seeds on four different soil types, each symbolizing four ways human hearts listen to God. First, the hard heart is resistant to the Word and unwilling to receive it. Second is the superficial heart, relegating the Word to life's periphery. Third, we have a divided heart, chained by the busyness of life, the lies money tells, and the desire simply for other things. Last, he pictures the welcome heart, ready to receive God's word. It alone bears fruit (Matt. 13:1-23).

Elsewhere, He shows us a fishing net, full to bursting as it's dragged through the sea (Matt 13:47); a wolf disguised as a sheep tearing apart the flock from within (John 10:12); a weary traveler trudging through night's blinding darkness, only to lift his eyes and see on a hill the beautiful city of Zion, glowing in the distance with a brightness that beckons (Matt. 5:14).

---

8. Stuart Olyott, *Ministering Like the Master: Three Messages for Today's Ministers* (Edinburgh: Banner of Truth, 2017). The next few paragraphs draw from Olyott's thought.

Jesus tells of two men going to pray at the temple (Luke 18:10), a shepherd on the mountainside at day's end, separating sheep from goats (Matt. 25:32). They've been together all day, yet now they must part forever. He speaks of ten virgins—five wise, five foolish. Outwardly, they appear identical: dressed alike, they carry the same flasks, they do the same thing—sleep. And, what is more, they all await the same master, Jesus. Yet, look closer. They are as similar as salt and sugar: five are bound for heaven, the rest for hell (Matt. 25:1).

Jesus isn't the only illustrative preacher. Isaiah describes how sin scars the soul, like pustulating sores from the sole of the feet to the top of the head, all unclean (Isa. 1:6). He speaks of Israel like a stubborn vine that resists the efforts of the vine planter to bring a fruitful harvest (Isa. 5:1ff). He illustrates sinners like sheep wandering away from their master (Isa. 53:6). Children think of sheep as cuddly bedtime toys; God thinks of them as stupid animals, the kind who forsake a green meadow for a freshly plowed field just because they can.

Ezekiel also loved to preach with illustrations. He spoke of rebellious men listening to God with their ears switched off (Ezek. 12:2). See him smile as he describes the deadness of God's people like a valley of dry bones. And then, hear what a rustling and the rattling as God comes down in reviving grace, and all the bones spring to life as a mighty army.

Consider Amos' allegory of a man fleeing from inescapable judgment. It's as if he's running through a forest from a lion, only to confront a bear. Escaping the lion and bear, he gets home, slams the door shut, sighs with relief, and reaches for the light switch, only to find a viper lurking on the wall. There's no escape: it strikes; he dies (Amos 5:19).

Or take David in the opening verse of the Psalter, how he traces the soul's gradual departure from God, using three vivid verbs: "does not *walk* in the counsel of the wicked... does not *stand* in the way of sinners... does not *sit*..." (Ps. 1:1). Walking, standing, sitting—with each step, the foolish man becomes progressively bogged down along his chosen path. What a graphic image: At first, you may find yourself listening to the words of those on the highway to hell, but before long, as sin wraps its tendrils around you, if you are not very careful, you will find yourself laughing at those on the way to heaven. By contrast, another image is that if you listen to God's fatherly instruction (law), you will become like a verdant and fruitful tree planted by the refreshing streams of the water of life. If not, you'll become a very different sort of plant matter—chaff—inherently rootless, lifeless, weightless, and worthless, soon scattered and consumed by the fiery winds of eternal judgment.

Or Solomon, who illustrates the sluggard bolted to his bed, turning endlessly like a door on its hinges. Persist in such laziness, and you will find it has the rather nasty habit of catching up with one in a moment of disaster—when your poverty comes in like a mugger with a gun (Prov. 24:34). Then there's his stark imagery of infidelity: "The mouth of an adulteress is a deep pit; He who is cursed of the LORD will fall into it" (Prov. 22:14, NASB95). Notice how Solomon paints adultery not as the commencement of a man's downfall but as its capstone—God's crowning act of judgment upon a 'long disobedience in the wrong direction.'

To conclude, if you wish your congregation to see what you're saying, show them what they are hearing. This shouldn't be an occasional trope. Make it habitual until they can't help but *see and feel* the truth you want them to grasp. Consider the Russian sniper Vasily Zaytsev, immortalized in *Enemy at the Gates*. His father taught him to shoot wolves through the eye to preserve the pelt. In like manner, if we aim to capture sinners, learn to aim at the eye. You might want to give the sheep a few warning shots but shoot the wolves through the eye.

Rhetorical Skill (Oral Style)

In the sermon, two voices are constantly in play: the voice of God and the voice of man. Scripture honors both sides of this dynamic. Take, for example, Luke's description of two fruitful days of preaching. In the first description, he explains why so many Gentiles came to faith in Jesus Christ. The secret lay behind the preacher in the electing grace of God: "And when the Gentiles heard this, they began rejoicing and glorifying the word of the Lord, and as many as were appointed to eternal life believed" (Acts 13:48).

A few verses later, Luke sees a more down-to-earth explanation for the compelling sermon: "Now at Iconium, they entered together into the Jewish synagogue and spoke in such a way that a great number of both Jews and Greeks believed" (Acts 14:1). So many people responded in faith to the apostolic message because Paul and Barnabas "spoke in such a way" that they felt compelled to respond. Paul describes the same dynamic in his first epistle to the Corinthians:

> If, therefore, the whole church comes together and all speak in tongues, and outsiders or unbelievers enter, will they not say that you are out of your minds? But if all *prophecy* and an unbeliever or outsider enters, he is convicted by all; *he* is called to account by all, the secrets of his heart are disclosed ... (1 Cor. 14:23-25).

Notice the human element at play here: "If all prophesy and an unbeliever or outsider enters, he is convicted *by all*, he is called to account *by all*"—not just by God—by all of you! Yet, behind the prophet's words, another personality is at work, revealing His presence, exposing hearts, reaching out to the darkness, and so, Paul says, the hearer will fall on his face, worshipping God and declaring, "God is really among you" (v. 25).

We should craft our pulpit speech to honor both sides of this dynamic. Wasn't that Peter's point? "Whoever speaks, is to do so as one who is speaking the utterances of God..." (1 Pet. 4:11, NASB95). To obey this command, we must consider what we say (words and sentence structure) and how we say it (tone of voice and rhetorical phrases). How we speak matters; Paul knew this. In his letter to the Corinthians, when he eschewed rhetoric, Paul wasn't arguing for careless preaching, as if our only role in preaching was to shovel truths haphazardly at our hearers, expecting the Holy Spirit to make up for our dull, lifeless efforts. In his excellent commentary on 1 Corinthians, David Garland points out that Paul's point here is not to condemn an artful, effective presentation of the Gospel, but the kind that focuses merely on tickling the ears of man, impressing the hearer and leaning upon human eloquence as the secret of our success.[9]

Praise God, the Holy Spirit makes up for what we can't do, but we should not expect Him to do what we won't do or are too lazy to do! I remember hearing of a young student almost boast of his refusal to study to an older, wiser minister: "God has no need for my learning," the young preacher said. "Yes, son," the old man replied, "But he has still less need of your ignorance!" We might say the same about the study of rhetoric.

Paul was not a boring preacher. He could have just said, "You know God is very wise," but he did not. He said, "Oh, the depths of the riches both of the wisdom and the knowledge of God" (Rom. 11:33). Feel the pathos here. How are we to accomplish this effectively? While this is neither the time nor the place for an extended treatment of rhetoric, here are some fundamental guidelines:

First, we should preach in the oral style, which means using plenty of short sentences (ten words or less) full of non-technical, vivid, everyday words that most of our hearers will understand. Our pulpit speech should be clear, simple, and straightforward. Say what you mean and mean what you say. As one wit put it, "Instead of describing a tertiary number of visually impaired rodents, we should probably just say, three blind mice!" Dr. Reeder was supremely gifted here. Listen to his preaching; you will hear a natural cadence and rhythm in almost every sentence, compelling an audience to listen. Sentences need to sound well if they are to be heard well. Many men struggle to do this through a keyboard, making their pulpit speech sound clumsy, complicated, and hard to follow. If you are writing a manuscript, speak as you type or type as you speak. I have known some preachers pace around their office, preaching their sermon into a voice recorder, which they then type up later.

---

9. David E. Garland, *1 Corinthians*, Baker Exegetical Commentary on the New Testament (Grand Rapids, MI: Baker Academic, 2003), p. 82.

Second, the active voice should be used whenever possible lest the congregation be confused by lengthy sentences filled with passive verbs. No! Don't confuse your people with long sentences full of passive verbs. Use active ones instead!

Third, remember the rule of threes. The human ear loves to hear things grouped in threes. God is holy, holy, holy. The Messiah's throne is high, lifted up, and greatly exalted. When God describes human evil, He often speaks of the triad of iniquity, transgression, and sin. In like manner, asking, "Are you discouraged, cast down, at the end of your tether?" sounds better than just one, two, or four phrases. Of course, as with any good thing, don't overdo this!

Fourth, rhythm and sound matter. English teachers always remind their students to write for the ear rather than the eye. This is especially true for spoken discourse. Preachers who rely on manuscripts must be careful here (see point #1). Using repeated language can help with rhetorical rhythm. Who can forget Winston Churchill's rousing speech: "We shall fight in France, we shall fight on the seas and oceans, we shall fight on the beaches, we shall fight on the landing grounds, we shall never surrender."[10] The repetition of "We shall fight" has a mesmerizing cadence that pulls the hearer in, preparing them for the climactic, "We shall never surrender!"

Fifth, learn to ask the congregation questions. Dr. Reeder did this constantly when he preached, keeping the listener engaged, forcing him to be self-reflective and to stay connected to the message. God loves asking questions: "Adam, where are you?"; "Who told you that you were naked?"; "Have you eaten from the tree from which I commanded you not to eat?"; "What is this that you have done?" (Gen. 3). Then, in the next chapter: "Cain, why has your face fallen?"; "Where is your brother?" (Gen. 4).[11]

Sixth, condense your words into short, memorable, well-balanced phrases. The Bible is packed with these—take the

---

10. Winston Churchill, "We shall fight on the beaches", Hansard vol 361, 1940.
11. To grow in your ability here, I commend an excellent book by John Carrick: *The Imperative of Preaching: A Theology of Sacred Rhetoric* (Edinburgh: Banner of Truth, 2016).

whole book of Proverbs, for example, not to mention the Book of Psalms: "For the LORD knows the way of the righteous, but the way of the wicked will perish!" Notice how the sentence begins and ends with a balanced contrast (parallelism). Paul uses the same technique constantly: "But I say, walk by the Spirit, and you will not gratify the desires of the flesh" (Gal. 5:16), or "Do not be deceived: God is not mocked, for whatever one sows, that will he also reap" (Gal. 6:7).

As with so many of the parts of effective preaching, Dr. Reeder was a master here. Some of the phrases he immortalized include:

- The root, the shoot, and the fruit of Christian growth.
- The importance of staying "On Mission, on message, and in ministry."
- We are called to be the light of the world, not the light of the Church.
- The Gospel is the Christian life's Foundation, Formation, and Motivation.
- The world is not your measuring stick; it's your mission field.
- You'll never be outside His secret will if you are inside His revealed will.
- How does the world measure effective ministry? Nickels, noses, and noise!

Following similar principles, Donald Macleod spoke of Christ's three "becomings": "He became flesh. He became Sin. Then, before it was all said and done, He became cursed." Macleod also had a memorable way to describe the incarnation, adapted slightly here, "Without ceasing to be what He had always been, He became something He had never been before."[12]

The Puritan Thomas Watson described the cross as "An ocean of wrath without a drop of mercy." In like manner, he spoke of the terrible scramblings when a rich miser dies: "The worms are scrambling for his body; his family are scrambling for his money; and the devils are scrambling for his soul."[13]

Some of my attempts to stand on Harry's shoulders and follow his example include:

---

12. Donald Macleod, *The Person of Christ*, ed. Gerald Bray, Contours of Christian Theology, (Downers Grove, IL: InterVarsity Press, 1998), 186.

13. I heard these quotes long ago, and can't quite place their original source.

If we are to live a way we have never lived before, we must learn to think a way we have never thought before.

In Ephesians 4:17 and the following verses, Paul outlines the three steps of worldliness as empty heads, hard hearts, and filthy lives.

You can't climb Jacob's ladder with golden weights tied around your ankles!

Effective preaching comes from the heart of God, through the heart of the preacher, and to the heart of the congregation.

Powerful Application

Preaching isn't preaching until it gets to meddling. We must not be content with a surface-level approach, but we must rub the truth of God's Word like ointment into the soul. To do this well, the preacher must be a skilled student of the human heart and the well-beaten paths leading away from Christ to the citadel of self. He must be adept at applying the truth of God to his own burdens, problems, disappointments, doubts, and fears. To be effective in the pulpit, the pastor must supply precious remedies to Satan's devices. He must know how in every temptation, as Thomas Brooks put it, Satan presents the bait and hides the hook; how he presents the passing moment of greater weight than eternal glory; how he fights tooth and nail to keep us off our knees; how he strives to undermine our assurance; how he works to attack weakness, spread doubt, and sweeten sin.

Effective application often comes to mind if we remember to ask the right questions: Why do I struggle to believe this truth? How does this passage rebuke me? How does it set my thinking, speaking, and living straight? How could this truth help me to grow as a Christian? What relevance does this truth have to the unbeliever: the hardened, skeptical unbeliever, the complacent unbeliever, and the awakened unbeliever? What about the Christian? How does this truth apply as they mature from child to teen to college student, young married, and finally to parent? How will this truth help those struggling through a midlife crisis as life's morning turns to afternoon? What about those entering the autumn years of retirement or those winter years as they await the last enemy? Does it have anything to say to the depressed, discouraged, and downcast? How might this truth impact and encourage the tried and tested Christian? In many instances, to ask these questions from the text is to answer them.

The sermon must overwhelm and conquer the status quo—which in pig Latin means "the mess we are in!" Truths are to be enjoyed, promises trusted, commandments obeyed, warnings heeded, and threats are to be taken seriously. Above all, Christ is there to be known! Sometimes, the most effective application comes as we paint Christ's glory, beauty, and kindness before the hearer—leaving him saying, "Hallelujah, what a Savior!"

Experiential Delivery

As things appear to me, the great need of the hour is for preaching that moves the affections—preaching that comes from the heart of God, through the heart of the preacher, and to the heart of the congregation.

As we approach any text of Scripture, four affections must be considered. The affections of God Himself, the affections of the human beings in the passage (including the man Christ Jesus), the affections of the preacher, and finally, the affections of the hearer. Let's consider these one at a time.

First, the affections of God. Say, for example, we are preaching John 3:16; we should meditate on the astounding love of God for a world lost in the darkness, a world that hates Him. These are not easy people to love: they love darkness rather than the light (John 3:18), are dead in transgressions and sins (Eph. 2:1), and are ruled and governed by lust (1 John 2:15-17). As you muse on thoughts like these, pray your heart will burn.

Suppose the text has darker overtones, like the outrage of the Spirit (Heb. 10:29). In that case, we should consider the appalling ingratitude of a professing Christian, so eager to get away from God and out of the Church that he is ready to trample the Son under foot to reach the exit. Meditate on this until you feel some measure of outrage yourself, and also conviction at times (hopefully long in the rearview mirror) when you have committed this same sin yourself.

Second is the affections of any human beings in the text. Is Jesus reaching out His hand to touch a leper? Feel Christ's compassion for this man. This was not an easy move for Christ. From His earliest days, His mother, Mary, had conditioned the Messiah to touch neither unclean things nor unclean people. To do so would have contaminated Him. "Son," she would have told Him, "Touch a leper, and you'll become a leper." Touching the leper was a Gethsemane moment for Jesus. He had to steel Himself, reach through His godly revulsion of uncleanness, and touch this man's dirty head with His own clean hand. Think about this until you feel it deep down in your soul. How do we feel in such moments? Do you find it easy to touch unclean things, like cockroaches? It is not easy for us, and it was not easy for the Savior.

Why did Jesus touch this man in the first place? After all, He didn't need to touch him with His hand; He cleansed him with His word. Could it be that Christ wanted to show the man, more than His willingness to receive Him, that He was willing to become him (2 Cor. 5:21)? What compassion, gentleness, and meekness welled up in the Savior's heart at this moment!

We should also try to put ourselves in the leper's shoes. What was it like to be a leper in the first century—cut off from God, from kith and kin, and from hearth and home? Imagine the day he discovered the cursed spot, his wife's reaction, his children's fear, the priest examining him—with all the compassion of a vet examining the dead carcass of a rat! Why did the leper say, "If you are willing, you can make me clean!" What fears lay behind this question? Questions like these prepare us to preach a compassionate Savior to those who desperately need Him.

We should, thirdly, consider our affections as preachers. Let Jeremiah's testimony be the target after which we aim: "If I say, 'I will not mention him, or speak anymore in his name,' there is in my heart as it were a burning fire shut up in my bones, and I am weary with holding it in, and I cannot" (Jer. 20:9).

So many forces should conspire to move the deep wellsprings of a preacher's soul. We should be affected by the weightiness of God. Looking into the bright abyss of the divine majesty, with Augustine, we should find ourselves saying, "I can see the depths. I just can't see the bottom!"[14] We should also feel the glory of Golgotha. As Professor Fred Leahy described Gethsemane, "[The Cross] is not a place for hurried theological tourism. Here, the believer must linger, watch, and pray."[15]

We should also be affected by the task at hand and by our inability to accomplish it. The goal of the pastoral office is not to make sermons, entertain goats, or enliven what might otherwise be a relatively boring thirty-five-to-forty-minute segment of the service. No, we are called to bid dying souls, live; blind souls, see; deaf souls, hear; lame souls, dance; and the willing slaves of sin, be free. And all we have to effect this change are words. If this knowledge doesn't move us to cry out to God for help from the sanctuary, I am not sure what will.

Every preacher should also be deeply moved by the vast and solemn scenes of final judgment—first for ourselves and then for our hearers. This was the thrust of Paul's final counsel to his young understudy, Timothy:

> I charge you in the presence of God and of Christ Jesus, who is to judge the living and the dead, and by his appearing and his kingdom: preach the word; be ready in season and out of season; reprove, rebuke, and exhort, with complete patience and teaching. For the time is coming when people will not endure sound teaching, but having itching ears they will accumulate for themselves teachers to suit their own passions, and will turn away from listening to the truth and wander off into myths. As for you, always be sober-minded, endure suffering, do the work of an evangelist, fulfill your ministry. For I am already being poured out as a drink offering, and the time of my departure has come. I have fought the good fight, I have finished the race, I have kept the faith. Henceforth there is laid up for me the crown of righteousness, which the Lord, the righteous judge, will award to me on that day, and not only to me but also to all who have loved his appearing (2 Tim. 4:1-8).

---

14. Augustine of Hippo, *Sermons*, The Complete Works of Saint Augustine: A Translation for the 21st Century, ed. John E. Rotelle, (New City Press, 1991), 3.2.108.

15. Frederick Leahy, *The Cross He Bore: Meditations on the Sufferings of the Redeemer* (Edinburgh: Banner of Truth, 1996).

James' words should sear our hearts: "Not many of you should become teachers, my brothers, for you know that we who teach will be judged with greater strictness" (Jas. 3:1). Notice he does not say, "Were it not for the doctrine of justification by faith alone in Christ alone we should be wary of entering the pastoral ministry; for were it not for the cross, we would receive a stricter judgment." There are no ifs, ands, or buts in James' language. It is a sobering statement.

Third, we must also be affected by our message. As with nature, so in grace, the river rarely rises higher than the spring. The sermon will rarely affect the people more than it has affected the preacher. The preacher must, therefore, feel himself confronted by the Divine majesty, overwhelmed by His limitless being, stretched and enlightened by His truth, enticed by His goodness, sobered by His warnings, arrested by His justice, stunned by His wisdom, and enthralled by His glory. Sincerity is key. The best way to sound enthralled with God is, quite simply, to be enthralled with Him. If we are to preach the loveliness of Christ, we must first sense and taste some of that loveliness for ourselves. Our Sermon must, therefore, have answered questions we ask, solved problems we face, eased burdens we carry, warmed the coldness we feel, and conquered the doubts with which we wrestle. The last thing any of us should feel in the pulpit is nothing.

The surest path to feeling God behind the sacred desk is to meet Him on our knees in the study. As Charles Simeon observed, "No amount of homiletical technique can make up for the want of a close, personal walk with God."[16] As Dr. Reeder liked to remind us, "When it comes to Christian ministry, godliness trumps giftedness all day, every day, and twice on Sundays."

As a rule, only when the sermon becomes a felt reality for us will it become a felt reality for our hearers. It is almost impossible to pretend genuine earnestness. How many of us could go home now to our house and pretend to call our wives and children to

---

16. John Stott's introduction in *Evangelical Preaching: An Anthology of Sermons by Charles Simeon*, ed. James Houston (Vancouver: Regent College Publishing, 2003).

escape the flames and run for their lives? Why? Well, because our houses are not on fire. But if we smelt the smoke, saw the flames, and felt the heat, the emergency would lend a natural, earnest eloquence to everything we said. This is the grand secret of moving men to God: we must first be moved by God and to God ourselves. Until that happens, our words will sound like one raising the alarm over a pretend fire. Baxter described the dynamic well:

> What! Speak coldly for God, and for men's salvation? Can we believe that our people must be converted or condemned, and yet speak in a drowsy tone? In the name of God, brethren labour to awaken your own hearts, before you go to the pulpit, that you may be fit to awaken the hearts of sinners. Remember they must be awakened or damned, and that a sleepy preacher will hardly awaken drowsy sinners. Though you give the holy things of God the highest praises in words, yet, if you do it coldly, you will seem by your manner to unsay what you said in the matter. It is a kind of contempt of great things, especially of so great things, to speak of them without much affection and fervency. The manner, as well as the words, must set them forth....[17]

Finally, under this head, as we preach, we should consider the affections of our hearers. We must persuade their minds, awaken their consciences, stir their hearts, and storm their wills. To do this effectively, we must know our people. It is very difficult, if not actually impossible, to preach regularly to people you are not pastoring. Like shepherding, preaching is a hands-on job; it cannot be done at a distance.

We must also feel our union with our people in Christ. In a way far beyond my capacity to describe, their burdens really are our burdens. We should preach to our people the way we pray for them—remembering their cancer is our cancer, their spouse suffering the early ravages of Alzheimer's disease is our spouse, their struggle is our struggle, and their pain is our pain. We must

---

17. Richard Baxter and William Orme, *The Practical Works of the Rev. Richard Baxter* (London: James Duncan, 1830), 14:183.

preach to help them—to make every burden lighter, every promise sweeter, every shadow just a little bit brighter.

It is tough to communicate like this while reading a manuscript. If preaching is to be a heart-to-heart business, it must surely be a face-to-face—an eye-to-eye business. If we can't remember what we want to say, how on earth are the people to have any hope of remembering it? Many, no doubt, fear that preaching extemporaneously will mean sacrificing the quality of the content—and, let's be honest, it will. But, they fail to consider that preaching from a manuscript will almost inevitably mean sacrificing something even more critical—the note of personal communication. When most men read from a manuscript I feel as if I am being spoken at, as if the preacher is talking to everyone in general and no one in particular. Compare that to Daniel Webster's desire: "When a man preaches to me, I want him to make it a personal matter, a personal matter, a personal matter." Please speak *to* your people, not *at* them. You must look them in the eye and speak from your heart to do this.

A Prayerful Preacher

As we have repeatedly said in this essay, the best preparation for helping men towards a close walk with God is to walk closely with God ourselves. I never tire of hearing Alistair Begg summarize his method of sermon preparation: "First, I think myself empty, then I read myself full, I write myself clear, I pray myself hot, and then I let myself go."[18]

Let me leave you with a delightful quote from E.M. Bounds:

> The preacher may feel from the kindling of his own sparks, be eloquent over his own exegesis, earnest in delivering the product of his own brain; the professor may usurp the place and imitate the fire of the apostle; brains and nerves may serve the place and feign the work of God's Spirit, and by these forces the letter may glow and sparkle like an illumined text, but the glow and sparkle will be as barren of life as the field sown with pearls. The death-dealing element lies back of the words, back of the sermon, back of

---

18. Alistair Begg, *Preaching for God's Glory* (Wheaton: Crossway, 2010).

the occasion, back of the manner, back of the action. The great hindrance is in the preacher himself. He has not in himself the mighty life-creating forces. There may be no discount on his orthodoxy, honesty, cleanness, or earnestness; but somehow the man, the inner man, in its secret places has never broken down and surrendered to God, his inner life is not a great highway for the transmission of God's message, God's power. Somehow self and not God rules in the holy of holiest. Somewhere, all unconscious to himself, some spiritual nonconductor has touched his inner being, and the divine current has been arrested. His inner being has never felt its thorough spiritual bankruptcy, its utter powerlessness; he has never learned to cry out with an ineffable cry of self-despair and self-helplessness till God's power and God's fire comes in and fills, purifies, empowers. Self-esteem, self-ability in some pernicious shape has defamed and violated the temple which should be held sacred for God. Life-giving preaching costs the preacher much—death to self, crucifixion to the world, the travail of his own soul. Crucified preaching only can give life. Crucified preaching can come only from a crucified man.[19]

As preachers, we go forward on our knees or shall not go forward at all. For the health of our souls, the warmth of our words, and the vitality of our ministry, we must carve out space every day for unhurried time on our knees with the Father, through the Son, and by the Spirit. Although, at times, it can be surprising how well a man can seem to preach without such discipline, in a way that's 'better felt than telt,' the Sheep can always 'smell' a pastor who's been around the Good Shepherd.

Conclusion

In the life of a minister, you can measure the progress of self-crucifixion by whether the people leave the sermon impressed by the gifts of the preacher or with the glory of Jesus. Following John the Baptist, a crucified man should feel himself "decreasing" under the weight of glory until the congregation is left seeing none but Jesus only—Jesus, the heir of all things, through whom God made the cosmos; Jesus, the radiance of the glory of God and the exact

---

19. Edward M. Bounds, *Power through Prayer* (Oak Harbor, WA: Logos Research Systems, Inc., 1999), found near the end of chapter two, "Our Sufficiency is of God."

imprint of His nature; Jesus the one who upholds the universe by the word of His power; Jesus; the faithful witness, the firstborn from the dead, and the ruler of the kings of the earth; Jesus, the sinner's friend, who laid down His life for us all; Jesus, who holds the keys of death of heaven and of hell; Jesus, whose face shines like the sun in its strength, whose voice is like the sound of many waters; Jesus, on mission, on message, and in ministry.

This will be my enduring memory of Dr. Reeder's ministry: when I listened to him, I heard a man point away from himself to Another. And when I came away from the message, I was not left saying, "What a great preacher!"—but rather, declaring with renewed abandon, "My goodness, what a Savior! Isn't He lovely!"

3

The Primacy of Lord's Day Worship

John E. Haines

"If I could get you to conduct the congregation the way you conduct the choir, we might get some worship going on in here!" He chuckled, swung his arm around my shoulder, and then, with the lowered but reassuring voice of a father coaching his son on the pitcher's mound, he instructed me on my primary biblical calling—to serve the congregation's corporate voice in worship. This was the first of many practical worship directives I received from Pastor Harry Reeder. I was a twenty-nine-year-old classically trained musician, who had little church experience and no theological training. Harry probably had no business hiring me; but he was the consummate talent scout, always searching for individuals who loved the Lord Jesus Christ, wanted to serve the Church, and were teachable (and I needed the teaching!). In my initial interview with the Session, I was asked if I had any exceptions to the Westminster Confession of Faith. I wasn't sure what the Confession was. "You have read it, haven't you?" asked a confounded elder. "Well, not for bedtime reading," I snickered alone. The room fell silent. Sensing that an interrogative brawl was about to erupt, Harry loudly asserted, "Men, I'm sure John is committed to receiving the necessary theological training commensurate to his biblical calling." His direct and commanding stare at me evoked my involuntary response, "Yessir, absolutely!" I was enrolled in seminary shortly thereafter.

The Biblical principles of my calling as a worship leader were a recurring theme of Harry's mentorship. He considered a formal education in Reformed theology to be foundational, but his personal instruction was pragmatic. He focused on the practical matters of worship where theology is expressed through Godly leadership. This essay will focus on three of those over-arching biblical principles of worship leadership: (1) holiness; (2) the Lord's Day; (3) shepherding souls.

Practicing Personal Holiness

Harry modeled holiness, but he made frequent, direct, and solemn exhortations to us as young ministers. In my first interview with him, we met in his car in the parking lot of a Denny's in South Carolina: "John, before we go any further in this process, I need to know that you've made obedience to the Lord from His Word, a *lifestyle*. As a worship leader, Satan is going to put a target on your back. I need to know now if you have anything in your life that would disqualify you from public ministry."

Harry never revisited that question. However, he began each of our weekly worship planning sessions by asking about my marriage. He considered the marital relationship as the holiness barometer. He would reference Paul's exhortation in Ephesians 5:25, "Husbands love your wives as Christ loved the Church and gave Himself up for her." Or he'd say, "John, the most important gift you'll ever give to your children, is how you treat Jenny. That will determine whether the faith you confess publicly is what they will own personally." Harry quizzed each member of the pastoral staff with the same questions in their individual meetings. The weekly group meetings started in prayer, most frequently on our knees, followed by the same questions and exhortations. Harry was predictable and repetitive. A person could ask, "When did Harry get down to the business of ministry planning?" For Harry, a character of holiness in obedience to the Word of God *was* the business. From there, the necessary planning followed.

If Harry considered marriage the true measure of a pastor's personal holiness, then the honoring of the Lord's Day is the public measure. Harry was a man of principle. In fact, he was annoyingly principled. And he disciplined himself to live scrupulously by every principle he believed. I remember an elder grumbling one time about Harry's decision on whether to wear a robe or not. He complained, "To Harry, everything is a principle!" But the principle of principles, the non-negotiable principle of life, was honoring the Sabbath, the Lord's Day. Harry delighted in the Lord's Day like no one I've ever known. His delight was contagious. He poured out as much time and energy preparing for the evening sermon as he did the morning, and he demanded of me that I do the same with the music. We strived together for the same standards of excellence, but the services differed in directional emphasis. In the morning, he crafted a Reformed liturgy structure that emphasized the Lord's transcendence. In the evening, the liturgy emphasized His immanence.

Honoring the Lord's Day

Harry loved all the Lord's Day services, but he had an affinity for the evening service. That affinity easily overruled many ideas and initiatives that Harry sensed encroaching that would bring any competition with true biblical worship. A couple of times in the early 1990s, the church tried to raise several million dollars for a sanctuary, with only a modicum of success. So, the Session decided to hire a nationally known and highly successful church fundraising consultant. He was a tall-strutting Texan who wore expensive boots, a huge white cowboy hat, and possessed a Texas-sized sales personality to go along with it. He was inspirational and brought energy to what had become a stale campaign. Everything seemed to point toward the beginnings of a highly successful initiative. Then, one day while glancing out the window of the choir room, I saw him leaving the building across campus where Harry's office was located. He was walking slowly back to his car, slump-shouldered and dejected looking—like a teenage boy who got dumped by his high school sweetheart. He drove off, and we never saw him again. Months later, I had the nerve to ask Harry, "Whatever happened to that guy?" The Harry-esque look of determination suddenly set like concrete on his face. With pursed lips, raised eyebrow, and his head cocked slightly my way, he said, "He didn't like the way I emphasized the evening worship. It was getting in the way of his ability to raise funds." And as you can imagine, that was the end of that. Two years later, by the way, we were breaking ground on the new sanctuary, with a Sessional call to congregational fasting, prayer, and personal commitment. Adults and children alike gathered outside to pray and solemnly place stones onto an "Ebenezer Pile," where they had inscribed their names and commitment Scriptures. That pile remains behind the sanctuary to this very day—a testament to God's faithfulness.

Next to actual worship on the Lord's Day itself, planning the Lord's Day service with Harry was the highlight of my week. I used to say there was so much energy as we met in the small McDonald's "dining room," that the tables started shaking. However, it wasn't just creative energy that we experienced, but the energy that came from the Holy Spirit filling us as we prayed and read the Word. Harry would take me through his sermon highlights, and we would pour through liturgical Psalms and Catechism questions. This was far from being a stale meeting between a Sr. Pastor and the church musician where we checked the obligatory liturgy boxes. No, this was a meeting where, as creative as I was, as much as I loved worship, and as much as I was supposed to be the church worship expert—I was out-gunned, out-manned, and out-passioned by the Sr. Pastor! He loved everything in every element of every service. He was into every detail with profound delight. Some might think that made Harry a micro-manager, but he was far from it. Rather, Harry was the quintessential macro-manager, who loved both micro- and macro-worship planning. He looked at those who planned worship with him as worship soulmates. He loved being inspiring, and he loved being inspired. Colleagues of mine were sometimes in situations where they worked for Sr. Pastors who could suck the creative air out of a room faster than it could be replaced. What little inspiration existed in a planning session, there was even less present in the worship itself. These pastors did not share Harry's conviction of what the primacy of the pulpit was all about.

Harry's philosophy was simple: The primacy of the pulpit did not mean the primacy of the man. Rather, it meant the primacy of the Word and the Preaching of the Word. The primacy of the pulpit was the fulcrum on which the rest of the service balanced, like the Archimedes model. This is thoroughly Reformed. The pulpiteer, the man called to serve at the pulpit, was also called to serve the liturgy. In practical application, Harry was the true Worship Director. He had to be, because as Sr. Pastor, who else could that be? Harry believed that the only logical way a Sr. Pastor could serve God's people well is by serving the liturgy well. The worship department's job was to serve the pulpit; and my job, technically speaking, was more accurately viewed as "Assistant to the Worship Pastor." My job was to assist the Sr. Pastor.

Other pastors and musicians I spoke with over the years would initially chafe at that description, but it worked for two reasons. First, there can only be one boss. The role of Sr. Pastor carries with it the responsibility to be the "boss," so to speak, of the worship. Harry took that role seriously. He recognized that the risen and ascended Christ was the true worship leader (Heb. 2:12), and that his job was to lead under Him faithfully. If he abrogates that role or assigns it to someone else, then someone else is at the helm. Second, it worked because of the operative word, "serve." If there were two words that Harry wore out like a pair of good old shoes, they were "serve" and "service." I coined an adage that summed up Harry's biblically-inspired philosophy of worship leadership: The worship department serves the Lord well, by serving His people well, by serving the pulpit well. Like any other professional relationship, we had our differences of opinion. However, it was the biblical principles of service, and of loving submission, that governed our leadership to reflect the beauty of unity and cooperation.

Our collegial relationship in worship planning was the envy of many of my colleagues. I cannot begin to count the times when, after a service or a concert, I was complimented on something that was sung or presented that showcased Jesus Christ, touched souls, and was magnificent in its presentation. I'd almost always respond with, "Thank you. That was Harry's idea!" But as excited as Harry would get with the music or creative ideas, these were not the basis for worship or its planning. Worship planning with Harry was built from the ground up on the Scriptures, which is true to our Reformed and Presbyterian heritage. This was a non-negotiable, and the principle of all principles! The Scriptures were foundational to begin, end, and permeate all worship planning.

Harry would, of course, frequently reference the Westminster Confession or the Shorter and Larger Catechisms. He loved the ancient Creeds and Confessions. He loved liturgy. He loved the magisterial Reformation. He loved anything that was rooted in the regality of Reformed tradition. But none of these things were the starting point for worship planning. Neither was his sermon, or the music, or the particular Sunday in the Church Calendar that we observed. His conscience was not bound by any of this. His conscience was bound to the Word of God alone. Scripture was where he moored himself. The entire service—every element, every hymn, every transition, every consideration for refinement or adaptation—had to pass through the filter of the Scripture's teaching. He had an instant, internal alarm system that sounded if he sensed something was not going to pass muster with the Scriptures.

Those of us who worked closely with Harry could see in his facial expression this instant notification in his conscience. We could see it as we presented new ideas or initiatives for worship. If Harry had a weakness, it was his love of new ideas and entrepreneurism. Whenever I would propose a new idea, if it passed Harry's Scripture sniff test, his face would light up like a kid in a toy store. His enthusiasm would ignite; he'd interrupt my presentation with his own; he'd augment and sometimes re-invent my proposal into something entirely different; then he'd suddenly look at his watch, and seeing he was now late for a meeting, he would abruptly close in prayer, tell me what a great idea I had and march off to his next appointment. Meanwhile, I was left drowning in a tsunami of directives, tasks, and a vision with far loftier expectations than I thought we could pull off.

If I made a proposal where he sensed the slightest potential compromise to the Scripture's commands, he would sit there listening, patiently listening, respectfully, with an agonizing attentiveness. As I talked, I knew this idea was probably destined for a Christian burial. When I was finished, he'd take a deep breath, look up thoughtfully, and say one of two things: "Mmm-hmm ... well, John, I love your enthusiasm and creativity ... but what about the Second Commandment? That's where I'm struggling a bit." Or, "I'm just wondering if this is something that would honor the Lord's Day ... it's the Fourth Commandment that I'm struggling with on this one, John." At that point, I could hear air hissing from my proposal like a new tire with a side wall puncture. Another great idea would be tossed out the back door (there's a big pile of those, by the way!). But what is important to remember is this: Harry was not the one who jabbed the tire but the Holy Spirit, with the Sword of the scriptures, in Harry's heart and mind.

Long before Harry was planning worship services, he had submitted to the tenets of Reformed doctrine, where biblical teachings about the Holy Spirit's work are pervasive. Question and answer 89 of the Westminster Shorter Catechism states, "The Spirit of God makes the reading, but especially the preaching, of the Word, an effective means of convicting and converting sinners." Harry believed that, since this was true, the entire service was made effective by the Holy Spirit. He believed that if the Bible and the preaching were to be in the vernacular of the people so that they could hear and understand the Holy Spirit, then the entire service needed to be in their vernacular.

I doubt anyone in our Presbyterian circles would take issue with that theologically since that's pure Reformed teaching. But in practice, Harry took issue with those who imposed their personal preferences on congregations, while calling them biblical principles. He believed that they were violating biblical principles in doing so. Yet, he also believed that the wise use of preferences was the key to touching souls in any church culture. Harry was the master of assessing cultural preferences and embedding them meaningfully and understandably within the liturgy. The elements of worship were vital and fixed, but the circumstances were flexible.

In our worship planning meetings, he labored over whether his sermon, the music, or the verbal transitions between elements were understandable to the average person in the pew. Every Monday, he made himself vulnerable to the three of us pastors in worship planning with, "Men, now I am not looking for compliments, please, I need some guidance here. Did you understand the final point of the sermon? Do you think the people got it, or did I not make things clear enough?"

After making himself vulnerable and taking whatever feedback we would give, he would look at me and say something like, "John, the music was great, but you need to remember that our people don't come to church necessarily prepared to receive what that set of hymns is about. I think you need to set the context of those hymns with a Scripture transition and a short, verbal directive that ties the previous and coming elements together in the liturgical theme." Or he would direct one of the other pastors to carefully pray and think through how their prayers, verbal transitions, explanation of the sacraments, etc., relationally move people. "We don't want to be talking just to talk," he would say. "We want to guide people with emotional intelligence from one element to another so that there is a congruence, a cognitive and relational flow."

I'll never forget how our meeting began the day after a major Christmas pageant: "John, that was simply the best Christmas program we have ever had. You really outdid yourself on this one, buddy." Then he looked at me with the look that I knew was going to be encouragingly, yet unequivocally directive and said, "Brother. Dear Brother. You spent a lot of time arranging and orchestrating that music, didn't you? It was simply superb!" Then he breathed deeply, and gently but firmly stated, "John, I want you to hear me now. The music was magnificent, but that style of music isn't who we are, and it isn't who Birmingham is. I need you to figure out how to speak to *this* musical culture, not just what you like. They aren't going to come out and hear the Gospel in this town for that kind of music. Now I'm not saying there's not a place for it, there certainly is. But this particular concert must draw people in for the Gospel. And the music that the people relate to will be the draw."

I don't think I've ever left a meeting feeling so good and so course-corrected for kingdom effectiveness. I was frustrated with myself that I'd been blinded by my own preferences. Yet, true to his mentoring style, he made a pest out of himself afterward in encouragement. He gave me a list of music that he knew would speak to the hearts of our people. And he taught me once again, even late in my ministry career, that the key to speaking to souls in their vernacular was serving within the context of cultural preferences. It was hard to pin him down on any liturgical or musical style preference because he so freely ministered in the extremes of traditional, contemporary, or blended styles. If he had a global preferential ethic, it was that shepherding en masse was communicated lovingly through humbling oneself to the preferences of the people.

The Importance of Shepherding

Harry considered shepherding a mandate for himself and for every staff person. I remember thinking, "I'm the music and worship director, I don't have time to shepherd." He never instructed me in shepherding. He confronted me with names and situations at the beginning of most of our meetings: "John, did you visit George? Did you know he had surgery?"; "John, is Alice's son still in the orchestra? Have you followed up on him?" John this person and

John that person. As a pastoral staff person, you quickly learned two things about Harry and shepherding. First, whomever you visited, prayed for, emailed, or called, Harry had already been there. Second, you did not want to be in a meeting where you were caught not having an answer to Harry's question, "How's so and so?" or "Have you gotten to the Smith's home yet?" Harry rarely displayed a look of incredulity. But few things provoked it more than pastors and directors not shepherding their people. Many men who claimed not to have the gift for shepherding suddenly possessed it after being confronted on the matter by Harry.

Shepherding the people in each official or unofficial sub-group that stemmed from the Lord's Day corporate worship—whether it was the choir, orchestra, Sunday School, Bible Study, or recurring business team of some sort—was the lifeblood of the church. It was the lifeblood of corporate worship because Harry believed that all worship was fundamentally relational. If we loved the Lord with all our heart, soul, mind, and strength, and loved our neighbor as ourselves (Mark 12:30-31), then this command would be tangibly felt and seen in shepherding. There were no excuses for doing otherwise. Harry was the busiest pastor I've ever known. So no one could say, "I'm too busy." No one could say, "I'm not gifted." Because Harry, although a deep lover of people, was not the tenderest of hearts. Yet I never knew anyone who worked harder to have a tender heart.

Harry was a private man who didn't disclose a lot of information about the years before he became a Christian. But I used to tell people, "If you feel like a terrible sinner and you need a safe place to confide and receive wise counsel, Pastor Reeder is the man to go to." When I first came to Briarwood, Harry said, "John, the toughest thing about a church this size, is how to make it feel small." He knew I was committed to shepherding the music and worship ministry as he had taught and as my predecessors had done, but he wasn't taking any chances. My very first weekend on staff, he called me into his office on a Saturday morning. He sat with me for at least two hours, reading through every name on the choir, praise team, and orchestral roster, just to tell me who had lost a loved one, who had been in the hospital, who recently had a baby. Until the Lord took Harry to heaven, that shepherding meeting was the longest meeting I'd ever had with him personally.

Just three days before Harry went to be with the Lord, we had our final worship planning meeting with executive pastor Bruce Stallings, and associate pastor Benny Parks. We were concentrating on the services for Ascension Sunday. There was a knock on the door as his assistant, Marie, was reminding him that he was late for something. That was a regular occurrence. After closing in prayer, I asked, "Hey Harry, where are you off to, anyway?" I knew he'd just gotten back from preaching at the Ligonier Conference, was en route at some point to the Alabama State Capital to speak, and had radio spots he was having to record. I knew it was something important. "I'm doing a wedding in my office," he said. The three of us pastors said in unison, "What?!" I laughed as Harry was walking toward the door and said, "Harry! You minister to more people than anyone I've ever known. There has to be two of you!" Harry turned and gave the characteristic half grin and chuckle as he walked out the door. Those were the last words I said to him. A few days later, I received a call from pastor Parks to tell me Harry had gone to be home with the Lord. Even amidst the shock, the picture of him walking out and my words that followed came immediately to mind. But the other picture that came to mind was something that Harry didn't see. I had followed him out the door, stopping briefly to look down the hallway. Through the glass of the receptionist's area, I saw the couple. It was an elderly couple who had experienced significant grief, but to whom the Lord had given each other for marriage late in life. Harry was in his office, putting on his robe, preparing for the sacred ceremony, as if it were a formal wedding in the sanctuary. I remember thinking, "Who's ever going to know that Harry set aside his fancy schedule, to shepherd this couple today quietly?"

Yet, this is exactly what a faithful shepherd does. He counsels, marries, buries, baptizes, and disciples even when he thinks that no one is watching. Harry was this kind of shepherd. Though he was a sought after conference speaker and author, that was not the core of his ministry. Rather, the core of his ministry was modeling the Good Shepherd of John 10 for his congregation, day in and day out and Lord's Day by Lord's Day.

4

The Pastor's Passion for Evangelism

Lessons in Sharing Christ from Dr. Harry L Reeder

Derrick E. Brite

Perhaps since the time of the Great Awakening, the responsibility of evangelism has been segregated away from the everyday life of church members, and assigned to either those uniquely called and gifted for the task or to pastors of a local church. It is certainly true that pastors have a responsibility to evangelize; as Paul charged Timothy, pastors must "do the work of an evangelist" (2 Tim. 4:5). However, as J.I. Packer has correctly written, "Always and everywhere the servants of Christ are under orders to evangelize."[1] Thus, equipping the congregation for the task of evangelism is vital for the long-term health and vitality of the church. This was the Apostle Paul's concern in Ephesians, when he speaks of particular persons (apostles, prophets, etc.) equipping the saints for the work of ministry (Eph. 4:11). Therefore, this chapter will focus upon three key elements of evangelism in order to aid the pastor in equipping his church in this essential work:

---

1. J.I. Packer, *Evangelism and the Sovereignty of God* (Downers Grove: InterVarsity Press, 2008), p. 13.

the *message* of evangelism, the *motivations* for evangelism, and the *methods* of evangelism.[2]

The Message of Evangelism
What the Message Isn't

What is the message of evangelism? A perusal of some common practices could lead one to think that the message of an evangelistic encounter is a personal testimony. A testimony is a useful tool in the evangelist's toolbox, but to make that the primary focus or central message of evangelism is using the wrong tool for the job. A personal testimony is part of the *method*, not the message itself.[3] It is also not obedience to God's moral law. I recall an encounter with an older man who told me his strategy for evangelizing a lost neighbor. He said, "I hand him a copy of the Ten Commandments and I tell him that if he will live by those rules, he'll be fine." What a terrifying and stunningly Christless presentation! For, it is not by the works of the law but by faith alone that we are saved (Gal. 2:16). This was precisely the deception that the rich young ruler was under in Luke 18: "All these I have kept from my youth" (v. 21). Yet, when Jesus called the young man to sell everything he had to follow after Christ, the rich young ruler went away sad. Why? Because his god was really his possessions. He found out that he had not really kept the law; rather he was guilty of breaking the first commandment. And as the brother of our Lord tells us, if you fail in one point of law keeping, then you have become guilty of breaking all of it (James 2:10). Unfortunately, unless Christ intervenes, this poor man will attempt to keep the moral law of God, only to one day have the same encounter with Christ that the rich young ruler had.

---

2. This entire chapter is meant to be practical instruction drawn from the teaching of Harry Reeder. Direct quotations from particular sermons are cited in the footnotes. Although we cannot give full justice to each topic and category presented here, the goal is to give short and practical helps for Christians and their pastors in the task of evangelism. For more study, I recommend two particular sermon series from which these chapters are built upon: *L.E.A.D. in Biblical Perspective* and *Project Andrew*.

3. We will return to the method of using a personal testimony below.

Of course, we should desire, work towards, and encourage moral reform and obedience to the law of God. However, this is a result of the Gospel, not the Gospel itself. To evangelize by proclaiming morals and obedience is to substitute the fruit of faith for the root of faith. Harry Reeder spoke clearly of the hope for and importance of revival in the midst of a decaying culture:

> Why is this important? It's important to me because I am praying for a Gospel awakening in our nation. Because I see this tsunami wave of secular humanism and moral relativism is sweeping across our nation. I know this will be destructive, for I can already see the destruction in families. There is a rising suicide rate and despair. You can't embrace the anarchy of sin and call it good without it having devastating effects. This tsunami wave will ebb someday. You cannot destroy the sanctity of life, marriage, gender, sexuality, and relationships without it producing devastation. What will be left in that day the wave will ebb?[4]

Yet, the danger of secular humanism and the need for reform is not the central message of the Gospel.

What the Message Is

So, what is the message of evangelism? The message, simply put, is the God of the message. It is nothing "except Jesus Christ, and him crucified" (1 Cor. 2:2). This is the central focus of the Christian life. Christ's substitutionary death on the cross in the place of a sinful people is why Christ came. This must be clearly explained in an evangelistic encounter:

> If somebody was to say to you, "I understand you're a Christian, so can you tell me the essential foundational truth of Christianity? Let me be more specific. You say that Jesus is the Son of God who came in the flesh, and this happened two thousand years ago. Would you tell me why? Just give me the bottom line, why did He come?" How would you answer that? It's a good question. It's one that we ought to be able to answer. Why did Jesus come? Jesus came in the incarnation of Christ. That is the Son of God

---

4. Harry Reeder, in a sermon entitled "Everyone Evangelizing Everybody Everyday: Matthew 13:1-8; 18-23" (November 10th, 2019).

in full humanity. He had a human mind. He had a human soul. He had a human body. It was the humbling of the Son of God, not by subtraction, but by addition, as He takes upon Himself a human body. We call this the incarnation. Emmanuel – God with us, God one of us, God among us, to take place of us. Why? To save us from our sins. That is the essential message of the gospel.[5]

It is only this message, the Christian Gospel, which will ultimately have a positive effect on society and bring the true fruit of repentance for a nation that has continued its slide into moral degeneracy, and it is only this Gospel message which can make the sinner acceptable and righteous before God on the day of judgment:

> Therefore there is coming a day where you can participate in the resurrection of the just. Why? It is not because of self-righteousness but because of a Divine righteousness. Romans 1:16-17 says: *"For I am not ashamed of the gospel, for it is the power of God for salvation to everyone who believes, to the Jew first and also to the Greek. For in it the righteousness of God is revealed from faith for faith, as it is written, "The righteous shall live by faith."* So that by His blood my sins are washed away, with His righteousness I am clothed, made acceptable and carried up to glory. God Himself did that for me when He didn't need me; He wanted me; and when I needed Him, I didn't want Him, yet this God has done that work.[6]

The Gospel message is so simple, yet so profound.

This is good news not only for the unbeliever, but also for the one evangelizing. By focusing exclusively on the Gospel as the core message of evangelism, the burden of producing results is removed from the evangelist. Any other message will stoke the fires of doubt and disappointment if a person does not respond to the call of Christ. The would-be zealous evangelist walks away, condemning himself while wondering if he had only been more intelligent, funnier, told another story, or been more engaging

---

5. Harry Reeder, in a sermon entitled "Your Sins Are Forgiven: Mark 2:1-12" (March 12th, 2023).

6. Harry Reeder in a sermon entitled "Christ's Call to Compelling Evangelism: Luke 14:7-24" (September 8th, 2019).

then maybe that sinner would have repented. This places an unnecessary burden on the Christian and fails to recognize the power and role of the Holy Spirit in the conversion of sinners. Rather, as Mark Dever points out, "According to the Bible, converting people is not in our power. And evangelism may not be defined in terms of results but only in terms of faithfulness to the message preached."[7]

The Motivations for Evangelism
Obedient Gratitude

What are proper motives for evangelism? Following the threefold structure of the Heidelberg Catechism—*guilt, grace, gratitude*—believers engage in good works, including evangelism, first and foremost, "so that we may testify, by the whole of our conduct, our gratitude to God for His blessings ..."[8] What are Christians grateful for? Simply, we are grateful for the Gospel of Christ, that while we were yet sinners, Christ died for us (Rom. 5:8). There is no greater gift to receive than salvation. Thus, gratitude for the work of God done in Christ on our behalf is the *primary* but not the singular motive for obedience.

Paul often structures his writings with the pattern of placing the indicative statements before the imperative statements. Or, put another way, Paul gives grand and glorious Gospel truths before he gives specific commands of obedience. In this way, he grounds the believer's obedience and sanctification in the truth of the Gospel itself. This is perhaps seen most clearly in the Book of Romans, where Paul reminds believers that since they have died with Christ, they must now live to God, considering themselves dead to sin and alive to God in Christ Jesus (Rom. 6:11). This argument is further brought out as he spends virtually all of the first eleven chapters expounding the Gospel before touching on

---

7. Mark Dever, *The Gospel and Personal Evangelism* (Wheaton: Crossway, 2007), p. 79.

8. Question and Answer 86 of the Heidelberg Catechism in *Liturgical Forms and Prayers of the United Reformed Churches in North America* (Ontario: The United Reformed Churches in North America, 2018), p. 237.

ethics. The believer must hear "there is now no condemnation" (Rom. 8:1) before he or she hears "present your bodies as a living sacrifice" (Rom. 12:1). As Robert Mounce observes:

> The dynamic of God's ethical instruction arises from its logical and necessary relationship to who he is and what he has done on our behalf. Many of the living religions have an ethical code that uplifts and inspires. Only the Christian faith, rooted as it is in a supernatural act that took place in history (the incarnation, life, death, and resurrection of Jesus Christ), has the ultimate moral authority as well as the effective power to transform human life according to the divine intention.[9]

We joyfully lay down our lives in service to the One who laid His life down for us. This is the pattern for the Christian life. And since there is no greater gift to be thankful for, then there is no greater way to express gratitude for that gift than by leading a life of faithful obedience in evangelism.

The Love of God

Closely related to gratitude is the love of God. God's love has been poured in our hearts through the Holy Spirit (Rom. 5:5). This undeserved love of God shown *to us* in return produces a love for God *in us* which then flows out to our neighbors *from us*. It is natural that those who have been shown the most love will then show the most love to others; and the best way to love others is by sharing the Gospel with them. Love for neighbor naturally flows from our love for God. Augustine helpfully puts it this way:

> Now you love yourself suitably when you love God better than yourself. What, then, you aim at in yourself you must aim at in your neighbor, namely, that he may love God with a perfect affection. For you do not love him as yourself, unless you try to draw him to that good which you are yourself pursuing. For this is the one good which has room for all to pursue it along with thee. From this precept proceed the duties of human society, in which it is hard to keep from error. But the first thing to aim at is, that we should be benevolent, that is, that we cherish no malice and no evil design against another. For man is the nearest neighbor of man.[10]

---

9. Robert H. Mounce, *Romans* (Nashville: B&H Publishing, 1995), p. 230.
10. Augustine, "Morals of the Catholic Church," in *The Nicene and Post-Nicene*

This is made all the more clear if we consider that this love shown to us by the Triune God is not something that can be earned. Rather, we love because He first loved us (1 John 4:19). Some may say this is an unconditional love, but this simply is not the case. As Harry Reeder rightly says,

> He didn't love unconditionally. Jesus loves you by meeting God's conditions to love a sinner.... God's love is unmerited, unwanted, relentless, and undeserved but it is efficient because God Himself met the conditions of 'holy, holy, holy is the Lord God Almighty.'[11]

There is no greater motive than the love of God in Christ which has met every standard of holiness and has now been imputed to us by grace alone.

A Longing to See His Churches Full

The renowned hymn writer Isaac Watts penned these words which express another heartfelt motivation for evangelism:

> We long to see Thy churches full
> That all the chosen race
> May with one voice and heart and soul
> Sing Thy redeeming grace.[12]

Christians are people who long to see churches filled to the brim with people singing praises to the glorious Triune God. In a world that is continuing its downward spiral into sin and rebellion, the idea that churches all around the country could once again be filled may seem like a pipe dream to some. Yet, the promise of evangelism is that God saves His people by the preaching of the Gospel. Evangelism does work, and the more a church is engaged in the ministry of evangelism, the more sinners will come to know Christ, and the more churches will grow. How beautiful a scene is a church filled on the Lord's Day, where tens, dozens,

---

Fathers, vol. 4, ed. Philip Schaff (Peabody, MA: Hendrickson, 1994), p. 55.
   11. Reeder, "Christ's Call to Compelling Evangelism."
   12. Isaac Watts, "How Sweet and Awesome Is the Place," *Trinity Hymnal* (Suwanee: Great Commission Publications, 1990), p. 469.

hundreds, or even thousands are united together in worshipping the God of heaven! Believer, do you long to see this? Do you long to see revival in this country? Then we must engage in the work of evangelism:

> If you want His church full, go to the highways and to the hedges. Not only go to the streets and lanes but go beyond the hedges. Purse them relentlessly. Go! Bring them to hear Christ so that seat beside you that's empty is filled with someone you brought to hear Him, with a compelling message, with a heart constrained by Christ and with the work of the Spirit of God working through you.[13]

Amen, dear believer. Go!

The Sovereignty of God

One may be led then to ask what relationship the sovereignty of God has to evangelism. "If God has already chosen the elect, then why evangelize?" is an oft repeated question by many from outside the Reformed tradition. Though well meaning, the question fails to realize that the sovereign Lord of glory has chosen to use specific means to bring about His chosen ends. God has ordained not only the ends, but also the means by which those ends come about. Consider what the Westminster Confession teaches in its chapter on *Of God's Eternal Decree*:

> God from all eternity did by the most wise and holy counsel of His own will, freely and unchangeably ordain whatsoever comes to pass; yet so as thereby neither is God the author of sin; nor is violence offered to the will of the creatures, nor is the liberty or contingency of second causes taken away, but rather established.[14]

Since God has chosen to use imperfect people to preach a perfect Savior, the Christian can have true confidence of success in evangelism. The sovereignty of God is not a deterrent, but rather a powerful motivator for the task. In fact, it is the sovereignty of

---

13. Reeder, "Christ's Call to Compelling Evangelism."
14. WCF 3.1.

God in grace which gives us our only true hope of success in the task of evangelism.[15]

The Methods of Evangelism

Understanding all that has been mentioned thus far, the next question that needs to be answered is, "How is evangelism properly done?" The aforementioned motivations have led some churches to adopt a "seeker-sensitive" approach, doing everything they can short of sin (and quite frankly, crossing the line into sin at times) to bring in people to hear the message. This approach, as well intended as it may be, fails to take into account that the methods cannot overshadow the message. Even the best of methods are but mere servants to the message. Confusing the two runs the risk of making the messenger the focus rather than the God of the messenger. Some have become so results-oriented instead of faith-oriented that almost any method can be justified so long as it brings sinners to Christ.

However, since success in evangelism is ultimately up to the Holy Spirit and not to the messenger, then we must realize that numbers are not indicative of faithfulness. One can present the Gospel clearly, and not have anyone respond. Even the greatest preacher who ever lived, the Lord Jesus Christ, did not always find success in evangelism. In John 6, Jesus performs the miracle of feeding five thousand people. Rather than being ready to make a commitment to Christ, the crowd is less than impressed, wanting more of the bread. Christ explains to them that He is the true bread (v. 35), and that unlike the manna given to their fathers in the wilderness, if they eat of the true bread they will never die (v. 51). And what are the results? "After this many of his disciples turned back and no longer walked with him" (v. 66). Do you see what happened here? Jesus performed a great miracle but the minute He began to preach the Gospel, everyone abandoned Him. Jesus let a mega church of five thousand people walk out the door! But the people did not want Christ, they wanted what they could

---

15. Packer, *Evangelism and the Sovereignty of God*, 104.

get from Christ. They wanted the gift but not the Giver. We must take this lesson to heart: do not value the method more than the message itself.

So, are there any methods or helps in evangelism that can be used rightly? The answer, of course, is yes. Here is some practical instruction from Harry Reeder:

Get a Testimony

Remember, your testimony is not a substitute for the Gospel, but can be a great bridge in order to get the Gospel to a person. A testimony is "bearing witness of what Jesus did in your life."[16] Testimonies are not all the same, nor are they the same length, but you can tailor your testimony to the occasion and time allowed. Reeder advises to have three testimonies. Note his practical advice:

> Take your testimony and develop it into what I call the elevator testimony. You ought to have a testimony that builds a bridge in three minutes to somebody. This is your short testimony. Secondly, get what I call a lunch testimony where you have about fifteen to twenty minutes to give your testimony. Thirdly, you have a long testimony, which is a polished testimony, where you spend about one third of the time talking about your life before Christ and two thirds of your life with Christ and what His grace has and is doing in your life. This is where in an evening you can share your testimony with someone.... People know you're a sinner so you don't need to revel in it and go through the juicy details of it unless they ask questions about it.[17]

The last sentence is key. Keep as little of you in it as possible, so that you may shine the light brighter on Christ. Many a testimony has fallen flat or been ineffective because the point of the story was the man and what he was saved from, not *who* he was saved to.

Get Equipped

Secondly, you need to become equipped with scripture. This means learning what Reeder called the "one verse evangelism." This means finding one verse which sums up the Gospel clearly

---

16. Reeder, "Everyone Evangelizing Everybody Everywhere Every day."
17. Ibid.

enough to be able to use, especially in the elevator testimony situation. So, for example, Romans 6:23: "For the wages of sin is death, but the free gift of God is eternal life in Christ Jesus our Lord." With this verse you can give simple statements to explain both the predicament that the sinner is in and the way that salvation is offered through Christ: "Here's where you are but here is where you can be. Praise God for the 'but' for he has intervened so you can have eternal life. Here is wages: sin and death but here is gift: God and life. Here's the bridge: Jesus Christ."[18] Scripture is the most valuable tool in the evangelist's tool bag.

Develop a Prayer Plan

Thirdly, and perhaps the most overlooked need, is prayer:

> Your prayer plan has two parts to it. One is pray for the people God is going to bring you. Currently I have about five people that I am asking God to give me an opportunity to talk to them about Him. Pray for God to give you "divine appointments." Pray for those God is laying on your heart to open the doors to them. The second part is they can't respond without a new heart so they need to be able to hear. They need eyes to see and ears to hear and you can't give them that so you're praying for the Holy Spirit to go before you to prepare their heart for the seed you are going to sow. You are praying for God to do a work of grace in their life.[19]

Be Practical

Fourthly, the Christian needs to be practical but not pragmatic. Following something he learned from Randy Pope, Harry Reeder utilizes the G.B.I. method—greet, befriend, invite:

> Treat people as if they are existing in front of you. Acknowledge them: "Hi there, how are you?"; "Where are you from?"; "What do you do?"; "How did you meet?" Be interested in them. Find out about them. Don't greet them and start telling them about yourself. You want to tell them about Jesus.[20]

---

18. Ibid.
19. Ibid. Perhaps you are one of the five that Harry had been praying for. Now is the time to come to Christ by faith.
20. Ibid.

These basic questions serve those evangelizing by helping them get to the 'next step' in the process, which is inviting their contacts to church or a church event.

This leads to another practical method, which is practicing hospitality.[21] "Go home, fill up the moat and put out the bridge ..."[22] Hospitality means inviting people into your homes, your lives, church, events, small groups, etc. Often times, the most organic opportunities for sharing the Gospel come in the form of hospitality. But, you may ask, what if you're one who is an introvert? Hand someone a book or a short but clear Gospel tract. God uses His Word, and He uses the means of the written word to bring sinners to Himself.[23]

Now What?

You may be asking yourself, but now what? Where do I start? A fitting close to this chapter is once again practical instruction from Harry Reeder:

> Start with your family. I thank God my parents made me go to church even though in the moment I didn't thank God for it because in the moment I was in rebellion, going the other direction. I got to the bottom of the barrel. Then I met Cindy and I had to go to church to date Cindy. I wasn't going to take her back to the church I had been going to because that would blow my cover and she would never date me again. I wasn't going to go to her church for various reasons, so I went and found a church for us to go to. It was just like the one my mom and dad took me to growing up. Start with your own kids, your family, your neighbors. Sow the seed everywhere. Jesus saves. Let's pray.[24]

---

21. Rosaria Butterfield has written about the way God used hospitality in her conversion. See Rosaria Butterfield, *The Secret Thoughts of an unlikely Convert: An English Professor's Journey into Christian Faith* (Pittsburgh: Crown and Covenant, 2012).

22. Reeder, "Everyone Evangelizing Everybody Everywhere Every day."

23. Some examples of short and helpful books to give someone are John Blanchard, *Ultimate Questions* (Darlington: Evangelical Press, 2013); Gabriel N.E. Fluhrer, *Alive: How the Resurrection of Christ Changes Everything* (Sanford: Ligonier Ministries, 2020); and John M. Frame, *Christianity Considered: A Guide for Skeptics and Seekers* (Bellingham: Lexham Press, 2018). No doubt there are more, but these three in particular stand out. Harry himself loved using Blanchard's book.

24. Reeder, "Everyone Evangelizing Everybody Everywhere Every day."

5

The Mission and Missions of the Church

Brian H. Cosby

Few utilized the memory tool of alliteration more than Harry Reeder. And of all his memorable alliterations, few stand out more than his frequent exhortation to the church to be *on mission, on message, and in ministry*. This call not only permeated Harry's long tenure in pastoral ministry; it also permeated his life. His commitment to local and global missions—which provided the contours of his message and ministry—drew from the deep well of God's Word and Harry's desire to see the preeminence of Christ magnified among the nations.

A Personal Tribute

I first met Harry as a nineteen-year-old freshman at Samford University in Birmingham, Alabama. It was my first Sunday, and several friends told me to visit Briarwood Presbyterian Church. As a typical college student, I arrived late and sat in the balcony. When it came time for the sermon, he asked us to stand for the reading of God's Word, and then he began. I was taken with Harry's expositional clarity, reverential sensitivity, and pastoral application. He preached the text—he preached *Jesus*—and my life was forever changed.

After the service that Sunday, as I was leaving the sanctuary, Harry greeted me. He told me of his mission trips to Uganda with my grandfather, Henry Schum, and his days at Covenant College with my mother. From that moment on, he never forgot my name. I joined Briarwood and, for the next eight years in Birmingham, Harry taught me, counseled me, prayed for me, and modeled Christian character. I recall his charge to me when he officiated my wedding in 2005 about my duty to love my wife as Christ loved the church. Eventually, I came under the care of Briarwood as a candidate for Gospel ministry.

Through my pastoral calls in Georgia and Tennessee, Harry continued to mentor me, as he did for so many others. He frequently visited the church I currently pastor, Wayside Presbyterian Church on Signal Mountain, Tennessee, to preach, speak to our men on leadership (with frequent mention of the Civil War!), or sometimes to simply pop in, with Cindy, for a surprise visit to worship with us. The Lord used Harry in directing me to my current call—which was a revitalization work—after attending a training that used his book, *From Embers to a Flame*. Since then, I've had the privilege of serving with Harry in the Gospel Reformation Network (GRN) and learning from his teaching and Christ-like example. I can say with confidence that no one has influenced my pastoral ministry more than Harry Reeder. I miss him, and I give thanks to God for his life.

Various "Missions" of the Church?

In a culture of confusion over the mission of the church, Harry provided penetrating clarity. Some have argued that the church's mission is cultural transformation, or social justice, or loving people through good deeds, or promoting church growth. But these, as Harry often argued, were simply *consequences* of the Lord's work in our mission, not the mission itself. The true mission of the church was much simpler, and much more biblically faithful.

If we're not careful, these other counterfeit "missions" can shape the church's *message*. Rather than making disciples through preaching the Gospel of Christ as the power of God for salvation to all who believe (Rom. 1:16), we begin preaching a pragmatic message, a therapeutic story, a moralistic triumphalism, or cultural accommodation. These messages distort the true message of God's saving grace for sinners through the life, death, and resurrection of Jesus Christ. In the end, those who preach counterfeit messages as *the* message in missions often create a syncretistic new religion altogether—something against which J. Gresham Machen warned a century ago.[1]

Ultimately, our mission and message find expression in the *ministry* of the church, what Harry described as a "W.E.L.L. Church": Worship, Evangelism, Loving, and Learning.[2] The goal of missions is not only that men, women, boys, and girls would come to a saving knowledge of the Lord Jesus Christ, but also that they would be gathered into local churches, established in the faith, and worship the true and living God. This takes ministry. Thus, ministry within local churches among the nations must be in view when we think about global missions.

It's not difficult to see in our own day the church's need for worship, evangelism, love, and learning. Thus, Harry's call for the church to stay *on mission, on message, and in ministry* is as important now as ever. In an ecclesiastical milieu where the church is being "tossed to and fro by the waves and carried about by every wind of doctrine" (Eph. 4:14), we need an anchor to steady us in our mission. And that anchor is found in the Great Commission.

The Great Commission

Harry writes, "No Bible passage informs our mission, and shapes our vision, more than the Great Commission in Matthew 28:16–20."[3]

> Now the eleven disciples went to Galilee, to the mountain to which Jesus had directed them. And when they saw him they worshiped him, but some

---

1. See J. Gresham Machen, *Christianity and Liberalism* (Sanford, FL: Ligonier Ministries, 2023).
2. Reeder, *From Embers to a Flame*, p. 200.
3. Reeder, *From Embers to a Flame*, p. 187.

doubted. And Jesus came and said to them, "All authority in heaven and on earth has been given to me. Go therefore and make disciples of all nations, baptizing them in the name of the Father and of the Son and of the Holy Spirit, teaching them to observe all that I have commanded you. And behold, I am with you always, to the end of the age."

The context of this passage follows Jesus' resurrection from the dead, but before He ascended into heaven. It's important to note that the Great Commission was given when the disciples were worshipping Jesus. The text says that when the disciples saw Him, "they worshiped him" (v. 17). Why is this important? Because Christ is worthy of all praise, and it is upon this wonderful truth that He commissions the church to make disciples among the nations so that the nations, too, might come to worship the King.

The Great Commission contains one key imperative, "make disciples," which is supported and modified by three participles: "going," "baptizing," and "teaching." As Harry once said, "The three participles are like the three legs of a stool, each supporting the seat of making disciples." Making disciples, then, forms the overarching mission of the church.

But before we look at the connection between the imperative and the participles, it's important to note Christ's authority in the text. God the Father was pleased to give His Son "all authority in heaven and on earth" (v. 18). Christ's authority is one aspect of His divine sovereignty, which is displayed in both eternal decree and temporal providence. God has declared the end from the beginning (Isa. 46:10), and He brings those decrees into time and space—what we call *providence*. Whether it's the moment of your regeneration or the sparrow falling to the ground (Matt. 10:29), God is in complete control over it all.

As the authoritative One, we can take comfort in the fact that Christ *is able* to do that which He promises. In other words, He is omnipotent. Jesus said, "I *will* build my church, and the gates of hell *shall not* prevail against it" (Matt. 16:18, emphasis added). At His ascension, He told His disciples, "But you will receive power when the Holy Spirit has come upon you, and you will be my witnesses in Jerusalem and in all Judea and Samaria, and to the end of the earth" (Acts 1:8). Why is this important? Because it is the biblical truth that Christ is sovereign that gives us hope and confidence that our mission will succeed! If Christ did not possess all authority—if He did not hold all power—we would have no hope that our mission would succeed in this world.

With Christ's authority in mind, then, how are we to make disciples of Jesus and fulfill the Great Commission? How are we to engage in global missions? The three participles help clarify our mission.

The *going* aspect of Christ's commission is that of being sent, which enlists our full activity and effort (we are not hyper-Calvinists!). God uses the preaching of the Gospel to save sinners. We plant and water, God gives the growth (1 Cor. 3:7). We preach the Gospel because faith comes by hearing (Rom. 10:17). God has ordained both the means *and* the end.

When Paul and Barnabas preached in Acts 13, the text says, "And when the Gentiles heard this, they began rejoicing and glorifying the word of the Lord, and as many as were appointed to eternal life believed" (v. 48). Paul and Barnabas preached; God saved. Likewise, the Lord opened the heart of Lydia "to pay attention to what was said by Paul" (Acts 16:14). Later, when Paul was in Corinth, Jesus came to him in a vision and told him to keep preaching. Why? He said, "[F]or I have many in this city who are my people" (Acts 18:10). God's Word goes out and will not return empty, but will accomplish the purpose for which it is sent (Isa. 55:11). The means by which God saves His elect is through the proclamation of the Gospel. Thus, our "going" involves our full activity in the means God has ordained, the means by which He saves His people.

The *baptizing* aspect of the Great Commission involves the gathering of God's people into the church. Sinclair Ferguson writes, "Being a Christian, by definition, involves belonging to the church—and that, in turn, means belonging to a particular church."[4] Baptism marks off God's people from the world and admits them entrance into the visible church, in which they avail themselves of the means of grace and where they enjoy the fellowship and communion of the saints. In short, baptism provides the context for making disciples. In a culture of hyper-individualism, especially in the West, baptism reminds us that though Christianity is personal, it's not private. God has designed the church as a means for our transformation and spiritual growth. We belong to Jesus, the Head, and because we belong to Him, we belong to one another in the body of Christ.

With relation to missions, then, the inclusion of baptism in the Great Commission reminds us that we are not to simply make individual disciples of Jesus, but disciples who belong to local churches. This reality is woefully neglected in modern missions movements, where the emphasis is on individual converts who say a "sinner's prayer." Rather, one of our goals is to see churches—may I even say *presbyteries*—planted and established among the nations.[5]

The *teaching* is not only the imparting of knowledge and truth, but is also life-transforming application. When people quote the Great Commission, they often leave out this transforming aspect, "teaching them *to observe* all that I have commanded you" (v. 20, emphasis added). Disciples of Jesus are not only to be hearers of the Word, but also doers of the Word (James 1:22). Their lives are to be transformed by the renewing of their minds, according to the truth of the Word (Rom. 12:2). If we don't preach "the whole counsel of God" in our mission (Acts 20:27), including the teaching to *observe* all that our Lord has commanded, then their sanctification and discipleship (and ours) will be hindered.

---

4. Sinclair Ferguson, *Devoted to God's Church* (Edinburgh: Banner of Truth, 2020), p. 1.

5. It is beyond the scope and purpose of this chapter to give any attention to the biblical argument for the Presbyterian form of church government. For an excellent study in this system of government, see Guy Prentiss Waters, *How Jesus Runs the Church* (Phillipsburg, NJ: P&R Publishing, 2011).

These three participles then—going, baptizing, and teaching—form the support for the imperative to make disciples. But there is one final element of the Great Commission that we must not overlook—Christ's promise. He says, "And behold, I am with you always, to the end of the age" (v. 20). Jesus' promise isn't only His abiding presence by the Spirit, but also His abiding power to accomplish the mission. He is our Immanuel, God with us, enabling us to fulfill our mission so that He would be glorified among the nations. It's a comfort and encouragement to know that, as we engage in the mission of the church to make disciples of Jesus, we are not alone. Christ will never leave us nor forsake us (Heb. 13:5). And because He has been given all authority, and possesses all power, we can trust His promise to be with us, even to the end of the age.

Defining the Mission of the Church

There are many good things the church can do in the world—feeding the poor, building houses, planting gardens, working to stop human trafficking, etc.—but what is the exclusive mission that Christ has given to His church? What are we, as Christians, called to do with the Gospel in the world?

From what we've seen in the Great Commission, which is in complete agreement with the rest of the New Testament, we may define the mission of the church in this way: *The mission of the church is to make disciples of Jesus Christ by going, baptizing, and teaching—to the glory of God the Father and by the power of the Holy Spirit—so that the joyful worship of God would spread to the ends of the earth.*

Or, to put this in terms of "global missions" specifically, we may summarize it this way:

> Global missions is the spread of the Gospel of Jesus Christ among all nations—faithfully making disciples and establishing local churches—so that all nations will glorify God and enjoy Him forever.

Jesus taught that the sign of the end of the age is the proclamation of the Gospel to all people: "And this gospel of the kingdom will be proclaimed throughout the whole world, as a testimony to all nations, and then the end will come" (Matt. 24:14). Because Christ has not returned, the mission is not finished. We still have work to do!

Persecution in the Mission of the Church

As we engage in the mission of the church, we should be mindful that we will face various levels of persecution. This shouldn't surprise us. Jesus prepared His disciples to suffer for their faith: "If they persecuted me, they will also persecute you" (John 15:20). The apostle Paul, who was no stranger to persecution, wrote to his son in the faith, Timothy, "Indeed, all who desire to live a godly life in Christ Jesus will be persecuted" (2 Tim. 3:12). The apostle Peter, who—according to tradition—was crucified upside down, instructed the exiles of the Dispersion, "Beloved, do not be surprised at the fiery trial when it comes upon you to test you" (1 Pet. 4:12).

The history of Christianity *is* a history of suffering—ridicule, ostracism, reproach, torture, imprisonment, and death. From the crucifixion of Jesus to the martyrdom of His disciples, from the sixteenth-century fires of Queen ("Bloody") Mary in England to the spearing deaths of the twentieth-century missionaries in Ecuador, the winds of Christian persecution have blown across every continent, in every generation.

Given this suffering and persecution in missions, it might be tempting to soften or tamper with the message—to recreate "Jesus" into a social reformer or attempt to lower God's standards of holiness and justice to "get people into heaven." But we must not capitulate nor compromise our message. For "there is no other name under heaven given among men by which we must be saved" (Acts 4:12). Jesus is "the way, and the truth, and the life"—and no one comes to the Father except through Him (John 14:6). Rather, when we suffer, we must count ourselves blessed: "Blessed are those who are persecuted for righteousness' sake, for theirs is the kingdom of heaven" (Matt. 5:10). If we are to be faithful in the mission of the church in making disciples of Jesus, we must have the courage to suffer.

Practical Take-Aways for Engaging in Missions

What are some practical "take-aways" (a phrase I learned from Harry) regarding our mission in making disciples among all nations? What can we be doing to lead others in the Great Commission?

First, ensure that your *motive* for missions is not mere "success", which is oftentimes referred to as the "Three Bs": budget, buildings, and bodies. Rather, we should strive for faithfulness to the God-appointed means of grace, ever looking to Him to provide the growth and fruit of our labors. *Success*-driven missions, and the immediate effect of comparing your mission work with others, only leads to either pride or despair; pride if it's going well, and despair if it's not. This type of motive is not only unhelpful, but dangerous. *Faithfulness*-driven missions, on the other hand, provides the comfort and blessing of knowing that—as we preach the good news of Christ—God saves and sanctifies His people. Christ is building His church, and the mission will be accomplished! We should view ourselves as "jars of clay, to show that the surpassing power belongs to God and not to us" (2 Cor. 4:7).

Second, *pray.* "Pray earnestly to the Lord of the harvest to send out laborers into his harvest" (Matt. 9:38). Pray for the salvation of the lost. Pray for the building up of the church. Pray that God would bring in the full number of the Gentiles, that all Israel might be saved (Rom. 11:25-26). Pray for those missionaries who make disciples of Jesus by going, baptizing, and teaching—that God would enable them by His Spirit to preach the unsearchable riches of Christ with boldness, clarity, and joy. Pray that local churches would be established among the nations, with qualified leaders and biblical worship. Why? Because God uses our prayers not only to draw us into deeper fellowship with Him, but also to accomplish His sovereign purposes. So plead His promises to Him with faith and expectation.

Third, *give*. I always appreciated how Harry *led from the front* in giving to missions. He and Cindy sought to increase their giving each year, which inspired me to give. Even if our offerings seem like meager "fish and loaves," God can multiply them in mighty ways. Moreover, giving is evidence of our dependence upon God; He uses our giving to increase our faith and prioritize in us what's truly important in life. God is the owner of all, but He has called us to be good stewards of those resources, so that the mission of making disciples continues to the ends of the earth. "For where your treasure is, there your heart will be also" (Matt. 6:21). If your heart is to reach the lost with the good news of Christ, your treasure will follow. Teach others to give toward missions—your family members and your church members. Teach them the importance of giving regularly, and not only at an annual missions conference. Teach them to give as a regular rhythm of Christian discipleship.

Fourth, and finally, *equip* the saints for the work of ministry (Eph. 4:12). This includes equipping the saints for the work of missions. Equip them with the tools they need—Bible knowledge, theology, and even serving as an example to them in evangelism as *you* engage in missions. Encourage them to speak truth in love (Eph. 4:15), and to be ready to give a defense of the hope they have in Christ, but to do so with gentleness and respect (1 Pet. 3:15). Prepare them to face rejection and persecution. Exhort them to avail themselves of the means of grace each week, especially in Lord's Day worship. Organize short-term trips so they may come alongside foreign missionaries for the purpose of encouragement and building up the body of Christ among the nations. Most long-term missionaries I know were called through short-term trips! These are all aspects of equipping the saints for the work of missions.

Our Hope in Missions

Harry often ended his sermons by painting a portrait of our future glory with the saints triumphant. I want to do the same here, because such a hope should gird up our souls—and give us confidence—in the calling to take the Gospel to the nations.

In Revelation 5, the apostle John gives us such a vision, but it doesn't begin with great hope. In fact, it begins with weeping. In John's vision, God holds a scroll that has seven seals, which signifies the execution of His perfect plan for the ages and brings all His purposes to pass. But "no one was found worthy" to open it (v. 4), that is, to carry it to completion. Hence, the weeping. Then one of the elders said, "Weep no more; behold, the Lion of the tribe of Judah, the root of David, has conquered, so that he can open the scroll and its seven seals" (v. 5).

John then looked for the *Lion*, but instead saw a *Lamb*—slain, but standing. The Lamb took the scroll, and the heavenly assembly broke out in a new song:

> Worthy are you to take the scroll and to open its seals, for you were slain, and by your blood you ransomed a people for God from every tribe and language and people and nation, and you have made them a kingdom and priests to our God, and they shall reign on the earth (vv. 9-10).

Two chapters later, we are told that the Lamb will continue His ministry among His people as their Shepherd: "For the Lamb in the midst of the throne will be their shepherd, and he will guide them to springs of living water" (Rev. 7:17).

What will take place in the heavenly assembly is the fulfillment of what the Psalmist had prayed for: "Let the peoples praise you, O God; let all the peoples praise you. Let the nations be glad and sing for joy" (Ps. 67:3-4a). Our desire for the nations is that they might come to know the Lamb who is worthy, and by so doing, praise Him as the King of kings and Lord of lords.

In reality, we today are to have something more than mere *hope* when we consider the future of missions. We are to have *faith*—"the assurance of things hoped for, the conviction of things not seen" (Heb. 11:1). We are not only to trust *in* the Lord, but to *trust* the Lord and His promises, because—

One day, the Gospel will be proclaimed to all nations, and Christ shall return.

One day, every knee will bow, and every tongue will confess that Jesus Christ is Lord, to the glory of God the Father.

One day, we will behold the reality that all of God's promises are "yes and amen" in Christ.

One day, we will join the heavenly assembly and praise the Lion and Lamb, who ransomed a people for God from every tribe and language and people and nation.

One day, the creation—now in bondage to decay—will be made new and the curse of the Fall will be fully and finally reversed, Satan will be cast down, and the thorns and thistles will be replaced by the evergreens of life and peace forever.

One day, the Lord will usher in the new heavens and new earth—and this present darkness will give way to light and life everlasting.

One day, the Lord will set a heavenly banquet before us, and we will feast in the house of Zion.

Dear friend, may we—with Harry Reeder before us—continue to be God's covenant people who are *on mission, on message, and in ministry*. And may we strive to spread the good news of Jesus Christ among all nations—faithfully making disciples and establishing local churches—so that all nations will glorify God and enjoy Him forever.

6.

A True Soldier of Christ

The Call of Christian Discipleship

Jon D. Payne

"To be a disciple of Christ is to be a soldier of Christ ... to enter a battle." These words, spoken by Pastor Harry Reeder in a sermon series on discipleship in the Fall of 2001, illustrate the true nature of Christian discipleship. They also express the pulsebeat of Harry's own life and ministry.

Harry was a courageous soldier of Jesus Christ, always willing and ready to take up the Word and enter the fray for the sake of the Gospel. Contending for the truth in a post-Christian culture is no easy task. Resisting the influence of progressive Christianity in the church is an unpleasant business. Pastoring a twenty-first-century church is not for the faint of heart. Attacks are frequent and fierce against those who choose to remain on the front lines. Even so, as a good soldier of Christ, Harry fought boldly, humbly, cheerfully, and tirelessly until the very end. The faithful pastor from Birmingham could have sincerely conveyed: "I have fought the good fight, I have finished the race, I have kept the faith" (2 Tim. 4:7).

In addition to being a genuine disciple, Harry was a cherished mentor and friend for over thirty years. I miss him dearly. His warm encouragement and godly advice were a welcome part of my week, along with his charming wit and dry humor. To know "The General", as many affectionately called him, was to be enrolled in a loving and continuous school of Christian discipleship. In every conversation, there was something to learn, a nugget of wisdom to consider. For these and other reasons, I am delighted to contribute to this *festschrift* celebrating Pastor Harry Reeder's life and legacy.

The Call of Discipleship

When considering the subject of biblical discipleship, a subject that Harry was passionate about, it is vital to establish from the outset that one does not become a true disciple of Christ through natural means. Disciples are not self-made. Indeed, nobody is a Christian disciple merely through human decision or an exertion of the will (John 1:12-13). No, in order to be a true disciple of Jesus Christ, one must be born again from above (John 3:3, 7). One must be supernaturally raised with Christ (Eph. 2:4b). The outward call to follow Jesus as Lord will never be obeyed apart from the inward, effectual, and irresistible call of the Holy Spirit. Why? Because in mankind's natural state, there is no spiritual life. None. There is only spiritual death. In his letter to the church at Ephesus, the apostle Paul reminds the early Christians who they once were before being saved:

> And you were dead in the trespasses and sins in which you once walked, following the course of this world, following the prince of the power of the air, the spirit that is now at work in the sons of disobedience— among whom we all once lived in the passions of our flesh, carrying out the desires of the body and the mind, and were by nature children of wrath, like the rest of mankind (Eph. 2:1-3).

Paul makes it clear that mankind's natural, fallen condition could not be worse. Each person's heart, mind, will, and affections are thoroughly corrupted by sin. Moreover, each is in bondage to Satan. Therefore, mankind will never choose God on their own. They will never autonomously *decide* to follow Jesus. Indeed, on their own, each will never desire a life of discipleship (Rom. 8:7-8; Eph. 4:18).

The Westminster Confession of Faith states that the "natural man, being altogether averse from [spiritual] good, and dead in sin, is not able, by his own strength, to convert himself, or to prepare himself thereunto".[1]

Thankfully, the wretched sinful condition of mankind is not the end of the story. "But God," the apostle Paul writes, "being rich in mercy, because of the great love with which he loved us, even when we were dead in our trespasses, made us alive together with Christ—by grace you have been saved" (Eph. 2:4-5; see also Col. 2:13-14). In Christ, sinners are raised from spiritual death to spiritual life. United to Christ, sinners receive a new heart, a renewed will, an enlightened mind, and new affections. It is with this new life in Christ that true Christian discipleship begins! Furthermore, it is *with Christ*—and never without Him—that disciples fight and persevere as soldiers to the very end. The Captain of salvation is always with His soldiers on the battlefield (Matt. 28:20), and they rely upon Him in every way. "Apart from me," Jesus declared, "you can do nothing" (John 15:5b).

It's vital to understand that discipleship begins (and continues!) by God's grace. Knowing this guards against a man-centered or works-based view of discipleship. To be sure, following Christ is demanding. It takes Spirit-empowered effort to engage in the battle. There is a real cost to genuine discipleship. But the serious demands placed upon Christ's disciples do not constitute a merit-based pathway to salvation. No, salvation is all of grace, and not through works of the law. Reeder explains that it's as if Christ says, "I have paid for your salvation in full. Receive the gift. Now follow me ... and here's the cost."

The Cost of Discipleship

John Paton (1824–1907) was a Scottish missionary to the New Hebrides Islands (modern-day Vanuatu). He is known for his passion for making Christian disciples out of a nation of violent cannibals.

---

1. WCF 9.3

When Paton first shared his desire to take the Gospel to the South Seas, many in the church were unconvinced. They even sought to change his mind. "What about your successful work in the Glasgow Mission?" they asked. "Why leave your work in Scotland when God attends it with such power? Aren't the spiritual needs at home important too?" Furthermore, many warned Paton of the dangers that he and his family would encounter. One man said to Paton: "The cannibals ... you will be eaten by the cannibals!" Paton's response is inspiring:

> Mr. Dickson, you are advanced in years now, and your own prospect is soon to be laid in the grave, there to be eaten by worms; I confess to you, if I can but live and die serving and honoring the Lord Jesus, it will make no difference to me whether I am eaten by cannibals or worms; and in the Great Day my resurrection body will arise as fair as yours in the likeness of our risen redeemer.[2]

The Scotsman and his young pregnant wife Mary Ann displayed hearts of true disciples. They counted the cost, and boarded a ship for the New Hebrides. As they left the bonnie shores of Caledonia to travel south, "Behind them was a homeland of lochs and glens, before them an island of spears and blood."[3]

It was not long after the Patons landed on the Island of Tanna that the cost of discipleship was deeply felt. After only three months, John Paton's wife and baby died of malaria. Paton buried them himself. He was shattered with grief. By God's grace, however, he persevered, fulfilling the Great Commission with an uncommon zeal for the remainder of his life. Paton's experience reminds us that, as Harry Reeder would put it, "Salvation is free, but discipleship costs."

Even so, a breezy and superficial approach to discipleship is prevalent in modern-day evangelicalism. The accent is placed on felt needs, consumer preferences, and safe spaces, rather than self-denial, spiritual war, and full surrender to Christ. The aim

---

2. Paul Schlehlein, *John G. Paton: Missionary to the Cannibals of the South Seas* (Edinburgh: Banner of Truth, 2017), p. 19.

3. Ibid.

is comfort, not sacrifice. The goal is self-preservation, not self-abandon, that is, a willingness to suffer and, if necessary, die for Christ. In a classic biblical text on discipleship, we learn that there is a cost to following Jesus.

> As they were going along the road, someone said to him, "I will follow you wherever you go." And Jesus said to him, "Foxes have holes, and birds of the air have nests, but the Son of Man has nowhere to lay his head." To another he said, "Follow me." But he said, "Lord, let me first go and bury my father." And Jesus said to him, "Leave the dead to bury their own dead. But as for you, go and proclaim the kingdom of God." Yet another said, "I will follow you, Lord, but let me first say farewell to those at my home." Jesus said to him, "No one who puts his hand to the plow and looks back is fit for the kingdom of God" (Luke 9:57-62).

In this passage, Jesus has three conversations with three different people along the way. In each exchange, we learn something important about discipleship. We learn that following Christ was never intended to be a broad and easy road (see Matt. 7:13).

Luke reports that as Christ and the disciples were walking along the road, someone said to Jesus, "I will follow you wherever you go." Now that's commitment to Christ, right? What pastor wouldn't want to hear that kind of devotion to Jesus? Should such a declaration be taken at face value? Our Lord didn't think so.

Jesus knew that the man's mouth was more eager than his heart. The truth is, he hadn't counted the cost of following Jesus. There were other reasons why he wanted to be near the Lord. Perhaps he witnessed the large crowds and wanted to be a part of the excitement. After all, Jesus's fame was growing in some parts of Galilee. Or maybe he was emotionally moved by Christ's powerful teaching. Perhaps he was amazed by Jesus' miracles, and wanted to see more. Whatever the reason, we know from Jesus' response that this man was not ready for the demands of Christian discipleship. Jesus declared, "Foxes have holes, and birds of the air have nests, but the Son of Man has nowhere to lay his head" (Luke 9:58). Discipleship is not like one might think it is. Even the Son of Man was without the creature comforts of common animals.

In the previous section, Luke reports that Jesus and His disciples were rejected by a Samaritan village. Indeed, they were denied both food and lodging (Luke 9:51-56). This was not uncommon either. Jesus was rejected in Judah, Galilee, Samaria, and in the town of the Gadarenes. In fact, His life began and ended with rejection. At His birth, He was turned away from the inn, and had nowhere to lay His head. In His death, He was rejected, scorned, and nailed to a wooden cross.

It's as if Jesus says to the traveler: "Do you *really* want to be my disciple? Do you realize that even I, the Son of Man, have fewer comforts than creatures in the fields and trees? Are you really committed to following me *wherever I lead*?"

Once again, being a follower of Christ is not easy. It was never intended or designed to be easy. Jesus was pressing this truth home to His first-century listeners, and to all of us! Darrell Bock writes: "Discipleship is a reorientation of life, involving suffering and perhaps death. If one is to go wherever Jesus goes, one must be ready for the rejection that he experienced."[4] Now, this does not mean that all Christians will endure the same level of suffering and persecution. Nor are all believers called to the darkest corners of the mission field. Some locations and callings are safer for Christians than others. Nevertheless, Christ's words still apply. Every Christian must be willing to forsake all earthly comforts to follow Jesus.

The person who approached Jesus in this first conversation boldly declared, "I will follow you wherever you go." But his heart was divided. He had no real intention of denying himself, taking up his cross daily, and following Christ (Luke 9:23). True discipleship is constituted of more than just words. Discipleship is a life devoted to Jesus, no matter what the cost is.

After the first conversation, there was a second. This time it was initiated by Jesus. "To another, Jesus said, 'Follow me.'" The

---

4. Darrell Bock, *Commentary on Luke*, (Grand Rapids: Baker Academic, 1994), p. 978

response of a genuine disciple would have been something like: "Yes, Lord, I love you, and will follow you without condition or qualification. Wherever you lead, I will go." But instead, he uttered, "Lord, let me first go and bury my father." Seems like a reasonable request. After all, shouldn't adult children honor their parents in life and in death? But Jesus says: "Leave the dead to bury their own dead. But as for you, go and proclaim the kingdom of God" (Luke 9:59-60). Some might consider Jesus' response as harsh. After all, shouldn't this man be allowed, even encouraged, to bury his father before following Jesus? As we take a closer look, the meaning of our Lord's response becomes clearer.

In Jewish culture, when a person dies, burial is required within twenty-four hours. Therefore, this man's father may have been elderly, and he may have been sick, but he was certainly not dead. If his father had died, he would have been in mourning and making necessary preparations for burial. He would not have been standing around talking with Jesus. No, the man's father was still alive. He may even have been in relatively good health. Therefore, the man's response revealed a reluctance to follow Jesus until all commitments to his earthly father were fulfilled. On the surface, this appears honorable. But Jesus unveils the fact that the man's highest loyalty and allegiance were to his family, and not to Him.

Family is by far one of the biggest obstacles to following Christ. It's a perennial problem in every culture. Jesus says that family should never rival true Christian discipleship. To paraphrase a well known saying from Basil the Great, the fourth-century Church Father: "A person who wishes to become the Lord's disciple must repudiate a human obligation, however honorable it may appear, if it slows us ever so slightly in giving the wholehearted obedience we owe to God."[5]

To be sure, it is never acceptable to dishonor parents in the name of Christian discipleship. What Jesus is referring to here

---

5. Saint Basil, *Ascetical Works*, The Fathers of the Church, vol 9, trans. Sister M. Monica Wagner (Washington: The Catholic University of America Press, 1962), p. 345.

is not parental disrespect, but whether one's ultimate allegiance lies with Christ or with family? True discipleship demands allegiance to the former. Loyalty to Jesus supersedes loyalty to family. Therefore, Christ exhorts the man to follow Him, and to let the dead bury their own dead. In other words, let his spiritually dead family members bury their physically dead family members. Now is the time to follow Christ and proclaim the good news of the kingdom.

Sometimes God provides living illustrations of biblical truth. In the mid-nineties, I made three mission trips to New Delhi, India, to work with Rev. John Dorsey. He was a friend to both Harry and me. The seasoned missionary had been laboring in northern India as a church planter and an educator since the 1950s. His love for Christ and His kingdom were second to none. During one of my visits, I was surprised to learn that he did not return home for his father's funeral. But I soon discovered that travel home and time away would have been too costly and disruptive to his Gospel work. He was, of course, very sad to miss his father's funeral. He simply knew where he needed to be; that is, in India, serving Christ and His mission.

In a sermon on discipleship, Harry shares a similar experience. His grandfather was in hospice and would soon be with the Lord. Though Harry had recently visited his grandfather, it was made known that his time on earth was short. The family was called in to say goodbye. However, Harry was scheduled to preach God's Word to a large gathering. Not sure what to do, Harry decided to call his grandfather. When Harry explained his situation, his grandfather said: "Don't leave your post."

The exhortation is for every Christian. While decisions in life for believers are not always straightforward, one thing is clear: we are to seek Christ and His Kingdom first (Matt. 6:33). We are never to leave our post. For the Christian, Harry reminds us, "No relationships in this world precede [our] relationship with Christ."

A TRUE SOLDIER OF CHRIST

Our Lord's sober words to His disciples in Matthew 10:34-39 are radically different than many of the superficial expressions of discipleship in the church today:

> Do not think that I have come to bring peace to the earth. I have not come to bring peace, but a sword. For I have come to set a man against his father, and a daughter against her mother, and a daughter-in-law against her mother-in-law. And a person's enemies will be those of his own household. *Whoever loves father or mother more than me is not worthy of me, and whoever loves son or daughter more than me is not worthy of me.* And whoever does not take his cross and follow me is not worthy of me. Whoever finds his life will lose it, and whoever loses his life for my sake will find it.[6]

Jesus' call to discipleship is unequivocal. So must be our response. Jesus said to the man in Luke 9:59, "Follow me." His answer—"Lord, let me first go and bury my father"—prioritized family over faith. Putting *anything* before Christ is discipleship on man's terms, not God's.

In a third conversation, someone addressed Jesus by saying, "I will follow you, Lord, but let me first say farewell to those at my home" (Luke 9:61). Similar to the previous request, on the surface, it appears sensible. What's the big deal, right? It seems reasonable to say goodbye to loved ones before leaving all to follow Christ. But once again, Jesus knows the state of the heart. He knows that the man's heart is divided. If he goes to say goodbye to his family, he will resist the life of Christian discipleship.

Jesus answers the request with an illustration from agrarian life: "No one who puts his hand to the plow and looks back is fit for the kingdom of God" (Luke 9:62). What's the point? In order to plow a straight furrow or trench through a field for seeding, the farmer must not look back. If he does, the furrow will be crooked. Instead, he must keep his eyes on a fixed and distant point, so as to furrow a straight line. Looking back will ruin the field.

Likewise, true disciples don't look back once they begin to follow Christ. They do not long for former days, or for those things that once stood between them and Christ. Rather, by

---
6. Emphasis added.

God's grace, Christ's disciples press onward, counting all things as rubbish in comparison to knowing Christ, and being robed in His righteousness through faith. Christ's disciples should not look back, but "strain forward to what lies ahead" (Phil. 3:8-9, 13). Disciples must not be like ancient Israel in the wilderness who, with rebellious hearts, longed for former times in Egypt. We must never look back, lest we plow a crooked path of compromise.

Followers of Jesus Christ are saved by God's sovereign grace, and called to a life of committed discipleship. Therefore, there must be no rivals to Christ; not even family. Jesus and His kingdom must be the disciple's highest priority. Harry often remarked that for the Christian disciple, "Jesus is not first on the list ... He *is* the list!"

The Means of Discipleship
Biblical discipleship begins with an efficacious call from above, and continues with the believer's Spirit-empowered commitment to count the cost. The sincere disciple is willing to deny self, take up the cross, and follow Jesus (Mark 8:34). Harry rightly states that true discipleship is "one-hundred-percent dependence *on* God, and one-hundred-percent devotion *to* God." These are key characteristics of biblical discipleship. The question remains, however: *how* does a disciple grow and mature? Through what means does a Christian soldier persevere on the spiritual battlefield? The answer is critical for comprehending the true nature of Christian discipleship.

In the Great Commission, Jesus commands the apostles to go into all the world and *make disciples*. He then provides clear instructions on *how* to accomplish it: "baptizing them in the name of the Father, the Son, and the Holy Spirit, teaching them to observe all that I have commanded ..." (Matt. 28:18-20). In other words, make disciples through the faithful ministry of Word, sacrament, and prayer; that is, through the divinely ordained means of grace (Acts 20:26-27; Acts 2:38; 2 Tim. 3:16-4:5; 1 Cor. 11:17-32). This is our Lord's strategy for mission and discipleship.

Isn't this precisely what we observe the apostles doing throughout the book of Acts? They were preaching, praying, teaching, baptizing, planting churches, appointing elders, shepherding, and administering the Lord's Supper. That's old-fashioned disciple-making! The apostles were not culturally-hip innovators, seeking to make disciples through worldly strategies and gimmicks. They were neither social activists nor political revolutionaries. No, they were "servants of Christ and stewards of the mysteries of God" (1 Cor. 4:1). Unlike progressive expressions of Christianity in our day, where we see the "invasion of the authority of the culture in the church," the apostles were committed to the countercultural ministry of the Word. Under their faithful leadership, the nascent church "devoted themselves to the apostles' teaching and the fellowship, to the breaking of bread and the prayers" (Acts 2:42).

The definite article (*the*) before each of the liturgical actions (i.e., *the* apostles' teaching, *the* breaking of bread, etc.) highlights the formal nature of these assemblies, led by the apostles in the context of the gathered church. It also demonstrates the nature of biblical worship. Disciples are made *in*, and not *apart from*, the worship of the gathered church. They are made through the divinely ordained means of Word, sacraments, and prayer.

To be sure, other avenues of Word-based discipleship are beneficial. Small groups, Bible studies, and one-on-one mentorship, for example, are legitimate modes of spiritual growth. But gathered worship on the Lord's Day, led by lawfully ordained ministers, is the highest form of discipleship (Acts 2:42). Public worship is the sacred context in which God promises to work.

His strategy for discipleship *is* the means of grace faithfully set forth. Indeed, Lord's Day worship is the Holy Spirit's workshop, and the means of grace are His tools for molding and shaping disciples into the image of Christ. It is through these effectual means that mature disciples are made, and Christ's spiritual benefits are communicated by grace, and appropriated through faith.

> The outward and ordinary means whereby Christ communicates to his church the benefits of his mediation, are all his ordinances; especially the Word, sacraments, and prayer; all which are made effectual to the elect for their salvation (Westminster Larger Catechism, Q/A 154).

Christian discipleship, therefore, is tied to the ministry of the church. It's not an autonomous endeavor. Disciples grow in community, and under the ministry of Word and sacrament. God's means of grace are irresistibly powerful, and made effectual by the Spirit, in the lives His elect. In Christ's school of discipleship, believers are saved and sanctified. Harry, in his preaching and writing, loved to draw attention to the lavish grace of the Gospel, and its power to transform sinners: "Praise God that His grace in Jesus Christ takes us right where we are, but never leaves us where we are — it changes us from faith to faith, victory unto victory, all the way to glory."[7] Yes— praise God, indeed!

Conclusion

Harry's understanding of the Christian life as a spiritual battle was chiefly informed by the Word of God. However, it was also shaped by his vast knowledge of the Civil War, and the myriad character and leadership lessons that have emerged from it. He always saw important events of the past as highly instructive for how we live (and lead) in the future.

Over the years, I had the privilege, along with a few dear friends in ministry, to travel with Harry to several historic battlefields dating back to the Revolutionary War. The General led us through the sprawling fields of Gettysburg, the beautiful grounds of Valley Forge, and many other sites, while giving military, social, political, and spiritual commentary on events of the past. It was all with the express aim to instruct, inspire, and encourage us to be good soldiers of Jesus Christ, and faithful leaders in His Church. Harry taught us that amidst the chaos and brutal casualties of war, it's vital that we trust in the Lord, put on the armor of God (Eph. 6:10-20), be strong and courageous, and "do the next right thing, in the right way, for the right reason." Harry taught us to be Christian soldiers. He taught us to be men.

> Stand up, stand up for Jesus, ye soldiers of the cross;
> Lift high the royal banner, it must not suffer loss:
> From victory unto victory his army he shall lead,
>   'til every foe is vanquished, and Christ is Lord indeed.

---

7. Reeder, *Embers to a Flame*, p. 71.

7

The Pastor as Shepherd

Jason Helopoulos

Some called him "Dr. Reeder," others referred to him as "General Reeder," but to me, he will always be "Pastor Reeder." Pastor is an old anglicized form of the Latin word for "shepherd." The Lord said, "I will give you shepherds after my own heart, who will lead you with knowledge and understanding" (Jer. 3:15). Pastor Reeder was such a shepherd. I've met few men who understood the calling as well as my dear mentor.

It is no small task to be a faithful shepherd among the people of God, and few things prove more rewarding in this life. Before we take a look at the three primary tasks of a faithful shepherd among the sheep of Christ, we first must identify the essential characteristic of a faithful shepherd.

The Essential Characteristic: Knowing Christ

If we are going to consider faithful shepherds, we will find help in Jesus' description of false shepherds. He provides a severe warning in John 10:1-5. There is no hesitation on our Lord's part, He calls false shepherds thieves and robbers. Too often, we have witnessed this in the history of the church. Men stand up front, speak soothingly, curry favor, and devour the flock of Christ. They appear as shepherds but are far from it. Christ clearly articulates what marks someone as a false shepherd: they don't enter by the door into the sheepfold (John 10:1).

Let's try to wrap our minds around the imagery here. In the Near Eastern world, sheep were, and still are, one of the great commodities. Of course, if people own sheep, they must take care of those sheep. Usually, the flocks were allowed to roam the pastures, but there were times when the sheep needed to be gathered together. In Palestine, shepherds collected flocks into a sheepfold. The sheepfold, created with a wall of rocks stacked and piled high, served as an enclosure for safety. To guarantee the security of the enclosure, brambles or thorn bushes were placed on top of the rocks. This added element prevented sheep from jumping out and also discouraged thieves from climbing in.

However, the sheepfold was not entirely enclosed. At least one opening or break in the wall remained, so that sheep could go in and come out (Psalm 121). The shepherd often stood in that opening during the day. At night, when the sheep were secure in the enclosure, it was routine for the shepherd to sleep in this opening. No sheep could wander out, and no enemies could burst in. The shepherd served as the door to the sheepfold. Jesus presents this illustrative image and declares that anyone who does not enter in through this door proves to be no shepherd of the sheep. "I am the door of the sheep," said Christ (John 10:7).

When we consider whether a pastor is worth following, the fundamental issue is not his humor, nor how interesting we find him, nor how nice he proves to be, nor how authentic he appears. The fundamental question is, "Has he entered through the door?" If he attempts to come to the sheep in any other way, over any other wall, through any other means, other than the door—you will know, because Christ proves to be very little to him. But if he has entered through the door, then the name of Christ will be on his lips because He dominates his heart. If that is not the case, the sheep must run for their own safety because he is no shepherd. He may tickle ears and stir affection, but he is damning souls.

The importance of shepherds entering through Christ, knowing Christ, and delighting in Christ cannot be overemphasized. Jesus makes an exclusive claim: "I am the door. If anyone enters by me, he will be saved" (John 10:9). Who we are matters even above what we are. In the Kingdom, if a pastor is not first a sheep, he cannot be a shepherd. Rather, he is a thief and a robber. Unconverted pastors, those who have not entered the church through Christ, are wrecking balls in the church. They destroy, damage, and ravage the people of God; they tear the church down from the inside.

For the Kingdom to prosper on earth as it is in heaven, it requires godly men who not only can describe Christ and debate the tenants of Christ, but who dwell with and delight in Christ, and their lives demonstrate it. Samuel Miller once said, "There is a power in consistent holiness, which belongs to nothing else beneath the throne of God."[1] Those who know and pursue Christ will prove the most able guides to Christ.

As I reflect upon Pastor Reeder, I often think about his "filing cabinet mind." He knew and loved a lot of things. In fact, I feel as though I could inquire of him about any subject, and he would search the filing cabinet of his mind emerging with three points, all alliterated. He was truly a unique man in experience and interests. I've sat for hours listening to him discuss the finer points of baseball. He grew up in a baseball family, played the game, and enjoyed it. But as much as he loved baseball, he loved military history even more. I've journeyed to numerous battlefields with him as my guide. Listening to Pastor Reeder describe the sorrows of the Continental Army at Valley Forge or the ferocious hand-to-hand combat of Devil's Den at Gettysburg will remain with me for life.

Yet, as much as he loved military history, he loved discussing leadership even more. In fact, I think much of his love for baseball and combat was his constant fascination with leadership. He studied leaders and committed himself to forming leaders. I happily sat at his feet as he shared not only his own stories, but those of generals, evangelists, missionaries, and pastors, all

---

1. Samuel Miller, *Christian Weapons not Carnal, but Spiritual*, (Princeton: Princeton Press, 1848), pp. 47-8.

the while teaching leadership principles. And, of course, Pastor Reeder loved his family more than any of these subjects. His consistent love for Cindy, his children, and his grandchildren were constant themes in conversation. Yet, when I think of Pastor Reeder, one love clearly surpasses all: his love for Christ. This glorious Savior and Lord captured his heart. I've known few that exemplified the words of the Apostle Paul better: "For me, to live is Christ, and to die is gain" (Phil. 1:21). Nothing rivaled Christ, and nothing received the devotion he reserved for Christ alone. That is what made him such a faithful shepherd—beyond anything else, he knew Christ. He had entered through the door. The faithful shepherd of God's people knows Christ.

A Faithful Shepherd: Knows the Sheep

An able shepherd of God's people not only knows Christ, but also knows the sheep. As leaders in the household of God, pastors simply reflect God Himself. We are shepherds, but only undershepherds of the Good Shepherd. And the Good Shepherd knows the sheep. "I am the Good Shepherd. I know my own and my own know me, just as the Father knows me and I know the Father; and I lay my life down for the sheep" (John 10:14-15). As the Good Shepherd knows the sheep, so the faithful shepherd among God's people knows the sheep.

In reflecting upon the connection between a faithful shepherd and sheep in the husbandry world, Laniak comments,

> Responsible shepherds know every member of their flock in terms of their birth circumstances, history of health, eating habits, and other idiosyncrasies. It is not uncommon to name each goat and sheep and to call them by name (John 10:3). One of the most striking characteristics of the shepherd-flock relationship is that control over the flock is exercised simply by the sound of the shepherd's voice or whistle (John 10:3; cf. Judges 5:16; Zechariah 10:8).[2]

---

2. Timothy S. Laniak, *Shepherds After My Own Heart: Pastoral Traditions and Leadership in the Bible* (Westmont: IVP Academic, 2006), p. 57.

The Shepherd truly knows and loves his sheep. As Sinclair Ferguson said,

> It is an important aspect of the New Testament's understanding of the Gospel that Christ not only draws us to himself by his Spirit's work; he also draws us nearer to each other. Our commitment to Christ always implies a commitment to Christ's people (Heb. 11:25-26). To love and care for his brothers is to love and care for him (Matt. 25:34-40).[3]

Paul will write to the Philippians, "My brothers, whom I love and long for, my joy and crown" (Phil. 4:1). What affectionate language pours forth from his pen! Paul knows them and isn't sheepish in stating or showing his affection for these sheep. In fact, he confesses that he is willing "to be poured out as a drink offering" (Phil. 2:17) for the sake of these Philippians. He saw his life in light of their lives. A shepherd's life becomes the flock.

I have a dear man in the congregation I serve who owns a sheep farm. I've visited him on occasion to watch him in action. Though, as a shepherd, he tends to hundreds of sheep, he knows them. He doesn't just know them generally; he knows them individually. Their routines, personalities, health, and proclivities are not shrouded from him. If one wanders, he notices. If sluggish, he recognizes. If ailing, he identifies it. He knows them. They are his sheep. When a disease ran through the lambs in his flock, I watched as he spent sleepless nights and long days caring for them. And each loss seemed to deal a blow. Of course, these sheep provide for his family, but more pulled upon his heartstrings than finances. It may sound odd to an urbanite like me, but what I palpably observed was his love for the sheep. They were known.

Pastor Reeder exemplified this kind of knowing. Each congregation he served from Florida to North Carolina to Alabama would testify that "he knew us and loved us." When I think of Pastor Reeder, three different remembrances flood my mind regarding his knowledge of the sheep. One was relayed to me, one he taught me, and one I witnessed firsthand.

---

3. Sinclair B. Ferguson, *Let's Study Philippians* (Edinburgh: Banner of Truth, 1997), p. 7.

The Lord, in His providence, called Pastor Reeder to serve larger congregations. On multiple occasions, I heard him say that he never aspired to serve a large congregation. Shepherding thousands necessarily takes a different type of ministry than pastoring dozens or hundreds. Though he loved the congregations he served, he often reflected on what serving a smaller congregation over an extended period of time may have been like. His simple desire to faithfully shepherd the sheep with true knowledge of each drove this reflection. Yet, Pastor Reeder, though he would have humbly aspired to do better, knew the sheep in these large congregations well. A longtime staff member of Briarwood relayed to me one day, "Jason, when someone from the Briarwood family is in the hospital, one of us goes to visit them. Almost without fail, Pastor Reeder has already been there." He knew his flock. He knew when they were ailing, and he knew how to minister to their need.

One of the ways he accomplished this monumental task was his commitment to praying for each congregant under his care. He taught me this practice in one discipleship meeting. I was seeking advice about caring for my own congregation, and he granted me a peek into his inner sanctuary of practice. "Jason," he said, "Cindy and I pray together through the entire congregation annually." This little instruction changed my shepherding. The Reeders uttered, not general prayers, but specific prayers for each member of the congregation. They solicited these prayers from members and prayed for them, by name. A shepherd who knows the flock prays for the flock. When they are on our hearts as pastors, they will be in our prayers as pastors. And when they are in our prayers as pastors, they will be on our hearts as pastors.

I also witnessed his knowledge of the sheep when visiting Briarwood on one occasion. Pastor Reeder and I walked into the building and through the halls of this evangelical cathedral. The sheer number of rooms and hallways amazed me. As we passed, various people were engaged in ministry, meetings, and conversations. I dare say that we did not pass one person or group of people without Pastor Reeder engaging them, most often by name. Little jokes and quick updates were shared. A gentle encouragement to "keep on" was offered. He knew the sheep. And the sheep knew his care. A faithful shepherd knows the sheep.

A Faithful Shepherd: Provides for the Sheep

A faithful shepherd not only knows the sheep but provides for the sheep. The people of God exist in the wilderness of this world. Like Israel in the desert, so the church in the modern world requires provision. If sheep starve, the responsibility lies with the shepherd, not the sheep.

In the ancient Near East, a shepherd needed to keep within a thirty-two-kilometer grazing radius of an adequate water source in cold weather and within twenty kilometers in summer months.[4] He made sure they possessed adequate access to a variety of vegetation. In fact, much of the shepherd's responsibility lies in providing nourishment for the sheep.

Christ alludes to the same for His sheep. When He restores Peter to service in that beautiful scene of John 21, it is no mistake that He says to him, "Feed my lambs," "Tend my sheep," and "Feed my sheep." Peter, by the grace of Christ, finds himself reengaged and renewed for service unto Christ. His love for Christ is to be demonstrated by his love for the sheep of Christ. And Christ charges Peter that this love shows itself in provision. The fundamental responsibility of the shepherd is to provide sustenance for the sheep.

We witness this throughout the Scriptures. In fact, God Himself provides as the shepherd of His people. In the most famous of psalms, Psalm 23, David begins with sound reasoning: "The Lord is my shepherd; I shall not want." Here is the fact: the Lord is my shepherd. And here is the implication: I shall not want. This is pristine perfect reasoning.

If the sovereign Lord of heaven and earth rules as my shepherd, I shall not want. This is an all-encompassing statement. I shall not want for anything. Why? Because my faithful shepherd provides.

---

4. Laniak, *Shepherds*, p. 54.

He provides for my material needs—food, drink, shelter, clothing, life. He provides for my emotional needs, social needs, and spiritual needs. Anything required for life abundant, He provides. Richard Briggs states it well when he says,

> Verse 1 points to letting YHWH decide what it is I need, in the very process of ensuring that whatever it is, I will not lack it.... Psalm 23 is partly in the business of training my sense of need to be better attuned to what God provides.[5]

As shepherds among the flock of God, pastors provide for the sheep in the name of Christ. And they do so by giving them the "Bread of Life." When Paul met with the Ephesian elders, he confidently asserted that he "testif[ied] to the gospel of the grace of God" (Acts 20:24), "proclaiming the kingdom" (v. 25), "declaring to you the whole counsel of God" (v. 27). And when he admonishes them to fulfill their duty, he warns of the wolves that would devour the flock, "speaking twisted things" (v. 30). The sheep require feeding, feeding with the Word of God. As he writes to Timothy, a shepherd among the sheep,

> preach the word; be ready in season and out of season; reprove, rebuke, and exhort, with complete patience and teaching. For the time is coming when people will not endure sound teaching, but have itching ears they will accumulate for themselves teachers to suit their own passions and will turn away from listening to the truth and wander off into myths (2 Tim. 4:1-4).

Faithful shepherds provide.

Pastor Reeder provided for the sheep faithfully. He truly loved the sheep of God by giving them the Word of God week in and week out. For Pastor Reeder, ministry in the name of Christ was simply ministry according to the Word of Christ to the people of Christ. He committed himself and the churches he pastored to feasting upon the expositional preaching of God's Word week in and week out. They received a steady diet of precept upon precept. He understood that "Christ and Him crucified"

---

5. Richard S. Briggs, *The Lord is My Shepherd: Psalm 23 for the Life of the Church* (Grand Rapids: Baker Academic, 2021), p. 73-74.

(1 Cor. 2:2) provided the nourishment sheep need yesterday, today, and tomorrow. In the pulpit, in the courts of the church, on his radio program, sitting on the board of Westminster Seminary, and every other endeavor he engaged in, the Word of God came to bear. Often, in these forums, he combatted the siren calls of our day to offer something sweeter to the ear. He continued to stand upon the Word, knowing the desire to find something more palatable for people in our day was a fool's errand. The sheep need the same unadulterated Word of God today, even as they needed it yesterday. His was a lifetime of simply proclaiming, sharing, and testifying to what God supplied to feed His people: Christ and Him crucified. A faithful shepherd provides for the sheep.

A Faithful Shepherd: Protects the Sheep

This leads to our final point. A shepherd not only knows and provides for the sheep, but protects the sheep. Sheep remain vulnerable. In Psalm 23, that great shepherd psalm, we see the shepherd carries a rod and staff. These two implements aided the shepherd in protecting the sheep. As Laniak comments, "The staff became a symbol for the protective presence of the shepherd" and allowed for peacekeeping among the flock. The shorter club or rod was used for defense and protecting the flock. These two implements represent two primary responsibilities of the shepherd— peacekeeper among the flock and protector from external threats.[6] Shepherds protect from harm within and protect from harm without.

Much of a shepherd's job consists of dealing with conflict. In the blink of an eye, a flock can become disoriented, disrupted, and dispersed due to conflict within or from without. There is a reason that much of the New Testament addresses conflict within the church and warnings about threats coming from the church.

Maybe the most common threat, but the one we least expect, is conflict within. Paul, in writing to the church at Colossae, instructs them about the virtues of Christ that are to adorn

---

6. Laniak, *Shepherds*, p. 56.

their lives. It fascinates me, that of all the virtues that Paul could have listed, he lists compassion, kindness, humility, meekness, and patience. Did you catch what is unique about these? Each virtue requires community. Many think the Christian life is just about them and God. But in Paul's understanding, in God's understanding, the Christian life is lived within the Christian community. And within that community, our lives are tested and tried. Holiness is not some mere private exhibition, but rather is worked out in relationship with one another.

Compassion, kindness, humility, meekness, patience—adorn yourself with them, Christian. Put them on. When at home, by ourselves, kindness and humility seem easy. But in community, they are tried. A soldier may excel on the gun range, but he demonstrates the true quality of his soldiering in battle when bullets fly around him, adrenaline pumps, and his life hangs in the balance. Compassion is easy to contemplate, quite another to show towards the one who fell into the same mess again. Kindness isn't difficult when I am separated from rude people. Humility comes easily when no one exists to compare myself with. Meekness seems simple when no one disrespects it. Patience appears effortless when no demands, solicits, or requirements come to bear. Where these marks are tested, biting among the sheep often erupts. The shepherds protect the sheep within by helping them manifest these virtues more and more, mediate conflict, rebuke where necessary, minister the balm of grace, and example before the flock a true love for and humility towards others.

The shepherd also protects from without. He provides protection from errant teaching by maintaining sound doctrine, administering church discipline, and giving wise pastoral counsel. He will not turn a blind eye to an error that disrupts the purity of the flock. He stands as a "watchman," always ready to defend the sheep from false shepherds or wolves who would enter.

As the Princetonian Samuel Miller once preached:

> [It is] necessary that all who profess to love the religion of Christ— and especially ministers, who are, by divine appointment, the official

conservators of evangelical truth—be constantly on the watch to mark these unhallowed attempts at mutilation and perversion, to guard those who are under their care against the insidious art of error, to distinguish with clearness between truth and falsehood, to recommend the one and denounce the other, and thus to hold fast and hold forth sound doctrine for the benefit of themselves and others.[7]

Let us always remember that we "keep watch over ... souls, as those who will have to give an account" (Heb. 13:17). On judgment day, as under-shepherds, we will stand responsible before the throne of the Good Shepherd for how we knew, provided for, and protected—not just the flock generally—but every sheep individually. Why? Because every sheep matters to Him. We will not give an account to the sheep, but to Him. As Albert Martin said, "We are to pass the time of our sojourning in fear, and we are to remember the charge that comes to us in the presence of God and of Christ Jesus who shall judge the living and the dead (Acts 10:42; 2 Timothy 4:1; 1 Peter 4:5)."[8]

As leaders in the church, our charge and responsibilities are great. As the Apostle exclaimed, "Who is sufficient for these things?" (2 Cor. 2:16). But where we began, we must end. Yes, the pastor serves as a shepherd. However, fundamentally, he remains a sheep under the care of the Good Shepherd. Again, Psalm 23, that great shepherd psalm, proves helpful. Notice that He leads us (Ps. 23:2-3). He does not drive me or you, He leads. He goes before, we trail behind. And we travel a well-worn path. Pastor Reeder would have appreciated thinking together about the old well-worn paths during Westward expansion (He loved history!). The Bozeman Trail or the Santa Fe Trail, or the Oregon Trail were not excellently paved roads laid down by the Federal Government. Rather, thousands of wagons, over time, headed in the same direction formed ruts in the ground. We possess such a path, a trustworthy way through the wilderness of this world.

---

7. Samuel Miller, *Holding Fast the Faithful Word: Sermons and Addresses by Samuel Miller*, ed. Kevin Reed (Grand Rapids: Reformation Heritage Books, 2018), p. 169.

8. Albert Martin, *Pastoral Theology, Volume 3: The Man of God: His Shepherding, Evangelizing, and Counseling Labors* (Montville: Trinity Pulpit Press, 2021), p. 43.

Other travelers walked this path before us. Pastor Reeder is one of the faithful who set out and finished their trek. Yes, we follow him, among others, but the significant imprint upon the path, what created the deep ruts that we can now slide our feet into, is the weightiest of men who walked this path before us—the Lord Jesus Christ, the Great Shepherd of the sheep. We follow Him. Our Shepherd leads us in paths of righteousness for His name's sake.

What He has called us to, He will equip and sustain us for. He knows us better than we know ourselves. Every failing we experience, He planned. Every insufficiency, He covers. Every need, He provides. He leads; we follow. He provides; we minister. He protects; we seek to be faithful. We pour out our lives, our very selves, for His people in His name. And the labor is worth all the cost expended. Edward Reynolds said it as well as any:

> Consider the weight and greatness of that Crown of Righteousness and glory which the Chief Shepherd reserves for all those who willingly and with a ready mind feed the flock of God. They who turn many to righteousness shall shine as stars forever and ever (1 Pet. 5:4; Dan. 12:3). What a glorious testimony will it be before the throne of Christ at the last day, when so many souls shall stand forth and say, "This was the hand which snatched us out of the fire, this tongue was to us a tree of life, his reproofs and convictions awakened us, his exhortations persuaded us, his consolations revived us, his wisdom counseled us, his example guided us unto this glory!" Some are apt to charge clergymen with ambitious pursuance of dignities and preferments; Behold here a preferment worthy the climbing after, a dignity worthy to be contented for, an apostolical ambition, as St. Paul's expression imports (Rom 15:20).[9]

The church is the flock of Christ. Pastors, these sheep do not belong to us; they belong to the Good Shepherd of the sheep. We simply care for them in this wilderness, with the pastures of eternity clearly on the horizon. There they will lie down in green pastures and be led beside still waters to dwell eternally with Him.

---

9. Edward Reynolds, *The Pastoral Office, Opened in a Visitation Sermon Preached at Ipswich* (London: George Thomson, 1662), pp. 44-45.

Even now, my dear mentor and friend, Pastor Reeder, basks in the glory of the Good Shepherd. And one day, all those sheep he cared for in the name of this Shepherd shall be gathered with him before the throne. On that day, his "joy and crown" will be manifest. And it will be manifest for all eternity.

8

Harry Reeder, The Consummate Biblical Counselor

Howard A. Eyrich

I became acquainted with Harry in Miami during his tenure at Pinelands Presbyterian Church, where I observed his revitalization of that church from a short distance. Since my ministry focus was biblical counseling at neighboring Granada Presbyterian Church, serving with Dr. Jim Baird, most of my contact with Harry was at Presbytery.

During the early years of planting Christ Covenant, our contact was occasional discussions of counseling situations and at the General Assembly. Also, during those years, my best friend's widow, a member of Wycliffe, kept me informed of his ministry. When this same widow's oldest son's wedding was to occur in the new sanctuary at Christ's Covenant, Harry extended to me the privilege of joining him in conducting the ceremony. This was an example of Harry's collegiality.

So why the title "Harry Reeder, the Consummate Biblical Counselor"? The title originated from the fact that Harry practiced biblical counseling. Anyone who heard him, whether from the pulpit, on the radio, in an organizational setting, or in personal conversation, sooner or later heard him mention his accountability group. This group consisted of four peers: Harry, Sandy Willson, John Wood, and Shelton Sanford. Accountability indicates a standard and a responsibility to hold each other accountable to the bar. That is the essence of biblical counseling from Genesis to Revelation, as God sets forth the standard. He keeps us accountable and teaches us to participate with Him in holding one another accountable (Gal. 6:1-5; Rom. 15:14).

Secondly, the title describes the core of Harry's ministry. "Hello, I am Pastor-Teacher Harry Reeder." While people generally refer to Harry as Pastor Reeder, his favorite self-designation was Pastor-Teacher. His biblical reference for the designation was from Paul's discussion of God's gifts to the church (Eph. 4:11), the latter of which he understood to be a hyphenated pastor-teacher. In another passage (Titus 2), Paul instructs Titus how to practice this gift and, in doing so, beautifully describes this gift in action: corrective shepherding through speaking, that is, teaching, which includes exhorting (coming beside to beseech, comfort, exhort, expressing a desire for change, entreat) and reproving (to reprehend severely, chide, admonish). Hence, biblical counseling is woven into the fabric of the shepherding aspect of this gift. Harry Reeder listened to his mentor, Paul, and displayed this gift in action, offering biblical counseling in every aspect of his ministry, as this essay will evidence.[1]

In the Pulpit

My tenure at Briarwood preceded Harry's by three years. Pam and I encountered expository preaching at every service in the twenty-four years of our concurrency. Book by book, verse by verse, and when necessary, phrase by phrase. Every sermon was, in part, titled "In Biblical Perspective." Harry never left any doubt in the

---

1. Six individuals have made invaluable contributions to this chapter. I tapped these people for two reasons. They either had extended *front-row seats* to observe the theme of the chapter, or they experienced specific biblical counseling from his lips. They are Bruce Stallings, Shirley Crowder, Lynn Downing, Alonza Jones, Tom Lamprecht, and David Eyrich. Without their cooperation, this chapter would be wanting.

hearer's mind regarding the inspiration, authority, and sufficiency of Scripture. Seldom, if ever, did he offer a sermon without some form of biblical counseling.

When a national or local crisis occurred, you could count on Harry to address it "In Biblical Perspective." He counseled from the pulpit, addressing thinking and emotions being experienced and coaching the congregation in processing the event through the lens of Scripture and the sovereignty of God. In like manner, he offered thoughtful, biblical counsel to the congregation when facing the personal crisis of heart valve surgery.

While many would not use the word *counsel* to describe his manner of leading Sunday morning worship, I certainly would view it through my daily counseling lens. Sometimes, it would be the application of a hymn by telling the story behind the hymn. Sometimes, it would be the comments around the word of pardon counseling through the affirmation of forgiveness.

Sometimes, he would counsel a specific audience. In one Sunday night sermon associated with the ordination and installation of officers, Harry was preaching from John 10. If you were an officer-elect, Harry counseled you. If you were an officer in the congregation and had not been biblically executing your office, Harry counseled you to repent. Harry had five points of biblical counsel by which to do a self-evaluation. They were:

1. A good shepherd knows his sheep.
2. A good shepherd sets the pace for the sheep.
3. A good shepherd tends and defends the sheep.
4. A good shepherd feeds the sheep.
5. A good shepherd is faithful in shepherding the sheep.

He closed this message with an appeal to King David that was an appeal to repent and implement the responsibility that accompanies ordination to office in Christ's church.[2]

---

2. Harry Reeder III, *I. What Does the Bible Say: Timeless Truth for Timely Topics in Biblical Perspective: Today's Leaders for Today's Church*, Briarwood Presbyterian Church, January 11, 2015.

One further illustration comes from sermon fifty-one of the series just cited. In this sermon, he addressed the essential nature of church membership from 1 Corinthians 12 and other passages. As he drew toward the conclusion, he assured the congregation that the preceding summarizes the dynamics of the church as God designed it. Any different approach is to say, "I did it my way." The appeal followed this counsel: "Don't try to live individually, independently, but live in Christ in the body of Christ manifested in the local church."[3]

Harry was passionate about evangelism and often came within a hair's breadth of executing a good Baptist altar call as he would counsel sinners to repent. But rather than inviting people to walk the aisle, he would offer biblical counseling growing out of the sermon and then appeal to those stirred by the Holy Spirit to make their way to the prayer team up front following the benediction.

In the Pastor's Office

My best illustration of his biblical counsel in the Pastor's Office is my own experience. During his first year at Briarwood, I was recruited by a seminary in another denomination. During an appointment with someone seeking pastoral guidance regarding that opportunity, he walked me through Acts 16:6-7. Harry concluded this review by saying something like, "I am sure you have prayed over this. Your wife has concurred. You told me that two other competent leaders have concurred. You have been in academics previously, so push onward, and the Holy Spirit will confirm or block the process." Leaving out the colorful details, the Holy Spirit did block the process through circumstances beyond my or the seminary's control. This occurred after I had already resigned from Briarwood and sought release from Evangel Presbytery.

I made another appointment with Harry as a parishioner, not a staff member. This is the way I opened the meeting: "Harry,

---

3. Harry Reeder III, *LVIX. What Does the Bible Say: Timeless Truth for Timely Topics in Biblical Perspective: What Does the Bible Say about Church Membership*, Briarwood Presbyterian Church, August 6, 2017.

I am here as a parishioner, not a staff member." After laying out the scenario, I said, "I am here today to ask if you might consider finding a place on your team for me?" He looked at me, smiled, and said, "There will be a place for you, but I am not sure what it will be." I responded, "Thank you. Whatever you and the Holy Spirit decide will be my assignment." He then commended me for being open to the Lord's leading, encouraged me, and prayed. He sent me off to reverse the process to rejoin the staff.

In the Staff

Biblical counseling, all too often, in the eyes of people, is relegated to a model that looks like therapy. And, yes, I have logged some 35,000 hours of counseling one-on-one (two or family), which is not too difficult when a career spans fifty years; however, biblical counseling for a man like Harry took place in every venue of life. I've seen him counsel someone in the hall. I've heard him tell accounts of an airplane encounter. I've watched him in staff meetings answer a question in a biblical counseling modality.

When Harry came to Briarwood, he, in effect, counseled everyone on the ministerial staff regarding the importance of being on the same page as a staff. How did he do that? He did so by interviewing each man. He completed each interview in a similar fashion. He offered this counsel: "If you find yourself not on the same page as my philosophy of ministry, please come and discuss this with me. If, after our discussion, you are still uncomfortable, let me know. You will have a job while I work with you to find a call you consider a better fit." They are not his exact words, since that memory is twenty-four years old. However, if you question others interviewed, they will confirm that those words are the essence of his counsel. Why consider this biblical counseling? For several reasons. First, it admonished us not to avoid dealing with an issue. Second, it invited honesty and transparency. Third, it exhorted us to avoid becoming resentful and developing a bitter spirit. Fourth, it was an appeal for righteousness.

My personal interview began with Harry having two of my books on the desk, laying his hand on them, and saying, "Howard,

I've read your books. I believe we are on the same page. If that is ever not the case, I expect you to come and discuss it."

In an interview with Bruce Stallings, Executive Pastor for most of Harry's tenure at Briarwood, who confirmed my observation, he recounted how Harry would listen as a person would present their case, such as being weary with a life situation, and then ask, "Let me ask you this. Why do you not love Jesus enough to do whatever was called for in the situation?" Then he would pause, letting the question hang in the air. He would then follow up with a biblical admonition within its context and frame it theologically and historically. Bruce continued, "Harry had an amazing gift of discernment. He was the best at counseling triage. He could get to the root of the heart problem quickly and discern if he needed to refer and to whom."

As we chatted, I sifted from our conversation; this same gift of discernment was observable in several discussions regarding staff. As staff changes occurred, Harry noted that the personnel change presented an opportunity to realign staff. He asked individuals to consider moving from their current position to the now-open one. He would then recite his analysis and give his biblical counsel for consideration.

Few people, over the past twenty-plus years, had the opportunity to observe Harry in action in an office environment more than Bruce Stallings. In my interview with Bruce, he shared two things with me. First, Harry was attentive to the folks within the office complex. He shepherded them, which, by its nature, includes biblical counseling. Second, in the same manner, with the support staff, from accounting or IT to maintenance, he could listen, make inquiries, quickly discern an issue troubling someone, and quickly move them along by offering biblical counseling.

There is another dimension of his biblical counseling in the office to be noted. From time to time, Marie, his Administrative Assistant, would schedule a meeting with him to transfer a counseling case to me. I found that he had an uncanny ability to analyze a situation. Harry expected me to do my analysis, and I did. However, while I may uncover nuances that fleshed out his analysis, he was always on target, and he realized that while he was competent to counsel, he did not have the necessary time to tackle an extended case and transferred it to me.

In the Classroom

I knew no one who had experienced the classroom with Pastor Reeder more than Dr. Lynn Downing. Therefore, I invited Lynn to contribute to this section of the essay. With a few exceptions, the following are his words describing Pastor Reeder as the consummate biblical counselor in the seminar classroom.

> I never had the privilege to sit under Pastor Reeder's teaching ministry in a classroom setting, academically speaking. However, I had dozens of opportunities to benefit from his counseling ministry to local churches in the United States and many other countries.
>
> The ministry context on these occasions was in conferences on church revitalization called *From Embers to a Flame*. These conferences were designed to drive home the point that a church's spiritual health and vitality are neither determined nor indicated by the *number* of people who attend that church. The biblical spiritual health and vitality level in the pastors, leaders, and church members indicates it.
>
> The primary biblical text for these conferences was Revelation 2:4-5, '... I have this against you that you have left your first love. Therefore, remember from where you have fallen, and repent and do the deeds you did at first, or else I am coming to you and will remove your lampstand out of its place—unless you repent.' The word "lampstand" refers to the local church's ministry effectiveness. This is, quite obviously, a solid instruction from Christ, the King and the Head of the Church. With the heart of a counselor, Pastor Reeder both passionately and compassionately challenged (think biblically counseled, and you would be correct) the attendees at these conferences with ten biblical strategies for restoring spiritual health and vitality to pastors, leaders, and members in local congregations. These had the ring of the biblical counselor assigning homework for the council lead to implement when leaving the counseling office.

Pastor Reeder's council for accomplishing Church Revitalization comes from the authority and the sufficiency of the Bible's instruction. He has used the ten strategies in his pastoral ministry with Christ-honoring success. So, what are these ten strategies to which I have referred?

Strategy #1. Connect to the past to learn from the past without living in the past. Here, he was repeatedly practicing God's counsel to His people. Remember to progress.

Strategy #2. He called for folks to engage in repentance. "Stay confessed-up and repented-up as pastors, leaders, and local church congregants" was his common homework assignment.

Strategy #3. Be Christ-centered and Gospel-driven in the entirety of your ministry. He often sounded like Paul counseling Timothy or Titus.

Strategy #4. Engage diligently and faithfully in Personal Gospel Formation in your own life as a pastor and the congregation's leaders by faithfully using the means of grace. This assignment was for their benefit, but also the benefit of those they would lead. At times, he sounded a bit like the pastor counseling a father. If you talk the walk, then walk the talk by developing your own spiritual life to be prepared to develop their lives and mentor them by example.

Strategy #5. Prioritize intercessory prayer in your life as a pastor, in the leadership, and in the congregation's members. Here, again, was a biblical counseling homework assignment.

Strategy #6. The primacy of the ministry of the Word through preaching. Marie Gathings, Pastor Reeder's long-time administrative assistant, has noted on more than one occasion that every time Harry preached, he did biblical counseling. He encouraged others to do the same.

Strategy #7. Staying on mission with a biblically informed vision for the life and functions of the church. While he gave this challenge from the teacher's podium, it was the same challenge he would give the husband in premarital counseling.

Strategy #8. The multiplication of servant leadership for the congregation. "Make disciples" is the essence of the Great Commission. Harry counseled and, in effect, gave this homework assignment at every Embers to a Flame conference.

Strategy #9. Small group discipleship – the biblical delivery system for effective discipleship.

Strategy number #10. Great commitment to Christ's Great Commission.

Strategies nine and ten are two sides of the same coin. His counsel was something like this. God did His part and has told you what your part is now; use every available means to get the commission done.

With a little sanctified imagination, you can hear the biblical counsel to husbands, wives, and parents regarding their relationships and parenting. As he noted periodically, the home is the seminary in the microsome, the church incubator of disciples, and the world is the target to be evangelized.

Pastor Reeder had a very high view of the importance of preaching, and he believed that every pastor, every church, and every church member must be developed to be Christ-centered and Gospel-driven. He also believed that we must practice preaching the Gospel to ourselves, and for Harry, that meant the whole counsel of God, along with preaching it to others.

He prepared for his preaching very diligently. He also listened diligently to the sermons of other preachers. For example, he once heard a sermon in which the preacher explained the meaning of ten biblical words that describe what Jesus did for us on the cross. He was so moved by the message that he couldn't eat the lunch that followed the service where the sermon was preached. He spent the lunch hour pacing and meditating on what he had heard.

His view of preaching was informed and deeply intensified by an earlier sermon he had heard (years before) on the "rhema" of Christ', e.g., in Romans 10:17. The original Greek term for "word" in 10:17 is not "logos" but "rhema."[4]

---

4. For further study, please see James Montgomery Boice, *Romans*, 4 vols. (Grand

Whether behind a lectern teaching, in a pulpit preaching, or a small group leading, Pastor Reeder was always doing biblical counseling because his view of the Word of God was that of Peter. It is sufficient for life (how we live in relationships, families, and society). It is also sufficient to develop a godly, spiritual life with God. Hence, it always calls for application and a means of implementation, which calls for biblical counsel.

I am thankful for the distinct privilege afforded me over nine years to have witnessed the riveted attention pastors and other church leaders gave to the Spirit-empowered counsel of Pastor Reeder's ministry toward church revitalization."[5]

He is now rejoicing in the Perfection of the Presence of The King and Head of The Church, Jesus Christ.

In the Session and Diaconate

Fresh Bread was the rubric he used to refer to his devotional before the joint meeting of the Session and Diaconate before they dispersed to conduct their kingdom business. This devotional usually had three components: encouragement, vision, and direction in daily and church life. These three components are the essence of biblical counseling. Hence, it is appropriate for the cooperate body of the Session-Diaconate or the individual member.

Casting the Gospel vision in this body for being good family leaders or good church leaders occurs regularly within biblical counseling. When I teach Introduction to Biblical Counseling, I point out that one of the flaws in many counseling theories is that the role of the counselor is limited to one dimension. In biblical counseling, the counselor fills multiple roles, one of which is being directive. Even in a devotional, Harry invariably fulfilled these three roles, with being directive as the concluding one.

Coaching the Session in developing white papers to provide the congregation with counsel regarding contemporary issues

---

Rapids: Baker Books, 2005).

5. For further study of Pastor Reeder's classroom-type counseling for and to the pastors, leaders, and members of local churches, please see his book, *From Embers to a Flame*.

is another significant way he offered biblical counseling for his flock and the church at large. One example is The Briarwood Theological Ministry Statement adopted by the Session at its June 18, 2019, meeting.[6]

"The Briarwood Statement is not meant as a full theological treatment of homosexuality generally, nor is it focused on the related but separate issue of gender identity," summarizes the statement, followed by ten affirmations and denials. The statement is posted on the church website and accompanied by Harry's pastoral letter, highlighting his biblical counsel. He writes:

> Therefore, together with theological clarity and ministry compassion, let us indiscriminately bring the Gospel to the lost and to each other so that those who hear by the power of the Spirit might leave the futility of trying to psychologically, cosmetically and culturally remove the shame of their sin, including homosexuality, and come to Christ, who is the Friend of sinners but who is no Friend to sin, and who can save you from any and all of your sins—homosexuality being no exception. Praise God, His Grace in Christ is greater than all of our sins and any one of our sins. The same answer for any sin is found from the same Savior of sinners.[7]

In Presbytery and General Assembly

Harry did not dominate the floor of the Presbytery. In fact, for a man in his position, he was circumspect. However, when he did speak, it was almost always to offer biblical counsel regarding an issue. What the Bible said about an issue was of the utmost importance, and the action that the Bible called for was always the desired outcome of his speech.

Here is an example. At a Presbytery meeting the year before the forty-ninth General Assembly of the PCA, a rather intense

---

6. As far as I can tell, there are seven Position Papers that Harry wrote offering biblical counseling, and the Session approved. The topics were: Sonship; Marriage, Divorce, and Remarriage; The Briarwood Statement on Homosexuality; The Role of Women in the Church; Boy Scouts of America; SCOTUS; and Deaconesses. For the paper on homosexuality, see: https://briarwood.org/wp-content/uploads/2019/06/The-Briarwood-Statement_June-2019.pdf

7. Ibid.

floor discussion occurred around Greg Johnson's book, *Still Time to Care*. Harry gave an impassioned speech pleading with the brethren to maintain a consistent biblical position regarding homosexuality. He was followed by another speaker arguing for a softening of the message to demonstrate compassion and appeal to the younger generation for the church. This dear brother implied that to follow the biblical counsel was to be compassionless. He confused emotional comfort and compassion. Harry took Peter at face value: "His divine power has granted to us all things that pertain to life and godliness, through the knowledge of him who called us to his own glory and excellence" (2 Pet. 1:3).

In Organizational Meetings

This past month, I attended a counseling conference where my long-time friend, Shirley Crowder, was the administrator. We had a little dead time, in which this chapter was mentioned. As we engaged in reminiscence, she shared the following incident, which displays Harry's ever-ready attitude of biblical counsel, in this case through prayer. It reminded me that I observed his mentor, Dr. Frank Barker, do something similar in a tense Session meeting some thirty years prior. Here is Shirley's account in her own words:

> With the death of Pastor/Teacher Harry Reeder, I have spent much time thinking about his impact on my spiritual life. My first "real" experience with him was when I was in a denominational-level meeting that was very contentious. I was the only woman in the meeting who had presented the information I needed to present. I won't go into detail about the behavior displayed other than to say it was disrespectful and arrogant. At one point, I had just about enough and leaned over to Pastor/Teacher Reeder, sitting to my right. I leaned over and said, "I won't stay and listen to this. I'm leaving." My right hand was on the table to help me push back my chair. Without hesitation and in one smooth movement, Pastor/Teacher Reeder put his left hand over mine, rose, and began praying. He prayed the Lord would forgive us of our sins: arrogance, bitterness, anger, mean-spiritedness. He quoted Scripture and implored the Lord to convict us of our sins and bring forgiveness and reconciliation to our hearts and

relationships. As he closed his very long prayer with "Amen," there was silence, except for the sounds of weeping. Several men were lying prone on the floor, asking God's forgiveness. The entire direction and tone of that meeting changed as repentant people honored God in their decision-making. Through the years, I would email Pastor/Teacher Reeder with a question or comment, and he was always very gracious to reply and offer me answers, encouragement, and biblical counsel for my ministry.

In the Broadcast Studio

I asked two people for input on this aspect of Harry's ministry. Tom Lamprecht was his sidekick on *Today InPerspective*. His response to my inquiry was that every broadcast session included biblical counseling. Below are his examples. The second person was my son, David. He has been an avid listener to *Today InPerspective* since broadcasting began in Birmingham. David is the sole proprietor of a landscape architectural firm and an elder in the PCA who gives us a layman's perspective.

David's Reflection and Comments

'Take every thought captive.' This phrase is that of battle. To take captive, to take prisoners, to take control of the battlefield is indicative of what I observed in Pastor/Teacher Reeder. Pastor Reeder was a bold, outspoken leader. He was 'in the fight'. He took his calling and mission very seriously, but I experienced firsthand his kind, attentive pastoral compassion as well. He was warm, charming, and kind on a personal level. I would say this is very uncommon in a strong leader.

From years of listening to *InPerspective*, I draw these conclusions about his biblical counseling beliefs—he believed we are in a daily spiritual battle internally and externally. As such, we should be prepared to confront the devil and our sins by using God's Word to take each thought captive on the day's battlefield. When wronged, we are to actively pray for the ability to forgive, knowing that it is our responsibility to forgive and act accordingly, trusting that the Holy Spirit (the helper) will make us do so, i.e., walk by faith. When we are wrong, he counsels us to pray for humility, seek forgiveness for our errors, and trust the Lord to handle the consequences or outcomes. The point is that we act in faith. We take the errant thoughts captive by appropriately applying all sufficient scripture to life contingencies.

Pastor Reeder would say, "Mortify or kill the 'old man' in us as we are new creations in Christ." Or, as I often heard him summarize his biblical counsel, "Get rid of stink'n thinking." This is the root of Biblical counseling. Harry offered the biblical counsel: God gave us a mind and His all-sufficient Word for teaching our souls to walk mightily and rebuking the errant, evil, sinful, selfish old man in us.

Pastor Reeder was as flawed as any man, but his gift for loving his flock in the church and on the radio by defining the enemy's lies was unique. His dedication to the faith was admirable and will be sorely missed. He has quit the battlefield and is at rest, but he has left us in good stead to do God's work in taking captives for Christ and winning over our hearts in obedience by following his biblical counseling example.

Tom Lamprecht's Examples

Dr. Reeder knew the Scriptures. If he had not memorized the exact verse that he wanted to point you to, he knew the book and chapter and would lead you to implement its intent for daily living.

Harry would put discipleship and biblical counseling in that same category. While he would have individuals in his office for private biblical counseling sessions, Harry proclaimed that if Christians would prioritize and be committed to corporate worship and discipleship in a Gospel-centered church and would implement in practice what was being taught and preached and counseled, then a large percentage of one-on-one crisis biblical counseling could be circumvented. Harry, like Jesus, would capitalize on events through which he could do Biblical Counseling. He termed it as gaining insight while on site.

As early as the 1980s, Harry began using the power of broadcasting, specifically radio. Whether *Fresh Bread*, a five-minute daily devotional, or *Today InPerspective*, which covered news stories through the lens of Scripture, Harry's function as a Biblical counselor was clear. He desired to get the listener to approach every facet of life, every news item in life, with a biblical worldview perspective that called for implementation in daily life.

Over the last few years of Harry's life, three categories of news stories seemed to dominate the hundreds of headlines that we covered: stories related to the LGBTQ movement, stories related to the culture shapers of society (media, big business, government, and academia), and stories related to all the aspects of the sanctity of life.

Harry wasted no time going to the common denominator in the three news categories. As the consummate Biblical counselor, he took the listener back to the Garden and the lie of Satan: "'You will not certainly die. For God knows that when you eat from it your eyes will be opened, and you will be like God, knowing good and evil'.... Then the eyes of both of them were opened, and they realized they were naked, so they sewed fig leaves together and made coverings for themselves."

If it was a story on transgenderism, it was a story of people shaking their fist at God and exclaiming, 'I will not accept how you created me, I am in charge, and I can become whatever I desire.' If it was a story on the culture shapers of society, it was the arrogant assumption that 'we, the elite of humanity, can be the savior.' If it was a story concerning the sanctity of life, it was sinful individuals striving to cover up the results of sin, even if it meant taking a human life.

As the consummate biblical counselor, Harry never left any news stories we covered without teaching, rebuking, correcting, and training in righteousness, thereby giving the antidote to cure the death sentence of sin—running to our Lord and Savior, Jesus Christ. Harry would always make clear that no matter how great one's sin is ...God's grace is even greater.

Harry would not end any of his *Today InPerspective* podcasts without including a postscript. That postscript was a simple reminder that it is faithful believers and faithful Gospel-centered churches who are on mission, on message, and in ministry, who are the couriers of this life-saving message that is desperately needed by a lost and dying world and the source of biblical counseling for confused and hurting saints.

In Consulting with Other Ministries

Harry has served on multiple boards of multiple organizations. I have chosen one illustrative example, local and counseling-oriented. I invited Dr. Alonza Jones to explain Harry's biblical counseling regarding an important organizational decision. The following is from Dr. Alonza Jones:

> Like the rare sighting of a soaring eagle in the foothills of Alabama, encountering Dr. Harry L. Reeder III was a once-in-a-lifetime experience for all who knew him. He has been described as a man's man, pastor's pastor, and leader's leader. He was all of those things. However, on one memorable occasion, we experienced him as the counselor to the counselors.
>
> The idea was simple. Biblical Marriage Institute (BMI)—a 501(c)(3) ministry founded by my wife Vanessa and me—would organize a major event involving churches and leaders from all four corners of Birmingham. Given the looming threat of marriage redefinition at the time, this plan would be a way to draw citywide attention to biblical marriage while introducing a unique start-up marriage ministry.
>
> Despite the newness of BMI, we were confident the event would be successful. Nevertheless, we decided to seek advice before moving forward. As trained biblical counselors and leaders of a ministry designed to help prevent marital and family breakdown, Vanessa and I relied on Proverbs 15:22, 'Without counsel plans fail, but with many advisers they succeed.' After a season of prayer, we could think of no one more qualified to give advice and counsel to us than Harry Reeder.
>
> Harry was serving as Senior Pastor at Briarwood Presbyterian Church. Though we were not members, we had a long-time connection with the church and a high level of respect and admiration for Harry. Vanessa worked at Briarwood in the early years of Harry's pastorate and often interacted with him.
>
> We called Harry's office, thinking it would be weeks before we got an audience with him because of his full pastoral and speaking schedule. To our surprise, he agreed to meet that week. A seasoned biblical counselor, Harry relaxed the atmosphere and drew our attention to his antique desk

and historic figures lining the walls of his office. We were impressed by the depth of knowledge of each man and his ability to quote their views on leadership. For a moment, it seemed we were on a history tour rather than an appointment to seek guidance. Within minutes, we were old friends. We sat, laughed, and talked. Harry leaned forward as we painted the picture of a grand event that would make a powerful statement in the city on behalf of biblical marriage, thereby bringing glory to God.

After we finished sharing our vision, Harry accurately restated what was presented and offered his thoughts. He skillfully asked questions without preaching, destroying our dreams, or crushing our spirits. It was clear. While the idea was good, its timing was premature for several reasons. Vanessa and I left the meeting relieved God had used Harry's insights to spare us from an ill-timed endeavor. We had been counseled by an intellectual who demonstrated the warmth and style of a country preacher. To us, something extraordinary happened that day. But to Harry, he was living out his calling as a loving pastor, leader, biblical counselor, and friend.

In this scenario, we observe the description of Harry, the biblical counselor counseling well-seasoned biblical counselors. He built involvement, gathered data, discerned the problem, confronted kindly, gave hope, and assigned homework to proceed at the appropriate time.

Conclusion

What made Harry such an effective counselor? And how can pastors and lay leaders follow his example? Ultimately, the answer is found in being a man saturated in the Scriptures. That is the true answer for what made Harry so effective, and it is the primary thing that must pervade our own counseling ministries. It is only in Christ that we find the words of eternal life (John 6:68). A deep and abiding love for the biblical text that has been cultivated by daily reading and meditation is what equips the counselor for any situation. Though the faces and times may change, the source of wisdom remains the same. Thus, whether you find yourself in the pulpit, a staff meeting, or even across from a board member of a 501(c)(3), you must draw upon the text of Scripture. As one dear friend has put it, "if you don't have a word, it's because you're not in the word." Harry was one who always had a word.

Postscript

It is a privilege to have the opportunity to contribute to this volume, honoring my colleague and my friend. As others read it, I hope they will be blessed, as was my friend, co-worker, and proofreader, Mrs. Tami Wells. She wrote, "… I did not expect to be so moved in reading it. I found counsel for issues I have been praying about. God works in beautiful ways as we serve Him … I never knew how much Harry loved us all and welcomed us into his life."

9

Life, Love, and Leadership

Kevin DeYoung

I suppose everyone is unique, but Harry truly was unlike anyone I've ever met. He was a powerful preacher—authoritative and gregarious, big in personality and passionate about the Gospel, funny and blood earnest all at the same time. But he wasn't just a gifted preacher and teacher. He was also an amazingly conscientious pastor—never forgetting a name, learning all he could about his flock, and constantly following up on church members. As everyone who knew Harry can attest, he seemed to possess indefatigable energy, not to mention a filing cabinet in his brain that could produce sermon outlines, the movements of Civil War regiments, and alliterative insights seemingly at will.

In many ways, Harry was a man's man: strong, athletic, and confident. But he was also a family man. Harry will be remembered by thousands, but especially by his wife Cindy, their three children—Jennifer, Ike, and Abby—and their many grandchildren. I will remember Harry as a Presbyterian Church in America (PCA) founding father, as a ministerial example, and as a friend.

A Faithful and Fruitful Ministry

Hardly a week goes by when I do not hear firsthand about Harry Reeder's ministry. Though Harry left Christ Covenant, where

I now serve as senior pastor, almost twenty-five years ago, the church still bears his imprint. Under the Lord Jesus, it's still in many ways Harry Reeder's church.

When Christ Covenant particularized as a congregation on December 5, 1981, the church had fewer than forty members and no pastor. At the time, Harry was leading a flourishing work at Pinelands Presbyterian Church in Miami, Florida. The PCA—less than a decade old—wanted to establish a flagship church in Charlotte. The aim was to plant a church that would plant a presbytery. Not surprisingly, the denomination wanted Harry to return to his hometown and plant this kind of church.

Harry was interested, but he soon discovered there was already a small PCA church in Charlotte, and Harry didn't want to plant a rival church to one that already existed. This humble hesitancy was all the encouragement Christ Covenant needed to aggressively pursue Harry to become its senior pastor. In February 1983, Harry and Cindy moved to Charlotte and began their ministry at Christ Covenant.

Harry left a thriving church of four hundred for a church plant in a trailer. But almost immediately, the church began to grow—tripling in the first three months, outgrowing their facilities the same year, adding a second service in 1987, moving into their first owned building in 1988, doubling again three years later, starting a Christian school in 1989, and then breaking ground in 1994 on the worship center where I now have the privilege of preaching. By the time Christ Covenant moved into its permanent home in 1997, the church had swelled to three thousand members, almost half of whom were children.

In 1999, Harry left Christ Covenant to become the senior pastor at Briarwood Presbyterian Church in Birmingham, Alabama. It may have been the only church that could have lured Harry away from the congregation and the city he loved so dearly. Briarwood isn't only a very large and generous church—it's also the mothership of the PCA, the place where the denomination began on December 4, 1973. Following Frank Barker at Briarwood was no small task, but Harry and Frank supported and encouraged each other admirably during the transition and over their many years together in Birmingham. For almost a quarter century, Harry preached the Bible—faithfully, fruitfully, forcefully—in what is one of our denomination's most important and influential congregations.

A Love for Leaders and for Leadership

For many ministers my age and younger, Harry became an implicit, and sometimes explicit, mentor. Like hundreds of others over the years, I traipsed across Civil War battlefields with Harry as he passed along the stories and leadership lessons he loved to share. He wasn't shy about stating his opinions, but he also was generous in passing out encouragement. Many pastors looked up to him for his theological clarity, his moral courage, and his resolute commitment to the "old paths" of preaching, sacraments, and prayer.

The PCA recently celebrated its fiftieth anniversary. It was strange not to see Harry there. As well as anyone I've known, Harry embodied the motto of the PCA: "Faithful to the Scriptures, true to the Reformed Faith, obedient to the Great Commission." That was Harry—all of him and all of it. He loved to teach the Faith, he loved to defend the Faith, and he loved to share his Faith. I'm sure I wasn't the only person to see Harry witness to the restaurant server or ask perfect strangers how he could pray for them.

Above all, Harry's legacy is the Gospel he preached so effectively and shared so frequently. But he also loved to teach and write about leadership. It was a topic near to his heart and central to his sense of calling. Anyone who knew Harry or learned from Harry on the topic, no doubt heard him talk about the leader's *character*, *content*, and *competency*. Or how the church must *define* Christian leadership, *develop* Christian leaders, and *deploy* them into the world. Or how the church that produces good leaders must be faithful to its Christ-given *mission*, *message*, and *ministry*. Or how the *principle leader* must mobilize *proven leaders*, who can equip *potential leaders*, who can reach out to *possible leaders*. That's how Harry's brain worked. He loved leaders. He loved simple, memorable outlines. And, yes, he loved alliteration.

Moses as Mobilizer

Like many other pastors, I'm sure, I think of Exodus 18 as one of the great chapters on leadership in the Bible. Of course, that's not all the chapter is about, or even the main point of it. But the chapter does contain a number of valuable lessons on what biblical leadership entails and what good leaders should be like.

Exodus 18 is a relatively simple story. Actually, it's two simple stories, both involving Jethro, Moses' father-in-law. The first story is about Moses and his family getting reunited (vv. 1-12). The second story is of Israel getting organized. Moses was acting as the supreme court for Israel. The job was wearing him out and frustrating the people. The situation was bad for everyone. Look at verse 17: "Moses' father-in-law said to him, 'What you are doing is not good. You and the people with you will certainly wear yourselves out, for the thing is too heavy for you. You are not able to do it alone.'" In effect, Jethro was telling his son-in-law, "Look, Moses, you are going to get frustrated because you are here from dawn until dusk, judging these cases. The people are going to get frustrated because there is such a backlog. Can't you see everyone is waiting for you? It's too much."

Think about it: there could be as many as two or three million people in Israel, and every time someone had a judicial case, they brought it to Moses. "Hey, my neighbor broke my wagon." "My cousin ripped my tent." "That man stole my cow." "She took some of my manna." "Your son was getting flirty with my daughter." "That family is encroaching on our land." "Their ox gored one of my sheep." I imagine those were the sorts of disputes that were brought to Moses constantly, and the whole nation had to wait in line while Moses consulted with them to give them an answer. "Listen boy, you got to work smarter, not harder. Teach them the statutes and the laws, and get some capable men to help you."

Amazingly, the system Moses established in Israel was not that different in basic organization from the American system. We have district courts, appellate courts, and the Supreme Court. The judicial system is also similar to a Presbyterian form of government, with a local board of elders (session), a regional body of elders (presbytery), and a national ruling body (general assembly). The Presbyterian system—*presbyteros* just being the Greek word for *elder*—is not only a good, common-sense form of government; it is eminently biblical.

Five Lessons on Leadership

But we aren't meant to simply imitate the system Moses set up. We are meant to learn certain lessons from the leaders who inhabited the system. Let me highlight five lessons on leadership from Exodus 18.

1. Good leaders show respect to others.

Moses is in charge of millions of people, and yet he's not too big to treat his family right. He greets Jethro, welcomes him in, and shows deference and respect. The great leader of God's people understands how he fits in a web of different relationships, especially within his family. Too many people, when they get to a place of social prestige, power, or privilege, feel like everyone ought to be subservient to them. They lord it over others. But Moses understood: "I may be the prophet of God's people—the one who God used to defeat the most powerful empire in the world—and the one who is single-handedly judging all the cases for an entire nation. I'm the one who they all look to for leadership. But here comes my father-in-law, and I'm going to show him respect."

There is a theme in this chapter that we can easily miss in the Western world, but that they wouldn't have missed in the Ancient Near East. Jethro is identified as Moses' father-in-law twelve times. The repetition communicated something important about Moses' identity. He was God's chosen instrument of deliverance; he was also a husband, a father, and a son-in-law. Jethro may have been a priest of Midian, but he was also the father of Moses' wife. That meant Jethro deserved honor and respect, even from Israel's national leader, and *especially* because Jethro was that leader's father-in-law. Even the most impressive leaders must understand that "leadership" is not their only calling or their sole identity.

2. Good leaders bear witness to God's work.

Notice what Moses wants to share once he and Jethro get caught up on each other's lives. In verse 8, Moses tells his father-in-law, "all that the Lord had done to Pharaoh and the Egyptians for Israel's sake." Yes, this was Moses' personal testimony, but the focus was on God, not on Moses. I hope that's what we do when we get to share about Jesus with someone. We may share our personal testimony— "Let me tell you what God has done in my life"—but the testimony should not be focused on our person. Anyone can share what Buddha has meant to him, or how yoga transformed her life. People are "transformed" by all sorts of things. We must share more than what has happened to us. We must share objective truths about who God is and what He has done.

What do you think of when you think of evangelism? Do you think of closing a sale or of twisting someone's arm to accept Jesus? Do you think of witnessing as an awkward attempt to steer every conversation back to a Gospel formula? Or do we think of bearing witness as nothing more (and nothing less) than sharing all that the Lord has done for the sake of his people?

Moses is a good example for all of us. "Let me tell you the great things that God has done," he relayed to his father-in-law. That's how hard and how simple evangelism is. "I've got really good things to tell you about this great God." That's the message good Christian leaders love to share.

3. Good leaders change (when necessary).

We get a glimpse in this passage of Moses' famous humility (see Num. 12:3). Moses listened to his father-in-law—probably a new convert to Israel's God, but still a spiritual novice compared to Moses. Moses explained what he was doing, but did not make excuses when challenged.

We have a great deal of freedom in life and ministry—not utter freedom, but a lot of freedom when it comes to strategy and structures. God doesn't spell everything out. We can take good advice from all sorts of places—from new believers, or sometimes from non-believers. We can even get good advice from in-laws. You'd think Moses would go back and say, "Zipporah, your dad is killing me. You've got to talk to him. This is really driving me crazy. He's always telling me what to do. I've had enough!" But Moses listens and does exactly as his father-in-law says.

Good thing, because Jethro happened to give really wise advice. Good leaders know when to change. That's hard for leaders because they are used to calling the shots. They grow accustomed to telling others what to do and how to improve. But godly leaders know they must never stop improving; they must always be open to change. If you are a leader reading this, consider, when was the last time you said to someone else, "That's a really good idea. Let's do it your way"? Or, "You know what? Your way of doing things is a lot better than the way I've been doing things"? If you've never said that to people, you're either God (let's cross that one off the list!) or you aren't thinking clearly. None of us have all the best ideas. None of us are so high and mighty that we don't have anything to learn from others.

4. *Good leaders delegate responsibility.*

If you care about people, you will always have work to do, because human beings never run out of needs. That means we need to know our limits. God is the only one in the universe who gets His to-do list done every day. Of all the wonderful things I've read from Calvin over my lifetime, this paragraph is one of the most encouraging:

> Therefore let all, whether kings or magistrates, or pastors of the Church, know, that whilst they strain every nerve to fulfill their duties, something will always remain which may admit of correction and improvement. Here,

> too, it is worthwhile to remark, that no single mortal can be sufficient to do everything, however many and various may be the endowments wherein he excels. For who shall equal Moses, whom we have still seen to be unequal to the burden, when he undertook the whole care of governing the people? Let then, God's servants learn to measure carefully their powers, lest they should wear out, by ambitiously embracing too many occupations.[1]

If that doesn't encourage you, then maybe this next sentence will. A little later in the same paragraph, Calvin offers this gem: "One ray of sun is not meant to illuminate the whole world." I love that line. Maybe it will stick with you. No matter how bright we may fancy ourselves, no matter how important we may consider ourselves, no matter how much we think may depend on us: "One ray of sun is not meant to illuminate the whole world."

Have you ever noticed that Moses is tired in both Exodus 17 and 18? In Exodus 17, he is tired, so two men lift up his hands and say, in effect, "Moses, you've got to do this. We'll help you, but you have to keep going." In Exodus 18, Moses is exhausted once again, but this time, he needs to be relieved of the work.

It takes wisdom to know the difference between "I just need a little support so that I can keep pressing on" and "I am doing more than I should be doing." It's not that Moses was incompetent or that the work was unimportant. Far from it. But he was only one man, and one ray of sun is not meant to illuminate the whole world. The critical work of rendering judgment for the nation did not depend upon Moses. God had another way, and a better way, to get the job done.

5. *Good leaders find other good leaders.*

In order to find good leaders, we need to know what we are looking for in good leaders. Thankfully, this passage gives us four criteria. Moses was told to look for (1) able men, that (2) fear God, are (3) trustworthy, and (4) hate a bribe. In other words, they were to be exemplary in relationship to the task at hand, in relationship

---

1. John Calvin, *Commentary on the Last Books of the Pentateuch*, trans. Charles William Bingham (Grand Rapids: Baker Books, 1999), p. 303.

to God, in relationship to others, and in relationship to money. This is what real leadership looks like, and what seasoned leaders look for in other leaders. Giftedness is not enough. Success is not enough. Competence and character are the irreducible minimum for godly leadership.

The Lesson Leaders Often Forget

While we are right to find application for leaders from Exodus 18, it would be a mistake to think the Holy Spirit inspired the passage primarily to give us something as abstract as "leadership lessons." The lessons are there, but if that's all we see in the chapter, we are missing the forest for the trees. We need to pull back and read the chapter in the redemptive-historical context of Exodus as a whole. And in doing so, we will find one more lesson for godly leaders—a lesson that many of us often forget.

As the Israelites made their journey from the Red Sea to Mount Sinai, God taught them something every step of the way. The Red Sea was the place of salvation. Marah was the place of testing. Elim was the place of rest. The Wilderness of Sin was the place of provision. Massah and Meribah were places of warning. Rephidim was the place of battle. Here in chapter 18, at the foot of Horeb, we have the place of help.

Don't miss the mention of Moses' sons in verses 3 and 4. He has two boys: Gershom and Eliezer. Those two names tell the story of Moses' life so far, with Gershom, which means "I was a stranger," and Eliezer, meaning "But the Lord has been my help." With the help of his father-in-law, Moses learns the lesson in Exodus 18 that God will help him when he reaches the end of himself. God has taught Moses: "I can take care of your food, your water, and your enemies." Now he teaches Moses what may be the most difficult lesson of all: "You are not indispensable; I can take care of my people."

It's a good reminder for parents, pastors, and any type of leader. Sometimes the hardest lesson to learn is that God can take care of the people that we love. Moses may have thought, "You can get water. You can send down bread from heaven. You can wipe out the Amalekites. But what about my family?" Well, God can take care of them too. God employs the wisdom of Jethro to free Moses from an impossible burden and to provide God's people with the structure they need.

There is a powerful connection between chapter 17 and chapter 18. In chapter 17, we see non-Israelites (the Amalekites) approach Israel with an intent to slaughter them. Now, in Exodus 18, we see a non-Israelite approach Israel, not to slaughter, but with great sympathy and a good system. God wants Moses—and Israel, and us—to see that He has multiple ways to care for His people. He can conquer the enemies of God (chapter 17) or He can convert them (chapter 18). Either way, God knows how to do for His people what they need to be done.

Blessed to Be a Blessing

There is one more aspect to the story about Moses and his father-in-law that we must not overlook. Let me finish here by suggesting one more parallel—this time not within the book of Exodus but within the Pentateuch. To see this connection we need to go back to Genesis 14 and a mysterious figure named Melchizedek.

Remember that context in Genesis 14? God gave victory to Abram over the nations (v. 17). Then, after that victory, Abram meets a man from a foreign nation: Melchizedek, the king of Salem. And what happens in the following chapter? The Abrahamic covenant.

Think about the same pattern unfolding in Exodus. We have a divine victory over the nations (i.e., the Amalekites) in chapter 17. Then we have the arrival of a sympathetic figure from the nations, Jethro, in Exodus 18. And, following Exodus 18, we have the Mosaic covenant in chapters 19 and 20.

There are other parallels we can point out between the two men. Both Jethro and Melchizedek were priests, both were foreigners, both met with Hebrew leaders after a victorious battle, and both men gave an almost identical blessing. Melchizedek declares, "[B]lessed be God Most High, who has delivered your enemies into your hand!" (Gen. 14:20), and Jethro declares, "Blessed be the LORD, who has delivered you out of the hand of the Egyptians" (Exod. 18:10). Both stories close with a reference to a meal, and both precede a major turning point in redemptive history—the Abrahamic covenant in Genesis 15 and the Mosaic covenant in Exodus 19 and 20.

So what does all of this mean? What are we supposed to learn from these connections?

When the Israelites were languishing as slaves in Egypt, they cried out to God, and "God heard their groaning, and God remembered his covenant with Abraham, with Isaac, and with Jacob" (Exod. 2:24). All that has taken place in the first half of Exodus has been in fulfillment of the promises that He made to the patriarchs. We can see a distinct pattern. God gives the Israelites victory over the nations, and then a great man from the nations blesses them. It happened with Melchizedek and it happened with Jethro. Why? Because God promised as much: "I will make your name great. You will be a great nation, and you will be blessed to be a blessing to the nations." That's the promise of the Abrahamic covenant.

When we come to Exodus 18 we see redemptive history repeating itself. Melchizedek roots his praise to Yahweh in creation. Jethro roots his praise in redemption. In one sense, Exodus 18 is an epilogue for Exodus 1–17 and a prologue for Exodus 19–40. The chapter is a turning point in the life of Israel. In the rest of Exodus, we see that Israel will have a special role in spreading the knowledge of Yahweh to the nations. This God—who promised to make His beleaguered people into a great nation and blessed them to be a blessing to all the nations—began the work through Abraham, and now continues through Moses.

Here's the point: the God who makes Himself known will be made known among the nations by *saving His people* and by *His saved people*. Exodus 18 is what connects those two themes. By sovereign grace, God had saved His people. Now, by the covenant keeping of this saved people, God makes His covenant mercy more widely known. This is what Christian leadership is all about. Israel's leaders were supposed to lead the nation that would lead others to consider Israel's God. Blessedness was meant to be a blessing. Their status as a holy nation was to make known the reality of their holy God.

10

Leading A Ministry Team

David Strain

Famously, Harry Reeder wrote that leaders[1] "are 'thermostats' rather than 'thermometers.' Thermometers merely reflect the environment around them, whereas thermostats change the environment.... A leader *influences others to effectively achieve a defined mission.*"[2] The pastor-as-thermostat metaphor reminds us that pastors are called to fulfill their ministries as part of a team of fellow leaders. It is his privilege and duty to set the spiritual and ministerial temperature of elders, deacons, ministry staff, and volunteers. Few have modeled this ideal more completely than Harry Reeder.[3]

---

1. In this chapter, I will refer to "senior leaders" and "ministry staff" or "teams" in an effort to address a variety of possible scenarios for Christian service, ordained and unordained, in which both men and women, staff and volunteers, are called to participate.
2. Reeder, *From Embers to A Flame*, p. 119. Versions of this definition appear in Reeder, *3D Leadership*, p. 36, and Harry L. Reeder III, *The Leadership Dynamic: A Biblical Model for Raising Effective Leaders* (Wheaton: Crossway, 2008), p. 43.
3. Dr. Harry Reeder mentored me, as he did with countless other young pastors, clearing his schedule to host me and answer my many questions. I was always helped by his seemingly limitless fund of anecdotes and outlines, typically alliterated, offering succinct and compelling counsel, especially on the subject of pastoral leadership. Touring civil-war battlefields or visiting civil-rights monuments over several years with a group of other young pastors, Harry never missed an opportunity to unpack the leadership lessons of history and bring them to bear on the demands of today's ministry in ways I will never forget. He was a pastor's pastor: teaching seminarians, mentoring young

The passage Harry named "the most important verse in Scripture about leadership development"[4] is worth reflecting on as we consider the priorities of leading a team. In 2 Timothy 2:2, Paul tells his protégé, "What you have heard from me in the presence of many witnesses, entrust to faithful men, who will be able to teach others also." The apostolic pattern is clear: Paul trains Timothy to train others, who in turn will train still others. Thus, "leadership development," in a New Testament frame, is an unending process of ministry multiplication. As Paul articulates here, two sides of effective pastoral leadership require attention. On the one hand, there is the ministry leader himself, and on the other, the leadership of the ministry that is entrusted to him.

The Ministry Leader

The exhortation to Timothy requires that ministry leaders must model what they seek to replicate in others. This call to model leadership highlights the centrality of character. Before practical tips or best practices can be considered, we must consider the who before we get to the *how*. When Paul mentions that his instruction to Timothy was "before many witnesses," the focus undoubtedly falls on the tried and tested, public emphases of his ministry, confirmed by the grateful testimony of the people of God.[5]

---

leaders, and training a generation for the work of Gospel preaching, church planting, and church revitalization. I owe him an incalculable debt, and this essay is a small token of my appreciation and gratitude to God for his friendship, example, and legacy.

4. Reeder, *From Embers to A Flame*, p. 120.

5. The phrase translated in the ESV, "in the presence of many witnesses," is διὰ πολλῶν μαρτύρων. Rendering διὰ here, as "in the presence of," is awkward, leading some to suggest the simpler, and more natural "through many witnesses." This creates its own problems, however, if it is understood to mean that Paul's instruction to Timothy was mediated to him second hand, by other "witnesses" and not directly by Paul himself. Given the close personal relationship between the two men, this hardly seems credible. A possible solution might be to understand that Paul's teaching was confirmed, reinforced, and supported "through many witnesses." It need not have been mediated to Timothy through them, second hand, but it most certainly was supported in its essential credibility and reliability by their endorsement. Thus, Timothy knew that what he had heard from Paul was not simply the apostle's own idiosyncratic, private ideas but the widely recognized and publicly supported truth of God, established "on the evidence of two or three witnesses" (Deut. 17:6; 1 Tim. 5:19; Heb. 10:28).

Timothy is to make this the center of his ministry, just as Paul did before him. But there is another facet of Paul's instruction here we should not miss. The open, public declaration of the truth also speaks to the matter of his *integrity*. These are twin concerns in Paul that are often found together. In 2 Corinthians 4:2, for example, Paul says of the ministry entrusted to him by the mercy of God, "we have renounced disgraceful, underhanded ways. We refuse to practice cunning or to tamper with God's word, but by the open statement of the truth we would commend ourselves to everyone's conscience in the sight of God." Here, the apostle rejects both manipulative cunning in his *methods,* along with any accommodation of the truth of Scripture to a private agenda in his *message*. Both who he is and what he says are open and above reproach.

All too often, in selecting and training candidates for pastoral office, the focus has fallen only on the accuracy and fidelity of the message. "Is this man orthodox and sound?" is indeed a question of vital importance, but it is utterly inadequate as the sole criterion of usefulness in the ministry. With it must come a second question: "Is this a man of proven integrity and deep honesty? Is he the real thing, or is he all talk?" A disproportionate concern with the question of orthodoxy to the exclusion of the question of integrity in screening candidates for Gospel ministry undoubtedly lies at the root of a great many instances of insecure pastoral leadership at the head of the team, and of festering ministry rivalries and resentments in the team itself.

But Paul insists on a different paradigm in his instruction to Timothy. The model is to select "faithful men who will be able to teach others also." The character of the man ("faithful men") as well as his orthodoxy and giftedness ("able to teach others") are both in view. And as Timothy looks for these things in others, he can look at his own mentor in the Apostle Paul to see them lived out in a ministry context. The point here isn't difficult, though its implications are profound: before a leader can entrust ministry to faithful men, he must *be* a faithful man himself. "Why are many not practicing 2 Timothy 2:2?" asks Tony Merida:

I am sure there are several reasons, but a few come to my mind. Mentoring is about relationships, and therefore many do not pour into others because it requires time, vulnerability, and trust – and the acceptance of the fact that inevitably someone will hurt you. Others do not practice this multiplying ministry because it is viewed as bonus work. How many pastors are asked by inquiring search committees, "Will you train other elders/pastors?" How many denominations keep count of mentoring relationships? Because we do not submit these things on our numbered lists, they are not deemed important ...[6]

To these reasons for why 2 Timothy 2:2 isn't widely practiced, I might add another: a generation is growing up without adequate mentors themselves. The ministry-multiplication chain described in 2 Timothy 2:2 needs only one broken link for the ongoing replication of new leaders to fail. As ministry becomes increasingly pressured, and the pastoral and leadership demands that ministers are expected to meet continue to grow, leaders sometimes retreat from investing in their team, simply as a coping mechanism amidst all their busyness. They expect the team to get on with the job while they focus on teaching and preaching. And in this way, the key leader stops coaching the team. The inevitable result is a crop of new leaders who have no, or what may be worse, very poor examples to follow.

The task of true pastoral leadership is demanding work. It requires the loving commitment of the mentor to the one being mentored. It involves personal vulnerability and honesty. And it takes a good deal of time. In my interactions with Harry Reeder, I was always impressed by the sheer volume of work he did. And yet, for all his busyness, what was more impressive was how much time, amidst that remarkably busy schedule, he devoted to being with people, investing in leaders, and equipping others. Harry knew that, in no small measure, people *are* the leader's work. If we are too busy to invest in people, we are just too busy.

---

6. Tony Merida, *2 Timothy*, in David Platt and Tony Merida, *Christ-Centered Exposition: Exalting Christ in 1 & 2 Timothy and Titus*, David Platt, Daniel L. Akin, Tony Merida eds. (Nashville, TN: B&H Publishing, 2013), pp. 162-63.

The Leadership of the Ministry

While Harry's emphasis on the character of the leader was paramount, his practical counsel on the nuts and bolts of effectively leading a team was invaluable. What follows is an attempt to distill some of those nuggets of Reeder wisdom that have shaped my own thinking about leading a ministry team.

The Four Cs

Harry was famous for alliterated points, and often summed up what he looked for in putting together a ministry staff team in four Cs: *calling, character, competency,* and *chemistry.*

First, he looked for evidence of a divine *calling* to the ministry in view. In the case of ordained staff members, this involved an inner sense of call, including a basic desire for the work ("If anyone aspires to the office of overseer, he desires a noble task ..." 1 Tim. 3:1). It also involved the outer call of the church, extended to candidates through the appropriate assessment and examination of elders.

Next, he looked for *character*, noting that the New Testament qualifications for office (1 Tim. 3:1-13; Titus 1:5-9) focus on the godliness of the candidate, listing only teaching and perhaps hospitality as areas of expected gifting and ministry. A man who is called but does not yet have the character will be a liability on any ministry team. The Lord may well desire to put them into ministry service in some capacity in due course, but until they meet the basic standards of New Testament holiness, they ought not to be included on any ministry team.

To a sense of calling, Harry added *competency*, by which he meant that good leaders look for the raw gifts needed for ministry in potential team members. We acknowledge that a person may indeed be called to some form of Christian service, and even be remarkable for their godly character, but a good leader of a ministry team is always concerned with matching the gifts of their team members to the needs of the ministry. Many teams devolve into dysfunction because good people, who want to serve, and should be serving, are ill-equipped to serve in the ministry area in which they are placed.

Faced with that problem, wise pastoral leadership ought not to move too swiftly to fire or replace the failing team member. It may simply be a matter of inadequate training. If that is the case, then the fault lies, not with the team member, who has been quietly toiling away as best they can in a role for which they are not properly resourced. The fault really lies with the senior leadership, who has asked this dear brother or sister to make bricks without straw. If, however, after all due training, and all appropriate resources have been supplied, the team member does not improve in their capacity to fulfill the mission they have been given, there are only two options remaining. Either they need to be kept as valued team members but moved into a different area of ministry for which they are better suited, or they need to be helped to move off the team altogether. This last option needn't be punitive or indicative of failure. It may simply indicate that the gifts and capacity of this team member do not fit the needs of the ministry and would be better deployed in a different area of service.

Finally, Harry talked about *chemistry*. In some ways this is the most overlooked, and yet the most pervasive element to assess in putting together an effective ministry team. There is an "x-factor", a hard to define sense of interpersonal connection, without which, even if all the other elements are present, a member of staff will not function effectively as a part of the team. A candidate may be called, godly, and gifted, but if he or she does not relate well to the team leader and the other team members, communication will be slow, trust will erode, and frustrations will arise. Hiring a staff member without attending adequately to the question of *chemistry* is to introduce the possibility of division into the team. The questions a good leader should be asking, as they consider a staff or volunteer team member are, "Do we *click*?" and, "How will this person click with the rest of the team?" Put differently, the question of chemistry asks, will this person *catalyze* shared ownership of the mission of this team, or will they *polarize* the team, creating silos, and reduce us to the pursuit of individual agendas? Chemistry really matters.

Hire to your weaknesses, not to your strengths
One critical mistake a senior leader can sometimes make is to look for people for his staff or ministry team who have the same skill set and personality type as he does. It is not uncommon, particularly in senior pastors who are deeply invested in the work of preaching and strategic leadership, to imagine that the best people with which to fill a team will be just like him, and be preoccupied with the same tasks and deploy the same skill set that he himself possesses. This is invariably a mistake. Remember Paul's rebuke: "If all were a single member where would the body be?... The eye cannot say to the hand, 'I have no need of you,' nor again the head to the feet, 'I have no need of you'" (1 Cor. 12:20-21). By hiring a staff team comprised of people whose main gifts and temperaments replicate his own, he dramatically limits the ability of his team members to fulfill their potential, since they will have to wait in line for opportunities behind the senior pastor.

Instead, a wise leader seeks and accepts the honest evaluation of his peers regarding his own strengths and weaknesses, gifts and capacities, and seeks to find team members who will work in conjunction with those aspects of his personality and ministry without excessive overlap. Of course, this requires deep humility on the part of the senior leader, who must learn to own his faults and limitations, and celebrate the ways his team members complement each other, supplying deficiencies, especially in the senior pastor himself.

One way to describe what he is looking for when building his team is *sympathetic contrast*. It *is* a contrast: all the team members are different in temperament, personality, gifts, and capacity. They do not approach problems the same way and they will not respond to people in the same manner. They do all share a deep sense of personal calling, but the work to which they are called is not identical to the senior leadership, or to each other. But, while it *is* a contrast, it must still be a *sympathetic* contrast.

Team members must know and embrace the assets and liabilities of all the members of the team. They must love and value the variety and diversity of gifts and graces on the team, viewing that variety as a strength to celebrate and an opportunity to collaborate, rather than a cause of jealousy or frustration. The senior leader can certainly foster this culture from the beginning by purposefully seeking sympathetic contrast in the selection and hiring of a staff team. And he must certainly foster this culture in the language, training, and ongoing development of the members of the team as they work together.

Ministry is to be given away, not hoarded

The New Testament word for "minister" is *diakonos*—sometimes translated *minister*, sometimes *deacon*, but the underlying idea is *servant*.[7] In Titus 1:1, Paul calls himself a "servant of God", as does James in the first verse of his eponymous letter, but the word this time is even more dramatic. Paul is a *doulos*—a *slave*. The point of both metaphors is obvious, yet striking. Leading a ministry staff cannot be about ensuring that everyone on the team makes the senior leader look good, as I once heard one senior pastor express his view of the role of the assistants on his team. It must be about the senior leader serving others as the Lord's bondservant. As a "slave of God" he has no intrinsic power or authority. His role is simply to advance the cause and interests of his master, Jesus Christ. What authority he has is, as the Book of Church Order of the Presbyterian Church in America puts it, "ministerial and declarative."[8] It is authority for service and proclamation only. The goal of ministry, in other words, is to give ministry away. It is to empower and equip others, that others might serve. As we've seen, this is the emphasis of 2 Timothy 2:2. Paul describes the priorities of ministry in very similar terms in Ephesians 4:11: Christ "gave the apostles, the prophets, the

---

7. E.g. Acts 20:24; Romans 16:1; Ephesians 3:7; 1 Timothy 4:6, etc.
8. The Presbyterian Church in America, *The Book of Church Order* (Atlanta, GA: The Office of the Stated Clerk of the General Assembly of the Presbyterian Church in America, 2023), Preface, Preliminary Principle 7; and BCO 11-12.

evangelists, the shepherds and teachers, to equip the saints for the work of ministry..." The ministry of pastor-teachers is to equip the saints for ministry in turn. Insecure and paranoid leaders see ministry as an instrument of control and a way to hold on to power. They use ministry to retain their position and status, often at the expense of other members of the team. But ministry in a truly apostolic vein is humble. It gives power away. It serves others, that their ministries might flourish. It is not threatened by the successes of other members of the team, but quietly works to ensure those successes, openly and cheerfully celebrates them, and claims them as wins for the whole team.

Pray for and with the team

Prayer is the minister's great work. Interestingly, it was the drive to preserve the centrality and priority of prayer amidst the growing demands of mercy ministry that led the apostles to create and empower a ministry team in Acts 6:1-7. Usually considered the foundation of the office of deacon, this passage describes the apostles' unwavering commitment "to prayer and to the ministry of the word" (Acts 6:4). Thus, delegated ministry in the New Testament was birthed in the context of the priority of prayer. Given this, it is hardly surprising that new ministry team members were set apart for their work by prayer (Acts 6:6; 13:3; 1 Tim. 4:14). Prayer, in the Bible, is the atmosphere and oxygen of ministry. It must be the non-negotiable priority of a ministry-team leader to pray for and with his team regularly. The senior leader should be able to look each of the members of the staff, or the volunteer ministry-team, in the eye and tell them that he has prayed for them personally, regularly, and by name. Doing so brings the additional benefit of familiarizing the senior leader with the needs of each member of the staff or team, which in turn will enable him to pastor and support them more effectively.

What's more, the senior leader should be the one taking responsibility to ensure the priority of prayer whenever the team assembles. Prayer should be on his heart, and it is his role to call the team he leads to engage in that vital work, insisting that it is the most effective way to advance the Gospel cause entrusted to them. Prayer, in the daily busyness of ministry, can feel like a distraction. We do not have time to pray. We have meetings to attend, decisions to make, events to plan, Bible studies to lead, disciples to make, and sinners to save! It is the senior leader's job to model and gently remind the whole team that apart from Christ we can do nothing (John 15:5). It is his role to bring people to the throne of grace, and insist that quality time taken to pray through the challenges, needs, and opportunities before them will be more effective than hours of prayerless strategic planning, or days of prayerless preparation, or the most compelling but prayerless presentation of biblical truth. What blessing can we expect from all our labor if we do not bow in the prayerful acknowledgement that unless the Lord builds the house those who build it, labor in vain (Ps. 127:1)? The senior leader will lead well when this is the concern that his team know burdens his heart.

Practice "Leadership by Walking Around"
Harry was often to be found wandering the halls, stopping at the study door of a pastor, passing the time with an intern, checking in with an administrative assistant. He was not sequestered behind closed doors, never seen unless to emerge on a Sunday to preach. He engaged in what he called "leadership by walking around." Leaders need to be visible and accessible. They need to care. But they also need to be *seen* to care. Good leaders make themselves available, not just on their own terms, and on their own "turf." I have a pastor on my staff who likes to say that good shepherds smell like sheep. They are always out among the sheep. But a good leader must not forget that his team members are his sheep too. He needs to pastor them, connect with them, shoot the breeze with them, so that they learn to trust him, and know he cares for them. What's more, "leadership by walking around" allows the senior leader to make his own assessment of what's happening, where people are, and what they are doing. It is one thing for a team member to talk over ministry in the senior pastor's study in a formal meeting. It is quite another thing, and may well yield

far more penetrating insights into the dynamics and needs of a team member, when that senior pastor sees them operate in his or her own working environment, where he or she feels most comfortable.

View Conflict as Opportunity

A conflict-averse leader is a contradiction in terms. I am not suggesting that good leaders enjoy conflict. In fact, if, as we face conflict, we do not feel some trepidation, some instinctive recoil at the possibility of giving offense, or of wounding another person, then we are dangerously calloused, and more likely to break a team and hinder its mission than we are to serve it well. And yet, good leaders learn to see disagreement over the best way to serve the core values and fulfil the mission of the team as healthy. Conflict between team members who honestly differ in their understanding or application of shared first principles can, when handled well, generate better understanding between team members and make the outcomes of the team's efforts stronger. To do this, the senior leader himself must be determined not to avoid points of difference, but to invite frank and open dialogue. He can foster a culture where team members are free to disagree, push back, and make their case. In this it is vital that he guard his own heart for defensiveness, and work to avoid identifying himself and his own worth with the acceptance by his team of his own ideas. He must model holding his own agenda with an open hand and willingness to have his mind changed. And he must be ready to meet, one on one, with team members who get defensive and retreat into silence or assert themselves aggressively.

A healthy team is one where all the members bring their thoughts, and are looking for pushback and welcome different approaches. A humble acknowledgment that "I may be too invested in this to be objective, so please help me think through the issues ..." invites the creative input of others and gives them permission to differ or bring critical insights that the team might otherwise have missed. Creating a culture like this takes practice. It needs to be named openly as desirable, and we need to acknowledge that we will not always do it well. We will step on toes, cross lines, hurt feelings, and bruise egos. But if the senior leader himself will keep short accounts with his team, seeking and extending forgiveness himself, and constantly naming the desire to build a team culture of healthy conflict and open debate, most ministry teams can achieve it.

Celebrate Wins

It is very important to the health of any team that each of its members know that the senior leaders value and appreciate them and hear them publicly say so. The Apostle Paul is often to be found describing team mates in glowing terms in his epistles. For example, in Romans 16:3 Paul says, "Greet Prisca and Aquila, my fellow workers in Christ Jesus, who risked their necks for my life, to whom not only I give thanks but all the churches of the Gentiles give thanks as well." In verse 6 he adds, "Greet Mary, who has worked hard for you." In Philippians 2:20 Paul says of Timothy, "I have no one like him, who will be genuinely concerned for your welfare. For they all seek their own interests, not those of Jesus Christ. But you know Timothy's proven worth, how as a son with a father he has served with me in the gospel." And of Epaphroditus, whom he names, in verse 25, "my brother and fellow worker and fellow soldier, and your messenger and minister to my need," Paul calls the church, in verses 29 and 30, to "receive him in the Lord with all joy, and honor such men, for he nearly died for the work of Christ, risking his life to complete what was lacking in your service to me." Paul is naming and publicly praising his team members to the churches, for the encouragement of the churches, and for the sake of the team members who must minister among them. Both the team and the church is helped when the senior leadership celebrates the wins and honors the team mates who have worked faithfully and well in Christ's service.

Practice Accountability

While good leaders celebrate wins on the team, they also must practice accountability. A staff or ministry team cannot succeed without it. Of course, the senior leader himself must be—and be seen by his team to be—accountable to the elders of the church. A man *with* authority who is not also *under* authority is a *liability*. The senior leader must also have the backing of his elders in the appropriate exercise of accountability. He cannot exercise authority he does not possess. But with these things in place, he must still practice regular meaningful accountability. He must have regular meetings with his team, collectively and individually. He must know the weaknesses and liabilities of each team member and openly address them in a spirit of encouragement, seeking to enlist the team member in addressing those issues over time. He must keep an accurate note of those discussions, and be ready to track progress, and encourage the team member for improvements noted. If correction is needed, it is the senior leader's role to offer it, and where necessary, to enlist key elders to assist him, should the message fail to get through. No-one on a ministry team should ever think themselves untouchable or beyond the need to give an account of how they spend their time.

Remember there are no bad teams, only bad leaders

One leadership principle I have heard that has stuck with me is that "there are no bad teams, only bad leaders." That is to say, if the team fails, a good leader does not blame the lazy team member or the dysfunctional staff person. He is accountable for the success or failure of the whole team. He has not communicated expectations appropriately. He has not invested time training and equipping for the task. He has not encouraged and challenged or exercised accountability and correction when necessary. But the success of the team or the failure of the team must be laid at the feet of the leader of the team. It is too easy for the senior leader to scapegoat a failing team member in order to excuse the team as a whole, or absolve himself of responsibility. But this is not a mark of a good leader.

Good leaders take responsibility for the whole team. That is undoubtedly a heavy burden. It is one Harry Reeder gladly bore, not because he believed himself always competent for every challenge, but because he believed himself called to do so by Jesus Christ, the King and Head of the Church. It is costly work. But it is necessary. When your team sees its leader take ownership of their mistakes, and bear the blame instead of them, they will be put in mind of their Savior, who loved them and gave himself for them. And they will love and trust that leader in turn.

11

The Church at Work

Church Governance

Fred Greco

As the other chapters in this book will testify, there are so many areas of Christian ministry in which Harry Reeder made his mark. He was a preacher, a leader, an evangelist, and a pastor. To know Harry was to know that he could, on a moment's notice, give you an alliterative outline on almost any subject! In addition to his own ministry, Harry poured himself into other men like me. He always had time to help younger ministers see and implement important aspects of pastoral ministry in their own contexts. Harry was never jealous of the success of others—in fact, he celebrated it.

One area in which Harry excelled that was not as visible as others was in the governance of the Church, or Church polity. I have had the privilege of teaching this subject at various seminaries and advising churches and presbyteries on polity matters. In this way, I have implemented one of Harry's favorite verses on mentoring and discipleship, 2 Timothy 2:2. Paul charges Timothy to transmit what he has learned to others for the greater benefit and continuation of the Church: "what you have heard from me in the presence of many witnesses entrust to faithful men, who will be able to teach others also." Harry was as active as anyone I have ever met in intentionally mentoring younger ministers and elders. He wanted the Church to benefit from what he had been taught. I recall hearing many times from him about his younger years and how men had poured into him—teaching him about ministry, the nature of the Church, and especially how to interact with other leaders in the Church. It may not be the first thing that someone thinks about when Harry's name is mentioned, but he was a true *churchman*. To that end, I would like to look at various aspects of Church governance that are important for any minister of the Gospel to know and to highlight how Harry set these forth in his ministry.

Being a Churchman

Church governance starts with understanding the nature of the Church. The general contours of the Church are set forth throughout the New Testament. The Apostle Paul calls the Church "the body of Christ" (Rom. 12:5; 1 Cor. 12:27; Eph. 4:12) and gives us a metaphor we can understand for the *connectedness* of the Church. Just as a body has many parts, so the Church has "many members," Paul writes. All of these members are part of a single body (1 Cor. 12:12), of which Christ is the Head (Eph. 4:15). This means that all members of the Church are connected to Christ. To be united to Christ means to be a part of the Church. The New Testament over and over again emphasizes that to be in Christ is to be a part of the Church. That is why Paul tells the Ephesian elders to "care for the Church of God, which he obtained with his own blood" (Acts 20:28). It is why Christ gave the Great Commission to the Church (through its leaders, the apostles), sending them to make disciples of all nations (Matt. 28:19). We should not be surprised that so much of the New Testament is letters written "to the Church" and "to the saints" (note the plural aspect) in various locations (Rom. 1:7; Eph. 1:1; 1 Cor. 1:2; 1 Thess. 1:1; 2 Thess. 1:1, etc.).

This means that believers live in a community that is greater than themselves. They are a part of the family of God, called to evangelize the lost and disciple other believers. As Cyprian stated, "He can no longer have God for his Father, who does not have the Church for his mother."[1] Or, put more bluntly, you cannot claim to love Christ and hate His bride, because Christ loves His bride. Because of this reality, leaders in the Church are called to work together for the greater good of the body of Christ. In the *locus classicus* for Presbyterianism, Acts 15, we see the apostles and elders gathered together to consider a matter of greatest importance: whether it was necessary to keep the law of Moses in order to be saved or whether the grace of God was sufficient (Acts 15:5, 11). The Church is a connected community that goes beyond individuals, or even local congregational expressions of the gathered saints. This is why we see Paul's co-workers Timothy, Tychicus, Mark, and others traveling from church to church to bring instruction, encouragement, and assistance. The PCA reflects this in its *Book of Church Order*: "[elders] must exercise government and discipline, and take oversight not only of the spiritual interests of the particular church, but also the Church generally when called thereunto" (BCO 8-3).

Harry exemplified this aspect of Church governance throughout his ministry. One might think that with all the responsibilities that Harry had in his local congregation, he would have had little time for the broader connectional Church. But this was manifestly not the case. Harry was an active member of his presbytery, serving and advising fellow churches and their pastors and elders. As significant as the churches where he pastored were, Harry knew that the Church of Jesus Christ was bigger. He was a *churchman*—always ready to lend a helping hand or word of counsel. This was also true on the denominational level. The PCA's General Assembly is the national gathering of hundreds of churches and thousands of elders. For many, it is a tedious time of hearing committee reports and contentious debate that "doesn't

---

1. Cyprian of Carthage, "On the Unity of the Church" in Fathers of the Third Century: Hippolytus, Cyprian, Novatian, Appendix, ed. Elexander Roberts, James Donaldson, and A. Cleveland Coxe, trans. Robert Ernest Wallis, The Ante Nicene Fathers, vol 5 (Buffalo: Christian Literature Company, 1886), 423.

reflect real ministry." But the connectional nature of the Church should remind us that we do not minister in a local vacuum; we are connected to the broader body of Christ. We are connected for the important work of planting churches, equipping and sending missionaries, and resolving difficult theological issues. Year after year, Harry could be seen on the floor of the General Assembly, listening to the debates and offering words of encouragement and wisdom. He had the privilege of serving our denomination as the Moderator of the Assembly in 2010 in Nashville, Tennessee. I still recall the grace, wit, and wisdom that Harry exercised in that role. It was a model for me, a younger minister, when I was elected Moderator in 2023. Seeing Harry serve the broader Church throughout his life was a personal application of 2 Timothy 2:2 for me. I have continued to encourage men younger than me to be churchmen—to be involved in the Church beyond the local congregation.

Governing in the Congregation

Presbyterianism is marked by connectionalism—the relationship that congregations have with each other in both a region (Presbytery) and nationally (General Assembly). But ministry starts in the local church. A pastor is called to lead his congregation in a way that honors the Lord and is for the benefit of the Lord's people. For this reason, church governance is not incidental to pastoral ministry in the congregation. As an elder, a pastor must work with other elders, deacons, and congregants so that all are pulling together on the same team for the same ends. We have a rough picture of what this looks like in the Pastoral Epistles of 1 Timothy, 2 Timothy, and Titus. Paul gives directions to his protégés about leading in their respective congregations. He would prefer to give them direction personally, "but I am writing these things to you so that, if I delay, you may know how one ought to behave in the household of God, which is the church of the living God, a pillar and buttress of the truth" (1 Tim. 3:14-15).

Biblical principles are crucial to leadership and governance in the local church. Far too often, leaders simply apply pragmatism or the latest corporate trends in a congregation. The first principle for leaders to remember is that *they serve*. It is important for leaders to know that they do not have all authority and that they should not expect the members of the church to bow to their every whim. The most fundamental authority in a local congregation, the ability to elect officers in the church, rests with the members of the congregation. We see this in Acts 6, when the apostles directed the members to "pick out from among you seven men of good repute, full of the Spirit and of wisdom, whom we will appoint to this duty [*i.e.,* the diaconate]" (Acts 6:3). The apostles appointed, but the members chose. This principle is put into action in the PCA (amongst other denominations) by empowering members of the congregation to nominate and elect their own officers (see PCA *BCO*, Preliminary Principle 6). Church officers must understand that they govern as *servants*, not as masters (Matt. 20:26). One practical outworking of this principle is that an individual's authority is very limited. An individual elder certainly can minister to members in the congregation through teaching and visitation; however, most ecclesiastical power is joint—that is, exercised in concert with other elders. All of us (even elders) have sinful natures we have to hold in check by God's grace, and so the Lord has designed His congregations to be governed by a group of elders who hold each other accountable.

A second principle of governing in the congregation is *humility*. Leaders must understand that the growth and success of the church do not depend on them but that they depend on the Lord. Jesus promised that the gates of hell would not prevail against *His* Church (Matt. 16:18). Don't forget that pronoun! The Church—in each of its local expressions—belongs to Jesus. He is capable of preserving her against schisms, heresies, false sons, and traitors (as the great hymn "The Church's One Foundation" puts it). Elders should not have an attitude that they should never be questioned and that the church is dependent upon them and their expertise. When the Westminster Confession states that councils may err (see WCF 31.4), included in that statement are the most local of councils. When those who govern in the congregation take to heart their own limitations and weaknesses, the strength of Jesus is evident (see 2 Cor. 12:10). I recall an example of this which Harry included in his book, *Embers to A Flame*. It occurred when Harry was the pastor of Pinelands Church in Miami, Florida. After reading the minutes of the Session, Harry saw ways in which the elders had not led the church in a Biblical way. The elders met and discussed the matter, which led to their admitting their faults and instituting a process of seeking forgiveness from former church members.[2] It would have been very easy for Harry to lead the church without humility and to assume that because the Session was in charge, they did not need to answer to anyone. But instead, Harry took the Biblical approach to governing with humility. The result was not a pragmatic increase in membership (as Harry writes, "out of four hundred calls, only four families came back to the church"), but the Lord was honored, and as a result, Pinelands was blessed.

A third principle of governing in the church is *orderliness*. It has been said that a Presbyterian's life verse is 1 Corinthians 14:40, "all things should be done decently and in order." The modern church often mistakes spontaneity and disorder for spirituality. There is a suspicion about any structure in a congregation—church committees are often thought of as contributing to the decline of a congregation. The Bible, however, takes a different view. Paul left Titus behind in Crete specifically so he could "put what remained into order" (Titus 1:5). This was Paul's pattern—as he and Barnabas traveled through Asia Minor, he appointed elders in every church so that the churches would be organized and strengthened (Acts 14:23). Orderliness in a congregation also has the benefit of engaging and involving the people of the church in the work of ministry. It has been well said that when something is everyone's job, it becomes no one's job. By establishing order and structure in a congregation, leaders can cultivate accountability and zeal for ministry. When pastors, elders, and deacons have the view that they must do all of the work of ministry, they deprive others of the blessing of service in the kingdom. Paul makes this

---

2. Reeder, *From Embers to A Flame*, p. 42.

point when he writes that the calling of church leaders is to "equip the saints for the work of ministry" (Eph. 4:12).

I remember the time when I and a member of my staff took a trip to Birmingham to meet with Harry and various members of his staff at Briarwood. Our church was trying to formulate a plan to organize our ministries and involve more congregants in the ministry. We had grown out of the initial phase of our church, during which the vast majority of work in the church was done by the pastors and a few leaders. As we grew, the church started new ministries and had new opportunities to disciple members and serve the community. We knew that we could not continue to operate as we had in the past and be effective. So our session asked Harry if he would be willing to help us to understand the organizational structure and principles at Briarwood, knowing that it would not transfer 1:1 to our smaller church but that we could apply their principles in our context. Harry graciously gave us access to his staff and met personally with us for two days, describing in detail how church committees were set up, how ministry teams reported to the session for accountability, and how new members were encouraged to get involved in the work at Briarwood. This was vintage Harry—rather than saying he was too busy, or that our church wasn't large enough to benefit from Briarwood's structure, he took the time to help us govern our church well.

Putting First Things First

Another important aspect of Church governance is something that we might not expect: understanding that Church government is not a first-order issue of the faith. Not every doctrine is of equal importance. Paul sets forth the doctrines that are most vital: "I delivered to you as of first importance what I also received: that Christ died for our sins in accordance with the Scriptures, that he was buried, that he was raised on the third day in accordance with the Scriptures" (1 Cor. 15:3-4). All teachings in the Bible are important and worthy of our study but some doctrines are more important than others. People of goodwill may have differing opinions on the subjects of baptism, the contour of the end times, and also the proper government of the Church, and still remain Christians. We can debate each other and even believe that others are wrong without anathematizing them. This would not be true of other fundamental doctrines like the Trinity, or the Deity of Christ, or the resurrection. To deny such doctrines would be to show oneself not to be a Christian.

Historically, theologians have referred to this as the distinction between a doctrine that is necessary to the being of a true church (*esse*) and a doctrine that is necessary to its well-being (*bene esse*). Each are found in the Scriptures, but a departure from teachings only necessary to the well-being of the church does not cause such a church to cease to be a church at all. The nineteenth-century Presbyterian James Bannerman put it well:

> What is essential to its existence as a Church, is something very different from what is essential to its perfection as a Church; and although a departure from the standard of the Word of God, either as to creed or outward administration, may be in itself sinful, and must, like every departure from Scripture, be injurious, yet it may be an error neither so fundamental nor extensive in its character as to imply, on the part of the Christian society which has been guilty of it, a forfeiture of its Church state, leaving its ministers without authority to preach, and its ordinances without virtue to bless.[3]

One does not need to be a *Presbyterian* in order to be a Christian. A church may survive (and even thrive!) with a less-Biblical model of government. Unlike first-order (*esse*) doctrines like the Trinity, we can recognize that Church governance, while important, is not essential.

Why is this the case? First, we acknowledge that the Bible contains a lesser amount of information on the subject of Church governance. Unlike the doctrine of justification by faith alone, which is set forth by direct statements in Scripture—"For we

---

3. James Bannerman, *The Church of Christ: a treatise on the nature, powers, ordinances, discipline, and government of the Christian Church*, 2 vols., (Edinburgh: T&T Clark, 1868), 1:57.

hold that one is justified by faith apart from works of the law" (Rom. 3:28), and "since we have been justified by faith, we have peace with God through our Lord Jesus Christ" (Rom. 5:1), to name but two—Church governance is understood typically through good and necessary consequence from the Bible. Passages such as Acts 6 or Acts 15 describe how the early Church operated; the Pastoral Epistles contain instructions regarding government; and even Old Testament accounts such as Exodus 18 (Jethro's advice to Moses about governing) give us principles by which to govern the Church. This fact leads to differing interpretations as to the nature of church authority, the level of organic connection between local congregations, and a variety of expressions of practical leadership.

Second, this requires us to rely on the Holy Spirit to lead His Church. The Bible is not a step-by-step "how-to" manual that we can follow in order to have success in governing the Church. We must do the hard work of studying Biblical principles and applying them to the context of the local church. We must trust the Holy Spirit to guide us into all truth (John 16:13) and give us the wisdom we need to serve God's people. But this does not mean that the Church is governed by its leaders sitting around and waiting for a mystical moment! The Spirit of God illuminates the minds of leaders and sets their hearts on the things of God. We trust that if leaders cultivate a culture of prayer and seeking the Lord, He will answer their prayers and give the wisdom that comes from above (James 3:17). In the well-known passage in Matthew 18, where Jesus tells the disciples that "where two or three are gathered in my name, there am I among them," many assume (wrongly) that Jesus is talking about a prayer meeting. The idea is often advanced that this text proves that even the smallest of church gatherings (two or three) are important to Christ, and He is present. But a closer look at the context of the passage shows us that Jesus is talking not generally about Christians gathering, but about an aspect of the governing of the Church, namely, church discipline. What our Lord is telling us is that He is present in the work of governing the Church, and we should both expect that and *rely* on that. Reliance on the Lord gives encouragement and confidence to those who govern.

Third, acknowledging that Church governance is not a first-order doctrine allows us to work alongside those who differ from us. I firmly believe that the Presbyterian form of government is both Biblical and the best expression of polity. But I have respect for those who have come to a different conclusion. A congregational church or a church governed on episcopalian principles is still a true church when it holds to the fundamentals of the faith. This means that those who are committed to Presbyterianism can work with non-Presbyterians on primary theological issues (*e.g.*, justification by faith alone, the inerrancy of Scripture, the Deity of Christ) and on the application of Biblical principles in our society (*e.g.*, the definition of marriage).

Harry's life and ministry reflected the truth of putting first things first. He was a committed Presbyterian and often quipped, "You can get into heaven and not be a Presbyterian, but do you really want to risk it?" At the same time, his main focus was bringing people to Christ and discipling them. That meant staying "on mission, on message, and in ministry" as he so often said. One of Harry's principles was, "I will go wherever I am asked if I can preach the gospel." That led Harry to a variety of venues and opportunities where Presbyterians seldom went. One example of this was the vibrant ministry that Harry and Briarwood had within prisons. At the Bibb County Correctional Facility, inmates were brought face-to-face with the claims of the Gospel. They put their hope in salvation by grace alone in the teachings of an inerrant and infallible Bible. Harry knew that what the inmates needed were the fundamentals of the faith. He did not dwell on distinctives like Church government—especially since those he ministered to were not in a local church!

Conclusion

I must admit that discussions about Church governance are not the most scintillating and sought-after of theological subjects. But if we understand that the Lord Jesus Christ came to build His

Church and that He loves His Church, we will love the Church too. We will understand that a practical way to love the Church is to lead her in a way that benefits and blesses the people of God. Leadership, for good or ill, has consequences. Harry understood this and was passionate about emulating great leaders and teaching principles of leadership. Whether it was military leadership, political leadership, or ecclesiastical leadership, Harry was a student who put what he learned into practice. We ought not to neglect the importance of proper governance in the Church. The Church of Jesus Christ is worth our efforts and our commitment.

12

Christian Education

The Leadership and Legacy of Harry Reeder

Niel Nielson

Harry Reeder's leadership and legacy for education, and specifically Christian education, grew out of the providential path of his own education—from his college years at East Carolina University where, he freely admits, his priority was baseball; and then at Covenant College where he first encountered the all-encompassing breadth and beauty of Christ's preeminence in all things; and then through his calling as a church pastor to lead and promote Christ-centered and biblically grounded schools and a theological seminary, all under the authority of the church; and then across the decades through his encouragement to parents to make the truth and grace and glory of Christ the centerpiece of their educational plans and aspirations for their children. Through all these stages and phases of life and ministry, Harry sounded a clear call for the priority of biblically grounded, Christ-centered, Gospel-fueled education.

My connection with Harry began shortly after I became president of Covenant College in 2002. Harry had arrived at Briarwood Presbyterian Church three years earlier, and because of the long relationship between Briarwood and Covenant,

I visited Harry virtually immediately. It was a delight to learn of his strong and clear Reformed biblical and theological convictions, his passionate embrace of his pastoral calling, and his wholehearted support for Christ-centered education. We met frequently throughout my ten years at Covenant to grow the crucial relationship between church and college, but, just as importantly, to encourage one another in our somewhat different but missionally aligned roles. Throughout those years, I came to lean on this biblically unswerving, clear-headed, articulate, and valiant champion for his penetrating questions, his sound counsel, and his encouragement to lead Covenant hard against the almost universal trend of Christian colleges and universities to drift from and eventually jettison their founding convictions. I treasure my friendship with Harry and, along with so many others, I miss him dearly.

In this brief essay, we will first follow Harry himself by considering the biblical foundations and motivations for Christian education that he considered most important. Harry was first and foremost a Bible man, and it was his relentless and spiritually instinctive pattern to always go to the Scriptures first to ground his thinking and practice firmly in God's Word. Harry believed that God has spoken clearly and powerfully and categorically about the responsibility of one generation to commend the mighty works of the Lord to the next, so that, by God's grace, children and children's children would walk in faith and faithfulness.

A great benefit of following Harry in his biblical expositions is understanding not only *what he thought* about Christian education, but also *how he thought* about it. Harry recounts that during a gathering of teachers when he was expositing a passage of Scripture, one teacher asked, "This is great, Harry, but when are you going to talk about education?" With his typical pastoral kindness but with absolute, even silencing, firmness, he responded, "Excuse me, but this is the very heart of education"—and carried on. For Harry, the Scriptures show us both what to think about Christian education and also how to think about it.

There is, therefore, no better way to honor Harry's leadership and legacy than to follow him through his explorations and expositions of Scripture and its implications and applications for Christian education.

Following this first and longest section, we will briefly consider several vital concepts in Harry's understanding of Christian education. Finally, we will get glimpses into Harry the leader and the man from others who knew him in the context of Christian education. (In most cases, his teaching on this topic occurred in "live" sessions, e.g., academic convocations, school staff gatherings, sermons, etc. This means that most of Harry's words on education are preserved in audio recordings and not in print—perhaps representing an opportunity for the valuable project of transcribing, editing, and publishing his work on the topic.)

Harry's Biblical Expositions
Psalm 1

Ask anyone who heard Harry speak about Christian education over the years, "What Bible passages did Harry regularly reference?" The response would always include Psalm 1. For Harry, Psalm 1, understood in its full biblical context, provides a sound basis and direction for parents and churches in their God-ordained educational calling.

First, Harry notes that Psalm 1 urges upon God's people the necessity of "putting off" before we can "put on"; we must walk away from the bad before we can walk toward the good. Thus, we must first recognize and avoid following godless counsel, giving ourselves to sin, and finally becoming scoffers at God's truth. Given how easily our minds can be captured by the ideas and ways of the world in rebellion against God, only God's wisdom will enable us not to be pulled by and absorbed into the world's ways.

Harry often rued the sad reality that many Christian parents are turning their children over to unbelievers for more hours than the parents themselves have with them, failing to recognize the ungodly counsel that is being infused into their children's minds.

In this context, I particularly mention Harry's extensive work on "Progressive Christianity," about which he spoke and wrote much. In calling out the motivation, mission, message, and ministry of progressive Christianity, Harry provided helpful resources for understanding the errors and dangers of this current trend—this failure to contend for the faith once and for all delivered to the saints—for Christian education. We can see ample evidence in the steady stream of formerly Christ-centered and biblically faithful colleges and universities as they embrace the counsel of the wicked, following and even promoting the way of sinners, and eventually take their place among the scoffers—more and more examples of what James Burtchaell calls "the dying of the light" on Christian campuses.

Harry repeatedly reminded his listeners that every communication on any topic has an implied or embedded world and life view, either God-centered or man-centered. This principle is especially significant for education—i.e., there is no such thing as spiritually and theologically "neutral" education, and there is no educational subject that eventually does not present the opportunity, indeed the necessity, for this either-or world view decision.

Our children do not begin life in spiritual neutrality, and neither do their teachers. By nature, they are all sinners in need of the cleansing blood of Jesus Christ and the renewing grace of the Holy Spirit. There is no neutrality—every human being is either a child of God or a child of the devil. This reality means that no aspect of education is outside the rule and authority of Scripture for Christians. Harry specifically recounted his own experience at Covenant College, where he saw that his history, biology, and philosophy courses were not "over here," while his Bible courses were "over there." Instead, the Scriptures grounded and framed all subjects, and all subjects were studied in submission to God's revealed Word.

In light of this, Harry noted several particular pitfalls even in Christian education:

1. *"Christian rationalism,"* which makes the mistake of starting with the elevation of reason and the capabilities of the rational human mind, fails to consider that our minds themselves are infected by the fall into sin. In Harry's view, human reasoning is a glorious gift of God, but is to be used as an instrument whereby our foundational faith seeks greater understanding and application in all areas of thought and life.

2. *"Pharisaism,"* which makes the mistake of trying to ensure that students don't do bad things and instead do good things, but without recognizing the fundamental need for minds and hearts to be transformed, to be made new by the saving grace of God and the supernatural work of the Holy Spirit.

3. *"Prideful intellectualism,"* which makes a mistake, analogous to Pharisaism, of focusing on academic achievement as the most important goal of education, failing to recognize the far more essential and eternal spiritual purpose.

(There is also what we could call *"prideful achievement-ism,"* whether in athletics, the arts, or business. Parents and Christian educators need to remember that there is a .003% probability that a student-athlete will play professional sports, but there is a 100% probability that that student-athlete will one day stand before the judgment seat of God. As Harry once put it, "It must not finally be about who goes where to college, or SAT scores, or sports championships. It must finally be about Judgment Day, and the wonder of hearing, 'Well done, good and faithful servant'" [Matt 25:23]).

4. *"Compartmentalization"* which makes the mistake of treating academic subjects and co-curricular activities as isolated units, each a world unto itself, fails to recognize their inter-connectedness under the authority of Scripture and the lordship of Jesus Christ. For Harry, whether in the classroom or on the playing field, mind, heart, and hands always work together as aspects of how God has made us.

So how did Harry advise that we avoid these pitfalls? Even as Psalm 1 first instructs us on what we must put off and walk away from, it also instructs on what we must put on and walk toward (v 2): delight in the law of the Lord, on which the Christian meditates day and night.

Harry frequently reminded his listeners that Christian education does not start with fear, neither fear of the devil nor fear of culture. Whatever you fear will most certainly control you. That is why Psalm 1 shows us the positive enterprise of educating toward godliness, rooted in God's perfect love and providence.

Those who delight in God's Word and ways, and whose minds and hearts abide with assurance in the good news of the Gospel and the hope of eternity with Jesus, are wonderfully described in verse three—Harry called this a "blueprint" for Christian education:

1. They are planted like strong trees, rooted and strong;

2. They live and grow by the nourishment of streams of living waters;

3. They bear the fruit of grace and truth and obedience in God's purposeful plan and timing;

4. They do not wither and die in seasons of struggle.

According to Harry, here is the spiritual design for Christian education that we should work toward, and the hope for students we hold in our hearts as parents, teachers, and church leaders. Our ultimate motivation must be that our children would grow into faithful and fruitful followers of the Savior, in wisdom and stature and favor with God and man, all for God's glory.

In one message, Harry referenced the story in Luke 2 of Joseph and Mary taking twelve-year-old Jesus to the temple, where, according to verse 46, He was "sitting among the teachers, listening to them and asking them questions." His parents guided him into the path of learning in a place where there were mentors to assist them in their parental task. And we read in verse 51 that, even as the very Son of God incarnate listened and learned, He "was submissive" to His parents. What an example for us of our calling as parents and educators so that we would lead our children and students toward maturity in Christ, wisdom, self-control, and faithfulness.

If this is our task and our goal, how do we do it?

First, Christian education requires Christian educators. We will come back to this again later in the essay. But for now, we must immediately admit that we cannot expect our children to avoid the counsel of the wicked or the way of sinners or the seat of scoffers without teachers, transformed by grace, who themselves are listening to godly counsel, and pursuing paths of obedience, and displaying honor and love toward God's truth and the ways of biblical faith. For Harry, Christian education rises or falls on the shoulders of teachers. Why? Here are three reasons:

> (a) Competent and earnest Christian teachers "know their stuff," and thus, they can instruct and mentor wisely and well.

> (b) With hearts fully given to Jesus, Christian teachers will live what they teach and will be models for their students of Christian thinking, Christian living, and Christian witness. As Harry put it, for the Christian teacher, "20% is what I say, and 80% is what I am and do." Or, in another place, teachers teach "by talking and by walking."

> (c) Finally, true Christian teachers are those who love to learn. Psalm 111:2 says, "Great are the works of the Lord, *studied by all who delight in them*." That delight drives Christian teachers to continue to learn, for when we quit learning, we forfeit the right to teach.

Second, Christian education requires an unswerving commitment to the truth of God's Word. Harry would point out that:

> (a) All truth is God's truth, for He is the only source and guarantor of truth.[1]

---

1. Consider the words of John Calvin, who says that "All truth is from God; and

(b) Everything in the Bible is true; therefore, we can trust it for guidance in every area about which it speaks.

(c) But not all truth is in the Bible, and so we apply our minds and imaginations to discover the implications and applications of Biblical truth for all areas of life and learning.

(d) And not all that people claim is truth is true. Just because someone says it is true does not mean it is God's truth, which Schaeffer called "true truth."[2] And so we continually test all areas of human wisdom and knowledge against the inerrant Scriptures.

So, how do we deal with truth claims? We check to see that there is no contradiction with the Scriptures, which provide sufficient information and a consistent framework to evaluate all claims to truth. It is the task of the Christian educator to prepare students to deal with all truth claims. In the modern university, given over not just to secular but often pagan ideologies, spirituality is in but Jesus and the Bible are out. How will our students deal with that, if not by the inerrancy, sufficiency, clarity, and integrity of God's Word?

Third, Christian education requires the hard work of integration for the sake of a unified, biblically interconnected world and life view, that we might see all of life through the lens, and according to the paradigm and framework, of the Scriptures, with Jesus Christ at the center. What we know about God and His holy words and mighty works from the Bible changes everything. First and foremost, students must know their God—Creator, Redeemer, Sustainer, Judge. They must understand the biblical doctrine of man—created, fallen, destined for either everlasting

---

consequently, if wicked men have said anything that is true and just, we ought not to reject it; for it has come from God. Besides, all things are of God; and, therefore, why should it not be lawful to dedicate to his glory everything that can properly be employed for such a purpose?" John Calvin, *Commentaries on the Epistles to Timothy, Titus, and Philemon*, trans. Willam Pringle (Grand Rapids: Baker Books, repr. 1999), 300-01.

2. Schaeffer first introduced this idea in *The God Who is There* (Downers Grove: InterVarsity Press, 1968).

punishment by God's just judgment or God's glorious presence by His redeeming grace.

Ultimately, in and through every subject and activity, students must know that Jesus Christ is all and in all. In Him are hidden all the treasures of wisdom and knowledge (Col. 2:3); He has won the victory, and in His coming again, the final consummation of the ages will arrive.

Thank God for Harry's exposition of and development from Psalm 1 for such a grand and compelling vision and mandate for Christian education. Next, and much more briefly, we consider three additional Bible passages which Harry exposited as instructive for Christian education.

2 Timothy 2:2; 3:14-17

In 2:2, Paul reminds Timothy of what he has heard from Paul, and in 3:14, he urges him to continue in what he has learned. This is a learning that has borne the fruit of firm belief. Students cannot and will not learn what they have not heard, and they cannot and will not believe what they have not learned. Harry wisely and rightly stated, "We cannot give our students faith, but we can give them the word of faith—who God is, what He has done, and what they need to know and understand in order to believe and obey." Our aspiration must be not only that our students would pass the test, get the grade, graduate, or be admitted to the best university, but above all, that they would "firmly believe."

For Harry, this word of faith—the truth of all the Scriptures—points us to the authority, sufficiency, and inerrancy of God's Word. Harry's view of verbal plenary inspiration included attention to every word and even to word order, to the original authors' intentional vocabulary and grammar and syntax—what Paul in 2 Timothy 1:13 calls the "pattern of the sound words that you have heard from me."

But then Paul continues in 3:14—"... knowing from whom you learned it ..." an explicit reference to the role of the teacher, whose identity, character, and trustworthiness matter. Timothy's teachers included Paul himself, but also his grandmother Lois and his mother Eunice, who both taught and modeled a "sincere faith."

In verse 15, Paul makes clear that this hearing and learning from godly teachers was not haphazard nor occasional. It happened continuously, even relentlessly, from youngest childhood all the way through what we would term elementary, secondary, and post-secondary stages, so that Timothy became "acquainted with the sacred writings." The Greek word translated "acquainted" does not suggest casual acquaintance, but a deep familiarity and personal understanding that could result only from years of persistent and thoughtful learning.

And it is that deep familiarity with the Scriptures that made Timothy "wise for salvation through faith in Jesus Christ"; hearing and learning that bore the fruit of firm belief, which is the only ultimate indicator of the effectiveness of Christian education, by the grace of God.

We cannot give our children and students saving faith; we cannot produce firm belief in them; we cannot see into their hearts. But we can and must look for indicators that our sovereign, gracious God has done and is doing His saving and sanctifying work in them. In our assessments and evaluations, both of students and ourselves, how might we be assured that our students are actually converted, that their hearts have been made new in Christ, and that they are growing in faith and faithfulness by the power of the Holy Spirit? Of course, only God truly knows for sure. But we abdicate our responsibility if we do not seek to know what is in their minds and hearts, as we teach them and walk alongside them through the years they are with us.

This short section of 2 Timothy 3 concludes with its most well-known verses—verses 16-17—so often ripped out of the context of the previous verses. Not so in Harry's hands. It is all Scripture, breathed out by God, that provides the necessary and sufficient resource for the lifelong and salvation-fruitful education that Paul has just described in Timothy's life: teaching, reproof, correction, and training in righteousness, in order to be complete and mature in Christ and fully equipped for every good work (2 Tim. 3:16).

Here is how Harry unpacked this holistic and mature equipping through Christian education:

1. The ability to observe life accurately and clearly through the frame of a biblical worldview. What is my framework for everything I see? Mountains, people, politics and justice, food, sport, business, family, healthcare, gender, and—yes—rainbows!

2. The insight to analyze thoughtfully all that we observe, to understand and organize and make careful distinctions, and to define what the problem is and what Christian and godly responses should be. (Harry offered the example of the twelve spies of Numbers 13, all of whom viewed the same data but brought back very different recommendations because of different world and life views.)

3. The ability to draw logical conclusions, to follow lines of arguments and lines of cultural development to see where they end up.

4. The wisdom and courage to respond to opportunities and challenges of life, including their own mistakes and struggles and sin.

5. The capacity to contribute to the ongoing formation of their own lives, rooted in God's breathed-out Word and ever-growing toward maturity in Christ until they see Him face to face.

What a valuable explication of Paul's words in 2 Corinthians 10:6 about taking every thought captive to obey Christ under His preeminent supremacy and authority over absolutely everything. Of course, this is possible only through the illuminating, sanctifying, and empowering ministry of the Holy Spirit.

Thus, for Harry, Christian education is:

1. Foundational and comprehensive for all of life—God's people would, according to the Great Commission, observe all that God has commanded.

2. Continual—as followers of Christ we never quit learning, for even as we can know God now intimately and truly, even in eternity we will continue to know Him better and more deeply and more sweetly, as Paul says in Ephesians 2:7: "… so that in the coming ages he might show the immeasurable riches of his grace in kindness toward us in Christ Jesus."

3. Directional—always toward Christ, wanting our students not primarily to love or like us, but to love Jesus, and to love Him not only through Bible classes and chapel services, but also through history and biology and mathematics. Dare we imagine that, as Harry put it, we could "turn an algebra lesson into an evangelistic crusade?"

Romans 12:1-2

Our children and students are living in a world designed with every effort and skill to make them ashamed of the Gospel. What can enable them not to be ashamed of the Gospel, in a manner similar to Paul, who virtually shouted in Romans 1:16, "I am not ashamed of the gospel!"?

According to Harry, it is the truth of Romans 12:1—the finished work of Christ, by the mercies of God. There is nothing needed in addition to what Christ has done. In Christ, believers have a new perspective, a new heart, a new record, a new family, a new life, and a new home—all is theirs in Christ.

In Romans 12 and following, Paul answers the question, "How do we live in light of Christ's finished work?" In Christian education, how do we build bridges in every subject and activity to show our students the "why-how-where-for what" implications and applications of Jesus' death, resurrection, reign, and return?

1. We sacrifice for him; we live a sacrificial life for him. Salvation is a free gift that costs us everything. So, Jesus is not

at the top of our priority list; Jesus is THE priority. It is not just Sunday but every day; not just church worship but all my life and work as worship. In view of Christ's finished work, we present our bodies to him—our earthy, concrete, day-by-day-by-day, embodied life.

2. Paul appeals to "you." This is personal—it is "you" Paul is addressing, not just the others. There is no way to avoid the command for every one of us to keep on giving ourselves to Christ, who is our life.

3. This sacrifice is a total commitment—unreserved, with no negotiation or excuses. For example, Harry mentioned pastors who would affirm their pastoral calling as long as God did not call them to certain places.

4. This whole-life sacrifice is doxological; it is worship. Our lives are to be a worship statement—whatever you do, in word or deed, do all to the glory of Christ.

5. This worship is "logical," as Harry understood the Greek word. This is Gospel logic; it is where the Gospel mercies of God logically and rationally lead us, the life-and-living conclusion to the "argument" of the Gospel.

6. This logical sacrifice involves, as we saw in Psalm 1, both a turning toward and a turning away, in this case, "Do not be conformed to this world." Do we fully realize what our children and students are exposed to virtually continually, by the ubiquitous presence and addictive power of social media, relentlessly recommending to them a world and life view utterly opposed and hostile toward God? Of course Paul's aim here, and our aim, is not that our students would be eccentric or cultural weirdos, but that they would be different for Christ, shining like stars in a dark and perverse generation.

7. Finally, how do we get there? By renewing our minds. Harry points out that this is a command in the passive voice: an

intentional aim on our part that we cannot do by ourselves, a command that we obey only by the grace of God.

What, then, does it look like to do Christian education rightly and well? It begins with a right view of God, a right view of man, a right view of sin, a right view of being right with God, and a right view of God's purposes for His creation, from the beginning all the way to the consummation—all by the mercies of God.

What outcome do we work for and hope for? That those we teach become worshippers of God in the gathered assembly and throughout their entire lives: living sacrifices holy and acceptable, not conformed to the world's wisdom and ways, transformed for fulfilling the will of God, and all that is good, acceptable, and perfect.

Our prayer is that when they leave our school, they know Christ, they know how to live for Christ, they know how to tell others about Christ, and they know how to enjoy Christ.

Daniel 1

The early chapters of the Book of Daniel tell the story of four students who changed a pagan world. They were physically of good appearance; they understood learning and how to learn; and had "presence," competent to stand before the king. They were prepared for a royal examination through which they bore witness to their unbending allegiance to God and His word rather than following the ways of the pagan world around them. And thus they were in fact the beginning of the loosening of the bondage of Israel in Babylon:

> 1. Young men who made the right decisions, for encouragement and challenge to those who had compromised, to show that faithful obedience to God does make a difference;
>
> 2. Young men prepared for what was coming—a lion's den and a fiery furnace;

3. Young men who stood firm as faithful witnesses before pagan kings so that even a royal God-hater would become a God-fearer.

We surely must imagine a time in the earlier stages of these young men's lives, before their years in Babylon. Indeed, like Timothy, they had, from childhood, become "acquainted with the sacred writings" of Scripture, which were then able to make them wise for salvation and faithfulness.

Like Daniel, Shadrach, Meshach, and Abednego, our young people live amid a pagan society that celebrates and codifies unbelief and immorality, calling truth falsehood and falsehood truth, and calling evil good and good evil. And we can hope that God will enable our young people, like Daniel, Shadrach, Meshach, and Abednego, as His prepared, uncompromising, and faithful witnesses in their day. By God's grace, who will they be?

1. They will be students who have trusted in Jesus as Savior and Lord. And so we must evangelize them, not with gimmicks but with the clarion call of the Gospel, so that with new hearts they would trust in Christ alone.

2. They will be students discipled with a Christian world and life view, so that they will recognize the winsome and tempting menu of the world and, with the mind and heart of Christ, will think biblically and respond graciously and firmly. This will sometimes involve cleverly creating solutions, as in Daniel 1, but never by cowardly compromise and capitulation.

3. They will be students who, when the world tests them, know who draws the line. For them, Babylon will not set the agenda but God and His Word, showing them how not to defile themselves but to do all things for God's glory.

4. They will be students who will not live in the "arrogance of independence," but will seek out and appreciate the covenant communities of faith and the band of brothers and sisters with whom they walk before the Lord. What a blessing, especially

during times of testing, to encourage one another together in the Lord.

5. They will be students who know and understand the ideas, worldviews, and life views of the unbelieving and pagan world around them. As Daniel and the others knew the literature and language and culture of the Chaldeans; as our spiritual fathers and mothers knew and understood the heresies of the early church, and the errors of Darwin, Hegel, Nietzsche—and Oprah!—so our students will be equipped to peel back the layers of false and pagan worldviews, to raise incisive and revealing questions, to show inconsistencies and contradictions, to point to the destruction to which such views inevitably lead—and then to point to Christ who is the wisdom and righteousness of God, and who alone is the hope of the world.

What a legacy Harry has left us in his biblical expositions in the context of Christian education. Presented in this essay is but a fraction of all that Harry spoke on the topic, yet it is enough to know without question what his convictions were, and then to follow in his footsteps joyfully and uncompromisingly in raising up generations of young men and women to know and trust and love and serve the Lord.

In the remainder of this essay, we will first briefly summarize several of Harry's key convictions regarding Christian education, some of which have already been mentioned above, and second, observe several qualities of Harry's personal leadership in an educational context.

Harry's Key Concepts
Christian Education and the Christian Parent
Harry was adamant that the final responsibility for Christian education does not fall to schools but to parents. He insisted as well that Christian education is mandatory for every Christian parent, and that it is the joyful privilege and responsibility of parents to train and educate their children.

This does not mean that there is only one mandatory "delivery system"; parents have the prerogative and responsibility to choose what they believe to be the best for their children. But if they choose public education, their diligence and vigilance must be multiplied, especially in our time when ungodly influences are so powerful. They must look for ways to ensure that their children are being fully educated Christianly, whether the particular school they attend is aligned or not with their own biblical, theological, and ethical convictions. Even so, Harry believed that faithful Christian schools, like Briarwood Christian School, were unequal in what they did and could do.

Harry often quoted Deuteronomy 6:7 to emphasize parents' responsibility: "You shall teach [God's Word] diligently to your children ..." But he also warned that parents cannot teach their children what they do not know in their own hearts. This parental responsibility can be fulfilled only as parents themselves are growing in the Lord and filling their own hearts with more and more of God's truth, grace, love, and glory.

Further, this responsibility is not limited to "spiritual" devotions or bedtime prayers. Rather, Deuteronomy 6 insists that parents must disciple their children to take God's Word into all of life: "... when you sit in your house, and when you walk in the way, and when you lie down, and when you rise."

Furthermore, Ephesians 6:4 commands fathers to bring their children up "in the discipline and instruction of the Lord." This implies not only biblical content, but also the order and regularity and range of discipleship, so that our children will develop a consistent and systemic world and life view, able to see all of life under the rule and reign of Christ. In this way, they will more and more immediately recognize and understand the radical either-or dichotomy between the counter-cultural claims of Scripture and Christ and the false and misleading claims of the world.

Parents may rightly seek out assistance from schools for this formidable calling to disciple their own children, so that they might extend their own influence through the schools' impact.

In this case, parents should ask, "What kind of educators do we as parents want to help us disciple our children?"

But parents always remain fully and finally responsible for any and all such assistance, and must choose carefully and monitor closely in order to fill gaps, to counter error, and to affirm good teaching and challenge bad teaching. And of course, parents must pray earnestly and support eagerly the teachers and schools, and also the churches, who are providing assistance. After all, Christian education is a spiritual and supernatural endeavor.

We should note that Harry strongly rejected the concept of *in loco parentis*, according to which parents look to the school to take their place, as desperately wrong-headed and dangerous, especially in our time when governments act to subvert and replace parental responsibility, and to take total control of our children not only in education but also in healthcare. Christian schools can also be viewed in this way, as substitute and surrogate parents, especially when the parents are able to trust rightly in the mission and convictions of the school. Whether with regard to Christian or public schools, *in loco parentis* represents an abdication of parents' own primary responsibility, and Christian school leaders must aggressively resist and counter this attitude.

Christian Education and the Christian Teacher

For Harry, the key component of Christian education is the teachers. Yes, facilities and leadership and curriculum matters, but teachers matter most.

What does it mean to teach Christianly? Harry referenced Deuteronomy 6:4 as the first and most important qualification of Christian teachers—that they "... shall love the Lord your God with all your heart and with all your soul and with all your might." Christian teachers must know and love and seek the truth that parents want their children to learn.

Again from Deuteronomy 6:

1. Teachers must instruct diligently (6:7).

2. This truth is to be incarnated in teachers' own lives, as they sit and walk, and in all their interactions with students, inside and outside the classroom (6:7).

3. This truth is to be the teachers' very identity, openly displayed in all they say and do, like signs around their necks and in the front yards of the homes (6:8-9).

In Harry's thinking, there is no higher calling than that of the Christian teacher, with its opportunity to shape and direct students' minds and hearts and hands, intellect and affections and behavior, for the glory of Christ.

Christian Education and the Home/School/Church Partnership

Harry always stressed the importance of alignment between home and school and church, partnering and cooperating for the sake of generational faithfulness. He noted that those who first came from Europe to the North American continent founded churches and built schools before they had even developed a dependable food supply. Three centuries later, the Reformed Presbyterian Church Evangelical Synod, initially with only 8,700 members, built both a seminary and a college, for the sake of this vital partnership among these three spheres.

In this partnership, while Harry did not insist on church oversight of Christian schools, clearly he favored that model and approach, as providing the original and final authority for the vision and mission and program of the school, and ensuring that the school remains faithful to its calling.

Christian Education and Culture

Harry was deeply concerned for the fidelity of Christians, churches, and Christian schools in the midst of a hostile culture. He was wary not only regarding subtle cultural influences but also about the direct encroachment of government (what is sometimes called "statism") and accreditation bodies into Christian schools.

He strongly encouraged Christian schools to free themselves from participation in and dependence on government funding.

His phrase "tweaks become torrents" was his encouragement to be attentive and vigilant even about what may seem to be small and insignificant things which may grow into larger challenges to the missional integrity of Christian schools. Harry himself served as a much-needed "early warning system" in recognizing and responding sooner rather than later to such emerging challenges. In all of this, he was not hesitant to describe Christians' relationship with the surrounding culture in terms of "warfare," and his continual encouragement was to "do what God tells you to do, trust the Lord, do not compromise for the sake of your own survival, and be ready to die for it."

With regard to seminary education, Harry believed that rigorous training in the Scriptures, centered on Jesus Christ, was sufficient for training competent pastors. He wanted pastors to be theologically and exegetically sound and deep, able to answer hard questions of faith and life with disciplined and learned minds. While he valued other academic disciplines such as psychology and sociology, he did not believe that seminarians need to have an "integrationist" education in order to be sufficiently and fully equipped for their pastoral leadership.

Harry the Leader and the Man

One of the pleasures of the assignment to write this essay was the opportunity to speak with others who knew Harry well in the context of Christian education. They offered wonderful glimpses into Harry as a leader and a man, glimpses which I briefly describe in this appendix.

The core of Harry's conviction regarding Christian education was the sovereignty of God over all things, and His speaking authoritatively and clearly and sufficiently in His Scriptures, for His own glory and the glory of the Lord Jesus Christ. "Harry went into every meeting with an unfair advantage: he believed in the sovereignty of God, and was therefore convinced that things will always unfold according to God's purposes and plans." His trust in God prompted him to quip, "You cannot worry yourself to a good outcome."

Harry's main focus was the spiritual health of the school; he avoided getting involved in administrative or management matters except when mission and theological issues were involved. When he did feel compelled to address such issues, his first step was always to try to understand what people were thinking and why they believed what they believed, even if he already knew that they were off-track. Then as needed he would take the mantle of leadership and deal with the issue, but always with the primary motive of love for Scripture and sound doctrine, and with a pastor's heart—"loving and kind but unafraid to stand for truth."

In his involvements in hiring and termination matters, he was "rigorous but not ruthless," uncompromising on doctrinal and character standards, concerned about competency and chemistry ("he particularly disliked prima donnas"), but always eager to help people develop in the right ways, so that they might find their places of fruitful service in the institution.

Harry was deeply committed to excellence in all aspects of the institution, not as an end in itself but in order to have a platform for speaking into the spiritual lives of all who were specifically attracted by excellence, especially unbelieving parents.

Harry always connected the mission of the school to Gospel evangelism, of course toward students but also toward their parents, and among his top priorities for all graduates of Briarwood Christian School was that they would be equipped and eager to bear witness to others, in word and deed, to the good news of Jesus Christ.

Given the breadth of his responsibilities, Harry was almost unimaginably accessible to people, and "he knew hundreds of people on a first-name basis." He was keenly interested in everyone, and took time to meet with, listen to, and counsel students and parents, teachers and administrators. He regularly attended chapel services at Briarwood Christian School, desiring to come alongside and "feel the spiritual heartbeat" of the campus.

Harry was by all accounts a master story-teller, and seemed to have an anecdote or a gem of history for virtually every topic and situation. His stories "enabled him to connect with everyone."

In all this, his aim was always not just the transfer of information, but the transformation of lives for the glory of Christ. "Harry had great content, but he knew how to turn it into inspiration and transformation." People saw this transformation in Harry's own life, and therefore wanted not only to learn from him but also to follow him.

13

Cultural Engagement as Spiritual Warfare

Lessons from Harry Reeder

Rob Pacienza

For years now, Bible-believing Christians have noticed the cultural ground shifting beneath their feet. By the mid-twentieth century, the great German theologian Dietrich Bonhoeffer spoke of Europe as a "world come of age," meaning that European societies had begun to manage life without thinking of God. During the ensuing decades, the United States increasingly followed suit, with godlessness permeating every sector of society and every sphere of culture.

The great sociologist Philip Rieff (1922-2006) explored this secularizing impulse in his magnum opus, *My Life among the Deathworks*.[1] In this work, he argued that the United States and Europe are in the midst of a historically unprecedented attempt to sever "sacred order" from "social order." By *sacred order*, he refers to a transcendent moral ordering of the world; by *social order*, he refers to how society organizes its cultural institutions to align

---

1. Philip Rieff, *My Life among the Deathworks* (Charlottesville, VA: University of Virginia, 2006).

with transcendent order. In other words, the West is attempting to cut ties with our culture's Judeo-Christian heritage.

This move is unprecedented because, historically, all civilizations have embraced the reality of a transcendent religious and moral order and have sought to align their cultural institutions—legal, educational, commercial, and otherwise—with that order. This process has occurred with a full awareness that what a society believes about God and morality will inevitably shape its cultural institutions, which, in turn, will inevitably shape society. Yet, many of the West's elite cultural influencers think our society and its cultural institutions are better off without the Judeo-Christian worldview.

Rieff, who himself lectured and spoke almost exclusively at elite cultural institutions throughout his career, was viewed as a traitor within academia because he detailed the negative consequences of this secularizing project and warned that the worst is yet to come. When a society severs ties with its transcendent religious and moral ordering, he argued, its cultural institutions and products become "deathworks." A secularized culture causes society to decay; however, a transcendently-ordered culture causes society to flourish.

Similarly, renowned Canadian philosopher Charles Taylor concludes that Westerners have learned to live within the "immanent frame," meaning that we, intentionally or unintentionally, live as if there is no transcendent supernatural world outside of our own.[2] Christianity has been displaced from the default position and is now considered implausible, unimaginable, and even morally reprehensible as a way of life.

Thus, American Christians—like the early church—face the formidable challenge of proclaiming the Gospel in a cultural context that views Christians and the church as outdated and even reprehensible. Yet, we must not despair. As Rieff declares at the end of his book, the world awaits "a people" who can help the Western world recover the frightening beauty of the "thou

---

2. Charles Taylor, *A Secular Age* (Cambridge: MA: Belknap Press, 2007).

shalt" and "thou shalt not." In other words, we face the perfect opportunity to shine the light of Christ into the darkness of our secular age, showing our neighbors the beauty of God's character and His moral law.

Equipping Christians toward this opportunity is a mission for which Dr. Harry L. Reeder was a perfect fit. I first encountered Dr. Reeder when I joined Briarwood Presbyterian Church as an undergraduate at Samford University in Birmingham, Alabama. Never had I encountered a man who preached with such authority, cared deeply and personally for every member of his flock, and was equally at ease interpreting Scripture *and* culture. During the ensuing years, as a fellow pastor in the Presbyterian Church in America (PCA), I had a front row seat to experience Dr. Reeder's leadership in our denomination. He was a fatherly figure to younger pastors, and, when our denomination was riven by theological crisis, we were always comforted to know that Dr. Reeder was leading the way in the battle for theological orthodoxy. He was one of my heroes and served as an earthly exemplar in the ministry.

Those of us who knew him well cannot avoid a sense that his life was cut tragically short, a sense that goes beyond the feeling always occasioned by sudden death. With our society at a turning point, seemingly ready to jettison its Creator and His benevolent law, Dr. Reeder had played the role of seasoned guide for many of us, pointing the way forward theologically and reminding us that the magnitude of our challenges is matched and exceeded by the magnitude of the God we serve. For instance, here is one of his many calls to the North American Church in the twenty-first century:

> As Christians, I want you to be equipped to move into every sphere of society – corporate America, political America, journalistic media America, the academia, the home or wherever you find yourself. I don't want you to go to any sphere of society thinking that sphere is the key to the hearts of men, women, and the culture. The answer is not in the next election or in the next corporate initiative. The answer is in the Great Commission, the Great Commandment and the Great Commitment of God's people to

evangelize, disciple and turn out Christians who are salt to the earth and light to the world. There is no one shot, no quick silver bullet that is going to turn it around. Now, can God bring a sweeping Gospel awakening? Absolutely. Do I pray for that? Absolutely, but in the meantime, I want to keep oil in my lamp and keep burning every day until the day He comes. That's what I believe God has called us to do.[3]

In this chapter, I will attempt to capture Dr. Reeder's approach to cultural engagement, which was built on the solid foundation of Christian Scripture, forged in the fires of spiritual warfare, and carried out with fervent prayer and unshakeable faith.

The True Story of Cultural Engagement

Two of the most important themes that drove Dr. Reeder's life were biblical authority and sufficiency. Repeatedly in sermons, lectures, and innumerable conversations, he reminded us that God's Word is the supreme norm for the Christian life, sufficient to guide us in every aspect of life. Thus, any discussion of cultural engagement must begin with the biblical testimony.

The word *culture* is found nowhere in the Bible, but the concept is woven into the fabric of the entire biblical narrative. The English word for culture is derived from the Latin term *cultura*, which means "cultivation." Literally, it was a farming term referring to how a farmer approaches the earth's raw materials to create a fruitful harvest. Metaphorically, however, the term refers to how a human being brings out the hidden potentials of creation to develop abundant harvests in art, science, education, politics, sports, entertainment, and more. Just as Adam was called to "till the soil," literally, we are called to cultivate the created order, metaphorically.

Thus defined, we can see that the concept of culture permeates the Bible. Similar to other theological terms such as "Trinity" or "theology", the specific word is absent in Scripture but present everywhere as a concept. From Genesis to Revelation, as the Bible

---

3. Harry L. Reeder, "God's Blueprint in Biblical Perspective: Foundations from Genesis (sermon, Briarwood Presbyterian Church, Birmingham, AL, September 2021).

wends its way through Creation, Fall, Redemption, and Restoration, we see that God created us as profoundly cultural beings.

In the beginning, God created the world from nothing and deemed it "good" and "very good" (Gen. 1:1, 4, 31, et al.). Moreover, He created human beings in His "image and likeness" (1:27). He called them to "be fruitful and multiply" (1:28), "till the soil" (2:15), and "have dominion" (1:28). Just as God creatively built the world, so we must creatively build society and culture. God's central calling for humanity is glorifying Him by living their everyday lives according to His word and will.

Soon, however, the story takes a dark turn (Gen. 3:1-7). Adam and Eve committed a great mutiny and each of us, in the wake of the first couple's sin, have likewise sinned against God. As a result, our societies and cultures are shot through with sin and its consequences. Whereas God intended for human culture—art, science, education, politics, sports, entertainment, and more—to glorify Him, it often glorifies the Evil One instead.

In response to Adam and Eve's sin, God pronounced a curse and offered a blessing (3:14-24). The curse is that human life and culture would be riven by pain and suffering. Yet, the blessing is that God would send a Savior, born of a woman, who would deliver creation from the grips of the Evil One (3:15). God kept His promise by sending His Son, Jesus, who was born of a woman, and whose life, death, and resurrection paves the way for our salvation (John 3:16).

Sadly, not everybody embraces the Son (John 3:18), and those who reject the Son find themselves in the services of the Evil One. Under his skillful guidance, they corrupt and misdirect every human society and culture. Even those who embrace the Son do so inconsistently and thus unintentionally serve the Evil One through sinful words and actions. Therefore, God's good world is now riven by strife, in which humans must pick their side. There is no middle ground, no demilitarized zone. Either we serve God, or we serve His evil nemesis.

More to the point, culture is an especially intense battleground in the broader war between light and darkness. The Evil One spreads his lie so effectively because he promotes it through every aspect of culture: books, movies, songs, political rallies, celebrities, coffee shop conversations, social media posts, and more. Thus, as Christians, we must counter his lies not only from the pulpit but in every sector of society and sphere of culture.

The True Architecture of Culture

God created us as cultural beings; the cultural aspect of our lives is so significant that it behooves us to explore the concept further. What is God's design for culture? What is the proper role of things like art, science, politics, education, sports, or entertainment? Dr. Reeder explored these questions often, and to these questions we now turn.

There is, in fact, a God-ordained architecture for human culture. Reflecting on biblical teaching and biblical patterns, the great theologian Abraham Kuyper employed a spatial analogy to explain culture: just as God created animals and plants "according to their kinds" (Gen. 1:11-12, 21, 24-25), with each kind unique from the other, so it is with culture. It makes sense to say that God created different "kinds" of culture, such as art, science, or politics. And these kinds can be referred to as "spheres."[4]

Kuyper noted that each sphere of culture has its own "center" or reason for being. For example, government and politics exist to achieve justice for the various individuals and communities under their purview. Science exists to expand our knowledge of the natural world. Sports and entertainment exist to give some relief from the demands of everyday life. And so forth.

Similarly, each sphere has a circumference that indicates the limits of its jurisdiction. Because the sphere of government and politics is designed for one purpose—to achieve justice—it must keep its nose out of the church's business, which is religion. Similarly, because the church exists to disciple people in a covenanted relationship with Christ and each other, it must not

---

4. Kuyper provides a succinct summary of his view of Christianity and culture in Abraham Kuyper, *Lectures on Calvinism* (Grand Rapids, MI: Eerdmans, 1931).

seek to rule the government or the nation. Thus, under God's sovereignty, each sphere is designed to flourish within its territory. God is sovereign over each sphere, but none of the spheres are sovereign over the others.

God created each sphere; each is corrupted and misdirected by sin, and each will be restored to perfection on the last day. But between the Fall and Christ's second coming, we are responsible for engaging the various spheres of culture and attempting to redirect them toward God's purposes. However, as we carry out this responsibility, the Evil One will oppose us at every turn.

The True Nature of Cultural Engagement

Dr. Reeder delivered a prophetic message to my congregation and the Institute for Faith & Culture just before his death. In this message, he declared, "Spiritual warfare is not a subset of the Christian life. It *is* the Christian life." He explained that the annals of church history are the record of God fulfilling His promises through His Son, promises against which the gates of hell will never prevail. Never has a more accurate word been spoken, and what Dr. Reeder noted about the Christian life in general is also true of our cultural engagement in particular: cultural engagement is spiritual warfare.

We have three enemies in this warfare: the world, the flesh, and the Devil. Each enemy is formidable and must be consciously countered. To these three, we now turn.

First, the world. The Bible uses the word "world" in several senses, two of which are relevant to the subject matter of this essay. On the one hand, the Bible reveals that God loves the world so much that He gave His Son to die for it (John 3:16). Indeed, God loved His creation so much that through His Son, He saves sinners and will one day restore the entire created order (Rev. 21–22). And if God loves sinners and the created order, we should love them also. On the other hand, the Bible tells us to "love not the world" (1 John 2:15-17). In this sense of the word, "world" refers to the sinful misdirection of God's creation toward Satanic ends. In summary, we should love the world God created and the image bearers He placed within it, but we should hate the Evil One and the way he perverts God's creation.

In this sense, we must cultivate a holy hatred of the world. As Christians, we are called to identify the ways Satan has twisted the spheres of culture toward evil ends and resist those perversions with all our might. In science, we oppose anti-theistic theories of the universe's origin. In entertainment, we fight Hollywood's promotion of the LGBTQ+ agenda. In politics, we resist the promotion of child killing in the name of "women's rights." And so forth.

Second, the flesh. As with the "world," the Bible uses the word "flesh" positively and negatively. On one hand, the Bible makes clear that God created human beings from flesh and blood; He loves the entirety of us, including both soul and body, and thus, we should love our souls and bodies. On the other hand, Scripture uses the word "flesh" to mean "sinful nature." God sent His Son to die on our behalf so that we may be set free from our sinful "fleshly" impulses, and in that sense, we must hate the flesh. We must live according to the Spirit rather than the flesh (Rom. 8:3-8).

One of Satan's favorite tactics is to turn God's people against God and each other. If he can seduce us into living according to the flesh, when in reality we have been set free through Christ's atonement, he achieves a great victory in his public relations campaign against God. Therefore, we must put our flesh to death (Rom. 8:12-14).

Third, the Devil. This Devil, the serpent of old, is the "ruler of this world" (John 12:31), with "world" meaning anything and everything that opposes God. He actively manipulates the world system to hide the truth about God. He blinds the minds of unbelievers so they cannot see the light of Christ (2 Cor. 4:4) and exerts every effort to darken the spheres of culture.

How do we consciously counter the Evil One? We recognize him for what he is—a liar, a murderer, and a thief (John 8:44). He is a *liar* who tells only one lie—that God should not be loved, trusted, or obeyed—but tells it in many variations. He is a *murderer* whose deepest desire is to rob us of eternal life. And he is a *thief* who conspires to steal every good gift God wants to give us. Thus, we must put on the full armor of God so that we can stand our ground, strong in the Lord and His mighty power (Eph. 6:10-14).

The True Obstacle to Cultural Progress

During the final years of his life and ministry, Dr. Reeder came to focus on progressivism as a demonic ideology and, ironically, given its name, the true enemy of progress. He was right, as I see it. Although the Evil One employs many ideologies in his service, progressivism, more than any other, shoulders the load. Therefore, in a chapter on cultural engagement, I would be remiss not to devote time to this ideology in its secular and Christian forms.

First, secular progressivism. Today's secular progressives are beholden to a man whose name most have never heard—Auguste Comte (1798-1857). Comte, a French philosopher, rejected Christianity and all of its doctrine but mainly focused his sights on total depravity.[5] Refusing to believe that human beings harbor evil in their hearts, he instead blamed religion and government as the root cause of war and evil. Thus, if humanity wishes to progress, we must pave the way for a world void of religion and borders. With religion and government thus weakened, Comte's new "religion of humanity," as he called it, would save the world through social justice.

Second, Christian progressivism. While today's Christian progressives peddle a deceptively softer, gentler poison than Comte and his atheistic counterparts, it is nonetheless deadly. Instead of abolishing Christianity and installing an overtly atheistic "religion of humanity," they modify doctrine and practice to advance a Christianity that is "culturally relevant." Instead of preaching doctrines such as individual depravity, they focus almost exclusively on "systemic evils" such as capitalism. Instead of upholding the Christian sexual ethic, they treat it as a

---

5. Comte's vision captured in Gertrud Lenzer, ed., *The Essential Writings: Auguste Comte and Positivism* (New Brunswick: Transaction, 1998).

wax nose, altering it to fit the preferences of the day. Having thus weakened Christian doctrine and practice, they set forth to save the world through social justice.

Dr. Reeder was a gimlet-eyed cultural analyst, and the connection between godless secularism and Christian progressivism was not lost on him. In a series of sermons and articles before his death, he warned the Evangelical and Reformed Church not to drink from their poisonous chalice. Whereas progressives are motivated to save the Evangelical Church from irrelevance by diluting the biblical message and embarking on a social justice mission undergirded by accommodative sexual ethics, biblical conservatives must be motivated to glorify the Lord Jesus by preaching the whole counsel of God and undertaking a holistic mission to make disciples in every sector of society and every sphere of culture.

Dr. Reeder was right. There is nothing "progressive" about today's progressivism. It is regressive to the core, hearkening back to the serpent's lie many thousands of years ago: "Did God really say?" Thus, we must wage war against the reptile of Eden while patiently, charitably, and faithfully calling our progressive neighbors to heed the word of the Lord.

The True Enemy and the Enemy's Prey

"The strongman has been defeated," Dr. Reeder declared in his last talk at Coral Ridge. "Go plunder his house." For some Presbyterians, this talk of spiritual warfare might seem overwrought. Yet, when Dr. Reeder often spoke of spiritual warfare, he did so based on biblical teaching and in accordance with Christians of every historical era. The Church has always understood that our war is not against flesh and blood, but against dark principalities and foreboding powers.

Dr. Reeder's view of spiritual warfare, based on Scripture as it was, differs significantly from the view of many American Christians today. There's no scarcity of spiritual warfare talk among certain segments of our society. But pay close attention, and you'll notice that rarely is this talk directed toward Satan or his demonic minions. Instead, it is usually employed to demonize unbelievers or Christians with whom we disagree. But Scripture never calls us to demonize unbelievers, only demons themselves. What's more, our demonization of unbelievers is diametrically opposed to biblical teaching about spiritual warfare: "For we do not wrestle against flesh and blood, but against the rulers, against the authorities, against the cosmic powers over this present darkness, against the spiritual forces of evil in the heavenly places" (Eph. 6:12). Put differently, "We do not wrestle against unbelieving Americans who oppose the Gospel and hate the Church, for even the most malicious of them could one day be our brother or sister in Christ; instead, we wrestle against demonic powers who are beyond redemption and are committed to our wholesale destruction."

Knowing this, we must be unrestrained in our war against the Evil One but biblically restrained in our approach toward unbelieving neighbors. In short, as we wrestle against political activists, social media influencers, or everyday neighbors who have fallen prey to the Evil One, we must not employ biblically indefensible tactics—expressing outrage over every infraction (James 1:20), being quarrelsome in disposition (2 Tim. 2:24), and mocking those who oppose us (1 Pet. 3:15; Col. 4:5-6). This is a spiritual war. It is Jesus who gives us our orders and rules of engagement.

Thus, we must wage war against the Evil One but be gentler toward his prey. Consider Jesus, whose final utterance included a plea for the Father to forgive His murderers, and Stephen, who did the same. This is how Christians are called to interact with unbelievers. Instead of fighting fire with fire—hatred with hatred—we douse the fire of human hatred with the flowing waters of Christian love. Instead of putting on worldly armor designed to castigate, humiliate, and isolate one's human opponents, we must put on godly armor meant to win them to Christ while fending off their Evil Overlord.

The True Strategy for Victory

The task we face is great. Indeed, we are in the midst of a great battle during this era between our Lord's first coming and His soon return. The world He created was replete with a "unity in diversity" of cultural spheres designed to glorify their Creator but is now corrupted and misdirected by the Evil One. This Evil One—liar, murderer, thief—now wages war by manipulating fallen image bearers into perpetuating his foreboding array of false and destructive ideologies. Chief among those ideologies is progressivism, a brilliantly constructed lie that locates evil in human systems rather than the human heart and promises salvation through social justice rather than sacrificial atonement. The Church must rise and resist.

Yet faced with so great a task, how can the Church possibly succeed? Indeed, the task is daunting, considering the relentless determination of our opponent and the seeming inertia of the contemporary Church. The magnitude of our task, however, is matched and exceeded by the magnitude of the God we serve: if God worked providentially through a stuttering felon, Moses, to defeat the world's most powerful king, Pharaoh; if He empowered a young sheep herder, David, to slay the lethal killer Goliath; if He emboldened a raggedy band of fishermen to kindle the fire of Christianity that would upend the Roman Empire, then He can uphold the Evangelical Church today as we wage war against principalities and power.

This was Dr. Reeder's conviction, and it should be ours as well. He set forth a battle plan for the Church today: wage war by means of Spirit and Word. Dr. Reeder would point to Paul's second letter to Timothy, and it will also be our text for this concluding section. Paul wrote from a Roman prison cell—probably a dank hole in the ground with no bed, toilet, or light—just before his death in AD 67, as Christians had become a convenient target for the pagan Emperor Nero. Thus, for an American Church today that faces the burgeoning power of pagan progressives and their elite power brokers, Paul's words are poignant.

By the time Paul wrote this letter to Timothy, he had been imprisoned, flogged, beaten with rods, stoned, and shipwrecked; he had spent sleepless nights, with hunger and thirst and cold (2 Cor. 11:23-27). He bore "the marks of crucifixion" on his body and found himself imprisoned in Rome, shivering and asking Timothy to bring his coat (2 Tim. 4:13). By this point, Paul probably realized that he would soon die and that he must pass the baton. Given the constraints of parchment and pen, he must communicate the "essentials" to Timothy, his successor.

His message to Timothy in 2 Timothy 3 is, "Timothy, if you are to weather the opposition that you certainly will encounter as a minister of the Gospel, you must build your life and ministry on the sturdy foundation that is the Word of God." He makes this argument using three observations.

His first observation is that the context of Christian ministry is one of opposition (vv. 10-12). He reminds Timothy that "all who desire to live a godly life in Christ Jesus will be persecuted." His second observation is that the opposition to ministry will come from within and without (vv. 13-15), both from impostors and evil men. The third observation is that our ministry's foundation must be the unshakeable Word of God (vv. 14-17).

This third observation speaks to God's special revelation through the Scriptures. The Bible, authored by God in confluence with chosen prophets, apostles, and their close associates is a sufficient guide for all aspects of the spiritual battle. Paul writes:

> But as for you, continue in what you have learned and have firmly believed, knowing from whom you learned it and how from childhood you have been acquainted with the sacred writings, which are able to make you wise for salvation through faith in Christ Jesus. All Scripture is breathed out by God and profitable for teaching, for reproof, for correction, and for training in righteousness, that the man of God may be complete, equipped for every good work (2 Tim. 3:14-17).

In this passage, Paul tells Timothy that the only way he'll be able to stand firm when opposed by evil men and impostors is to hold tightly to the Scriptures. Paul goes so far as to make up a word when he refers to Scripture as *theopneustos*, which is usually translated as "inspired" but is more accurately translated as "God-breathed." Scripture is the very breath of God. This is why Paul nowhere dissents from biblical teaching, whether doctrine, ethical precepts, or prophecy. Throughout the epistles, he treats Scripture as an utterly trustworthy record. So must Timothy, and so must we.

Thus, armed with Scripture and empowered by the Spirit, we have no reason to fear. The gates of hell will not prevail. Although we will suffer setbacks and at times the Enemy might seem to have the upper hand, we can rest assured that God will prevail. Ultimately, we will taste victory, but God will get the glory.

A Call to Action

In the face of these formidable challenges and the subtle yet pervasive spread of secular and progressive ideologies, the path forward for Christians is clear and unwavering. This path is not merely a cultural or social endeavor; it is fundamentally a spiritual warfare that demands a robust and determined response grounded in faith and the Word of God.

Throughout his ministry, Dr. Reeder offered several practical takeaways for God's people as we participate in this spiritual war against principalities and powers. Four of those takeaways seem especially relevant to our subject matter in this chapter:

First, we must be unflinching in our commitment to biblical authority. The historic hallmark of evangelical Reformed Christianity is its commitment to Scripture as the norm above all norms. Thus, together with our forebears, we must resist any movement—secular or "Christian"—that places cultural accommodation higher than biblical fidelity. We must be men and women of the Word.[6]

Second, we must be patient with our brothers and sisters in Christ who have been seduced into accommodating culture rather than upholding biblical fidelity. As Dr. Reeder put it, "We

---

6. Harry L. Reeder, "Christianity and Progressivism: A Pastor's Perspective", Westminster Theological Seminary Magazine, Volume 3, Issue 1.

must be patient, dialogue, and constantly committed to 'giving the judgment of charity,' yet unyielding in our commitment to God's truth." If God has been patient with us, in Christ, we must be patient with our brothers and sisters.[7]

Third, we must desire cultural transformation but refuse to make it the Church's primary mission. To paraphrase Dr. Reeder, God didn't commission His disciples to "turn the world upside down" but to turn sinners right-side up. Thus, we focus like a laser on our mission to make disciples and count it as "icing on the cake" when culture also transforms.[8]

Fourth, we must be ready and willing to enter the darkness of our culture for the sake of Christ and His Gospel. Dr. Reeder, in response to Jesus' ministry to the paganized communities of Decapolis, articulated this sacred calling when he wrote,

> Therefore, I have resolved that if I am free to preach the Gospel and advance its claims—then by God's grace there is no place I will not go; no person so lost that I will not pursue, no power so threatening I will not face while believing there is no person saved who cannot change and be changed by God's grace. So, if I am free to present the Gospel and its claims and the Gospel call to repentance, by God's grace, strength and power I will go.[9]

The essence of a proper response to the secularization of American culture, therefore, lies in the realization that our struggle is not against flesh and blood, but against spiritual forces that seek to undermine and distort God's truth. This understanding calls for a strategy that transcends mere human wisdom or effort. It requires a return to the core of our faith—the Word of God and the empowering presence of the Holy Spirit. Scripture, God-breathed and alive, provides the unshakeable foundation upon which we must build our lives, ministries, and cultural engagement.

By firmly grounding ourselves in Scripture, embracing the power of the Holy Spirit, and engaging with love and truth, we

---

7. Ibid.
8. Ibid.
9. Harry L. Reeder, "Where To Speak? What To Speak? When To Speak?", *In Perspective*, https://harryreeder.wordpress.com/2018/04/25/where-to-speak-when-to-speak-what-to-speak/, April 25, 2018.

can effectively wage and win this spiritual battle for the heart and soul of our culture. Therefore, we pray for victory, no matter how daunting the cultural challenges may be. The task is great, but our God is greater, and we are assured of ultimate victory in Him.

14

The Pastor's Personal Life

Sandy Willson

Harry Reeder was one of my closest friends. Ever. We sought each other's advice. Our wives and children love each other. We occasionally took family vacations together. We ministered as colleagues. He preached in my church. I preached in his. We worked together in global missions. I love him. One should not expect me to be unbiased when assessing Harry's personal life, or when using him as an example of godly shepherding.

Of course, only the Lord knows a man's heart, but one can confidently comment on the obvious outward evidences of a man's internal life. In my years of knowing Harry Reeder, I observed four fundamental categories of attributes in his personal life that made him an effective Christian pastor, as well as a wonderful friend and confidant.

Christlike Character

The most effective pastors are normally gifted in several ways. They are typically good thinkers, reasonably trained theologians and ethicists, solid communicators, reliable counselors, friendly networkers, decent mediators for those in conflicted relationships, missionally minded strategists, and effective leaders and managers of people. Very few pastors excel in all of these ways. But most pastors aspire to be as competent as possible in each of these areas.

Without a doubt, however, the one characteristic which always defines the effective pastor is an intimate, adoring, submissive relationship with Jesus Christ. Faithful pastors exemplify Christ. They wear His clothes. They speak His language. There is no substitute for this. Everything else is secondary. Christlikeness is, above all else, what Harry Reeder had and did.

Christlike Convictions

The pastor must be scrupulous in both conduct and conviction. Remember Paul's word to Timothy: "Keep a close watch on yourself and on the teaching. Persist in this, for by so doing you will save both yourself and your hearers" (1 Tim. 4:16). The conscientious pastor realizes that not only is he saved through faith, but that his congregation and community are profoundly affected by his personal faith. This, in part, explains Harry's zealous devotion to doctrine. Biblical doctrine. Systematic biblical doctrine. He knew, in a very real sense, his hearers' salvation depended upon it.

A pastor's commitment to the truth of God's Word is connected to his being a man of his own word. Harry was an honest man, even when the truth hurt, even when the truth embarrassed him. He took Christ and the Gospel more seriously than he took himself. We friends loved to make fun of him, because he, too, enjoyed laughing (or smirking) at himself. For Harry, truth trumped sentiment. Every time.

Christlike Conduct

Harry wasn't perfect. Nobody is. But Harry's friends know that Harry's first concern in his decisions was whether it would honor and glorify the Lord, according to His will revealed in the Scriptures. Nobody, not even his wife, Cindy, was more important to him. There was an earnestness, a determination, a courageous faithfulness in Harry's ministry that emanated from his grateful devotion to Christ as his Savior.

There was a lovely consistency in his conduct. If one heard him preach on Sunday, he or she would be impressed with his zeal for the Lord. If that same person had lunch with him on Tuesday or played golf with him on Saturday, they would find Harry to be the same man. His ministry was not a career; it was his life's mission.

One of the most frequent ways in which ministers of the Gospel fail in their conduct is in handling—or mishandling—criticism. Too often we pastors passive-aggressively avoid or marginalize our critics or rigidly defend ourselves when critiqued. We often fail to consider what elements of truth our critics are communicating to us. Many pastoral ministries have been decimated by self-justifying arrogance in this area of life, when our pride is disclosed to plain view. When criticized, Harry typically did several things that are noteworthy: he welcomed and listened carefully to his critics; he acknowledged where he believed they were correct and fair; he honestly disagreed with them when he thought they were in error; he gladly submitted to a third party opinion, if needed; he didn't think less of someone who gave him constructive criticism.

Harry often taught on the topic of Christian manhood. One of his favorite Scripture texts was 1 Corinthians 16:13-14: "Be watchful, stand firm in the faith, act like men, be strong. Let all that you do be done in love." Harry believed that the Christian man must conduct himself in a manner tough and tender, courageous and compassionate, strong and sensitive. The men Harry most admired embodied these dualities. So did Harry.

In Jonathan Edwards' magnificent sermon, "The Excellency of Christ," Edwards sets forth the greatness of Christ from Revelation 5 where Jesus Christ is described as both a lion and a lamb. How odd. Are there two animals more different than a lion and a lamb? And yet, Jesus is described as One who both ferociously defends His people and also gently cares for them, even to the point of laying down His life as a lamb.

Harry Reeder was a lion. He would go anywhere to proclaim the Gospel. From the Bibbs County penitentiary to the Alabama Legislature. No one was too lost for Harry. He saw straight through all the excuses and diversions and delays that men use to avoid their sinful condition and their need of Christ. He fearlessly shared the Gospel with all types of people. He also spoke out clearly about our nation's need of faith in Christ and genuine repentance. But he was also a lamb. He knew he desperately needed the Shepherd. Harry constantly depended upon Him, and he faithfully cared for Christ's little lambs by encouraging them to do the same. Harry was a tender warrior for Christ and His Kingdom. He was a Christian gentleman.

Christlike Commitment

Peter's instructions to shepherds are that we are to serve "not for shameful gain, but eagerly" (1 Pet. 5:2). The pastor, like every other Christian, must provide for his family (1 Tim. 5:8). The family must be assured that their husband and father has put the family's interests above his own and that he is devoted to their well-being. And yet, effective pastors are not driven by greed. They are not driven by a desire for comfort or personal entertainment. To the degree that a pastor seeks his own interests, he diminishes his ministry to others. I have always been impressed with Harry's generosity and readiness to sacrifice for the benefit of God's people. Peter said this is essential for effective shepherding.

These personal traits are invaluable for the pastor who wants his people to know and follow Christ. To lead others, the pastor must be the first in line to follow Jesus. If every segment of the pastor's life is aligned with Christ and the Gospel, he then is ready to say with the Apostle Paul, "Be imitators of me, as I am of Christ" (1 Cor. 11:1). Only then can he answer constructively the most important questions he will be asked about various spiritual, ethical, and theological issues: "So, Pastor, what do you do with respect to this issue? How do you approach it? Why do you do it that way?" Pastors must not only tell the truth, but also show the truth. If a man does not practice what he preaches, he and we would be better off if he ceased preaching.

Deep Roots

The personal character of the Christian is rooted in an intimate relationship with the Lord. This intimate relationship occurs through regular fellowship with Him through the means of grace which He has given us: prayer, the Word, the sacraments, and Christian fellowship. These ordinary spiritual disciplines are the means by which believers walk intimately with the Lord, become convinced of His unconditional love, and are deeply moved to become more like Him. Harry spent precious hours every week seeking the Lord through these gracious means. This alone explains his character.

Prayer

I don't know how many hours I've spent with Harry on our knees, but it was enough to know that Harry fervently believed in the power and the grace of prayer. To be prayed for by Harry was a great privilege. I know that Cindy and her family miss Harry for many reasons, but surely one of the greatest sources of sorrow is no longer hearing his voice interceding for them before the throne of God.

The Word

Harry knew his Bible. He believed it to be God's perfect Word. He believed that his first duty was to feed God's people with His Word. He remained a Bible learner to the end of his life. His sermons were always framed by biblical truth, suffused with biblical references, and full of biblical wisdom. Every Lord's Day he blessed his hearers with biblical insights pastorally urged upon them. The faithful pastor is determined to give his congregation the truth of God's Word precisely because, in that very Word, *the pastor himself* has discovered light and life. It is by personal spiritual experience that the pastor is motivated to exegete, to expound, and to apply faithfully the Scriptures for his people.

Sabbath

Harry devoted himself daily to the reading of God's Word and prayer. He also planned his times to be in conversation with the Lord. In recent years, it has become the practice of many pastors to take sabbaticals away from their ministries in order to recharge their emotional and spiritual lives. Often, these times away are like extended vacations for rest and relaxation. It seems to me that we pastors too often look forward to those extended breaks to recover from an otherwise frenetic, stressful, exhausting life. What Harry did was a bit different and, I think, healthier. He stayed restful. Harry was an extremely hard worker, but he was not emotionally and spiritually exhausted because he lived a disciplined, restful life—a true Sabbatarian life. To support his preaching and teaching ministry, which was very demanding, he planned weeks throughout the year to get away privately to read, study, pray, rest, and reflect. He didn't wait for a long sabbatical to rest and reflect. His life was suffused with proper rest and meditation on God's Word, bathed in prayer. Shalom.

Loving Friendships

Most pastors today report that they have no close friends in the church. This should be of grave concern to us. Our *whole business* is about relationships—first of all with God, secondly with other human beings. Our specialty is in promoting and facilitating relational reconciliation. The preaching of the Cross provides reconciliation with God and with our brother and sister in Christ. The Apostle John says, "And this commandment we have from him: whoever loves God must also love his brother" (1 John 4:21). Whoever is a true friend of Christ will be a true friend to Christ's siblings.

Harry made real friends on many different levels. He invested himself in others deeply and truly. Cindy was his closest friend, followed by his children and their families. The next chapter tells us about his family life, but I want to remark on one implication of his relationship with Cindy. But first, some background.

Forty-five years ago, as a third-year student at Gordon-Conwell Theological Seminary, I was trying to discern whether to accept a call to a solo pastorate in a small church or a call, as a staff pastor, to a larger church. So, I sought the advice of a wise, older pastor. He said many helpful things, but one piece of advice impressed me the most. He suggested that when I interview for a staff role and go to dinner with the senior pastor of that church, I should be sure that his wife is also with us at dinner in order to observe carefully how he treats her, since the way a married man treats his wife indicates the way he will treat you. The way we married pastors treat our brides is ultimately the way we shall treat His Bride. I've never forgotten that—which brings me to Harry and Cindy.

Harry and his Family

In thirty-seven years of close friendship with Harry Reeder, I do not recall one critical word about his wife. But I recall scores of compliments. He loved her, admired her, served her, depended upon her, trusted her, and defended her. In my observation, this is the way Harry related to Jesus' Bride. The two go together.

Harry was also close to his parents and his sisters. He was close to staff and elders. He was also close to other pastors. For over thirty-five years, I knew Harry as an accountability partner. We met regularly with two other men for twenty-four hours at a time. During our time together each man shared deeply about his personal experience with Christ, his family, and his ministry, after which the other three men would ask probing questions and give advice when needed. Then we would go to our knees and intercede for the brother who had just shared his needs with us. We also challenged and enriched each other's biblical interpretations, theological perspectives, cultural assessments, and leadership decisions.

Over the years we also made covenants with each other. We promised that if any of us were unfaithful to our wives, the other three men would do everything in their power to prevent him from returning to pastoral ministry. We agreed that if any of us viewed a movie or read things that were inappropriate, we would report that honestly to the group. We promised to pray for each other. We preached in each other's churches and regularly counseled one another in the midst of ministerial challenges. We occasionally vacationed together and jointly took our sons on father-son trips. We participated in each other's family weddings—and funerals.

On one occasion I was preaching in a city away from home. I was by myself in my hotel room. Some weeks beforehand, Harry had asked for my speaking schedule. I had barely hung my clothes in the closet, when the phone in my room was ringing. It was Harry. "What are you watching?" he asked. My hotel's TV service allowed for the playing of pornographic movies. Harry wanted to be sure I had nothing to do with it. I happily reported that I was watching the news. After I hung up, I realized what a great friend God had given me. And he proved it many times over. Pastors must learn how to make and retain real, authentic, mutually accountable friendships.

On a broader scale, Harry devoted himself to Christ's Church in the USA and around the world. He took a special interest in his own denomination, the Presbyterian Church in America, and devoted himself to her welfare. So often, senior pastors of large, influential, affluent churches lose interest in denominational affairs. They imagine that they have more important things to do. Harry took the broader Church very seriously, and, in the process, made enormous contributions to many of our lives and ministries. Naturally, some in the denomination at times disagreed with some of Harry's viewpoints, but nobody questioned his love and care for Christ's Church. Harry knew he stood on the shoulders of faithful saints who went before him, and he sought to leave a healthy church for those who would come behind him. And he did. None of that would have occurred had Harry not decided a long time ago to invest himself lovingly and deeply in the spiritual lives of other people.

Conclusion

One might ask himself, "Since I know that I don't have Harry Reeder's intelligence, leadership gifts, and communication skills, how in the world can I imitate him?" The answer is actually quite simple. It wasn't Harry's unique giftedness that made him who he was. It was his personal life. More specifically, it was his love for Jesus Christ. And we know, trust, love, and serve the same Christ. We are called to the same mission. We share the same destiny.

The real question is shall we seek Christ and His Kingdom with the intelligence, leadership gifts, and communication skills that He *has* given *us*? If we shall, there will be in us a Christlike character, deeply rooted in an intimate relationship with Jesus, demonstrated in loving, mutually accountable relationships with His people.

15

The Pastor's Heart for His Family

Jennifer Toomer-Hay and Bruce Stallings

I am often asked the question, "What is it like to be Harry Reeder's daughter?" My answer is always the same—"I don't know what it's like NOT to be Harry Reeder's daughter!"

After the death of my father, my brother, Ike Reeder (or Ikie, as I still call him), approached myself and Bruce Stallings and asked us to write the chapter in this *festschrift* on "The Pastor's Family." I realized that I had the opportunity to answer the question I have gotten for most of my life in a very real fashion. Bruce Stallings served as Executive Pastor alongside my Dad for twenty-three years. In those twenty-three years, Bruce arguably spent more time with my Dad than anyone else in Dad's life apart from my Mother. Bruce has thoroughly seen the inside of our family life and was a confidant to my Dad. As Bruce and I met together to prepare this chapter, he shared with me about many of the times Dad would "verbally process" to Bruce situations that were going on in my life and the lives of my brother and my sister, our spouses, and his grandchildren. As a family, we consider Bruce and his wife Sonya "family" ourselves. To share with you our perspective, insight, and stories on Harry Reeder's approach to "The Pastor's Family," as is founded in his biblical world-life view, is an honor we were humbled to accept and challenged to work through while in deep grief, emotion, and loss, grappling with

Dad's passing. Our heart's desire is that we can encourage the reader with Scripture, advice, and illustration which will help one grow as a parent and spouse.

> Hear O Israel, the Lord our God, the Lord is One. And you shall love the Lord your God with all your heart and with all your soul and with all your might. And these words, which I am commanding you today shall be on your heart; and you shall teach them diligently to your sons and shall talk to them when sitting in your house and when you walk by the way and when you lie down and when you rise up. And you shall bind them as a sign on your hand and they shall be as frontals on your forehead. And you shall write them on the doorposts of your house and on your gates (Deut 6:4-9).

Foundational Priority: Jesus

To understand the methodology and practices Dad employed inside our family dynamic, you must first understand how he thought. Dad was convicted through Scripture that every second of every minute of every day, every word, every choice, every intention, and every action was to be done in light of one single priority. The priority of a believer was always singular, never multi-level nor a numerical list of priorities. That single focused priority is Jesus.

All for Jesus. As young children, we were taught the Children's Catechism. I can still remember clearly sitting on the kitchen table after dinner as a four-year-old girl in our home on Carter Lane right beside Covenant College. After dinner, Daddy would sit me on the table and be in front of me in his chair and would repeat the Catechism questions. I specifically remember: What is the chief end of man? And I would reply, "The chief end of man is to glorify God and enjoy Him forever." This principle drove into the core of my father. It informed his entire existence and gave him unbelievable clarity around all spheres of life. It particularly informed how he approached his marriage and his parenting.

Marriage Foundation

This foundational priority showed up in many ways. The first clear action that ran through his life from his marriage in 1969 until his death in 2023 was an unwavering dependence on and consistent practice of prayer. Prayer enveloped our life as a family. We prayed constantly. We prayed as individuals, we prayed together, we prayed together as siblings, and Daddy and Mother prayed together. Every morning, sometimes visible to us as children if we were up early enough, Daddy and Mother prayed together. I can still see them standing in the kitchen holding each other and praying for the day to come and their family members. If we were around, we were brought into "the huddle" in those early morning hours. I remember seeing them even as a teenager and the sense of stability it brought me, knowing my Mom and Dad were in lockstep together before the Throne of God and each other. We prayed before every meal. We prayed in family devotions together every night.

As adults, we prayed together when we left a family gathering to go back to our own homes—every time. I can hear his voice now, "OK, kids, let's huddle up and pray." Our arms would lock around each other, and we would get in tight and pray. In our adult years, we came together in times of crisis, sickness, tribulation, and trials to pray. We'd set a time and meet at Mom and Dad's house, circle the wagons and go before our Heavenly Father with our intercession and thanksgiving. It was completely common to be in full conversation, and for one of us to stop and say, "Let's just pray right now." Dad and Mom modeled that, and then in our adulthood, the three of us picked right up on their practice. Prayer was as much a part of his life as breathing was. Dad believed and taught us that "the effectual fervent prayer of a righteous man availeth much" (James 5:16b, KJV).

Family Foundation

The second clear action that showed up in his life as part of his commitment to the foundation priority of Jesus was that he created an unselfish foundation of family. This family unit "looked" a certain way. If you were to whiteboard out how Dad saw the family, you would see a vertical line and a horizontal line with another vertical line underneath the horizontal line. The first vertical line represents an upward relationship between each family member and Christ. That line must be strong, steadfast, and immovable. The horizontal line would represent the husband and wife to each other. If you ever had the pleasure of hearing Dad preach at a wedding, you would know what I am about to refer to. As our friend, Rev. Neil Stewart, said after Dad's passing in a sermon he preached at Briarwood: "I last saw Harry performing a wedding in my church a few months ago, and as I sat and listened to him riff on marriage, I realized I had never preached a wedding in my whole life."

Dad articulated 1+1=1: "and the two shall become one flesh" (Gen. 2:24; Eph. 5:31). The husband and the wife must commit to Christ as their priority, not each other. When they find fulfillment in Christ, the perfect fulfillment to our souls, then they are free to love their spouse without any expectation of one's needs being made complete in them, for each party to the marriage is a sinner and will never be able to complete the other perfectly. Understanding Christ as the focus and priority liberates us to forgive each other and be forgiven. As a result, the marriage relationship is the core, and its byproduct is the children. The children never ever become more important than the marriage relationship.

Dad parented us in such a way that we knew Mom came before us, and the family as a whole was not centered around any one individual. I will quote my Dad here as I remember being admonished for teenage self-centeredness: "The family does not revolve around you, Jennifer. You revolve INTO the family." This illustrates the third vertical line: children are subordinate to their parents, not made into idols of the parents or placed ahead of the healthy marriage or ahead of Christ. I recall my brother Ikie being disciplined once by our Dad on our way to church (Ike got disciplined a lot more than once, but I will stick with just this illustration). As we were cruising down Providence Road West on our way to Christ Covenant Church for Sunday morning worship, Mother asked Ike some innocuous question, and Ikie responded with a flippant "Yeah." It is a wonder that the car didn't veer off the road because Daddy came across the front seat, and his booming voice said, "Son, don't you ever speak to your Mother that way. She was my wife before she was your Mother, and you will show her the respect of a yes, ma'am." In two sentences, he reminded us that she was more important than we were. We needed that reminder. Of course, then we all had to get our smiles together to walk into church (If you are reading this and you are a pastor with a family young enough to still be in the home, trust me, you are not alone in experiencing the trials of the car ride before worship).

I believe this grasp he had of the structure of the family is what led to him and Mother having such an incredible partnership and relationship when the house was empty, and the three of us had moved on to build our own families. They never lost sight of the core component of the "Reeder family," which was Harry and Cindy—THEN Jennifer, Ike, and Abby.

Focused Intentionality

Intentionality. If ever there were a word to describe Harry Reeder, it would be this one. Dad was consumed by intentionality. Everything he did had a reason and a purpose. Understand that this filters back to his priority of Jesus and glorifying God. I never knew someone could take so much about purpose from the short verse in Paul's message in the synagogue in Antioch: "For David, after he had served the purpose of God in his own generation, fell asleep and was laid with his fathers and saw corruption ..." (Acts 13:36). Dad believed God had given him a purpose and he knew the weight of his words, actions, and thoughts. He understood that time is short and that we must pour ourselves out like a drink offering. He did not want a second wasted that could be used for God's glory. His intentionality was remarkably apparent in his life with our family.

As Bruce and I shared these stories together and formulated the points we thought would be helpful, this part of this chapter stood out so much to us because it seems in our world today that people live life almost as if they were the tail of a kite, just being whipped by the wind, following "their hearts" and doing "what makes me happy." Dad's focused intentionality stood out in a world of amoeba-like creatures just shape-shifting through their existence.

Displays of Affection

Intentionality showed up in his physical displays of affection. Dad loved big, and he hugged big. He was never afraid or embarrassed to hug his wife or his children anywhere and everywhere. He would walk hand in hand with our Mother or us. I remember countless trips to SouthPark Mall, where we would visit his mother, who worked at Sears, and then window shop through the mall. His arm was around me or my sister Abby. Additionally, we were often embarrassed in those walks through the mall because he also had no shame and would sing loudly whatever song was in his head or make up his own words to a tune. You can imagine, as thirteen-year-old kids, how fun that was! But we felt safe, we KNEW we were loved, we knew he loved Mom, and he showed us all.

When I was a senior in college at Liberty University in 1992, I flew from Lynchburg, VA, to Philadelphia, PA, to meet my Dad. He was at Westminster Theological Seminary for meetings, and I was considering graduate work at WTS. This was my trip to visit the campus. There were no cell phones then, and my flights were delayed, so I called him in his hotel room from a pay phone in the Charlotte airport to tell him I would not be getting in until around midnight. He gave me very specific directions on how to exit the Philadelphia airport, where to walk to get on the subway, what stop I was to get off at, and then the streets I was to walk to get to the hotel where he was. I remember hanging up the phone and being so very scared because I did not think I could figure all of that out. I boarded my final flight and landed in Philadelphia. As I came off the airplane, I looked, and there was my Dad waiting for me at the gate (back when we could do those things). To this day, I can remember the rush of relief at seeing him there, all the fear of getting lost and not finding my way instantly escaping my body and him wrapping me up in his big bear hug and saying, "After I hung up the phone I realized you were probably going to end up lost in the middle of downtown Philadelphia at midnight and I knew I had to come and get you." It's silly now, but I remember tears flowing because I knew I was safe. The hug and his presence calmed my heart and settled my soul.

Discipline and Consequences

Dad was intentional about the non-negotiables. Many would assume we were raised in a rigorous environment. Truth be told, that was not the case. Dad and Mom did not believe in a lengthy list of dos and don'ts. The rules were not many, but they were not negotiable either. You told the truth. You showed respect to others. You obeyed when given an instruction or directive. You did not talk back. Honestly, that was about it, and when you begin to think it through, you understand that those basically covered it all.

When I graduated high school, I attended Liberty University. Liberty was a culture shock to me because upon receiving "The Liberty Way Handbook," I was overwhelmed by the number of rules I had to memorize and follow. Violating the rules of Mom and Dad's home absolutely had consequences, and they were intentional in delivering those consequences. They did not break, nor did they waver. They disciplined us with intentionality. As young children, we had "the rod" in our home, and it was used. If you go to my parents' home today, you can see the clear yellow fiberglass rod that was crafted by a member of our church in Chattanooga, Tennessee, and given to my parents as a gift. My Mother thought it would be a nice touch to paint our names on it in red fingernail polish. The number of times we tried to make that rod disappear is too many to count, but it always found its way back home and to our bottoms. And yet, even in the discipline of spanking, Dad always ended the experience with prayer—prayer together through repentance and remorse and prayer celebrating the sweet restoration of the relationship even after the breaking of trust through violating the rules. He modeled to us what it is like to experience God's perfect forgiveness that He gives to us as believers. When we grew out of the rod, discipline took other forms, but no matter what they chose to do, they were always consistent and always intentional with the express desire to draw out repentance and remorse ending in restoration.

Teachable Moments

The third area in which Dad showed intentionality was in what we called "the teachable moments." What is a teachable moment, you may ask? The answer is—every moment. When we ran together, we would talk about life, and he would teach us through those conversations. All three of us were athletes in high school and went on to be collegiate athletes. Our athletic activities were a treasure trove of teaching opportunities for him. Team sports brought the opportunities to teach us about self-discipline, commitment to team over self, loyalty, perseverance, selflessness, submission, humility, and other character traits. Our individual sports were the breeding ground for teaching us work ethic, determination, showing up when no one is watching, and finishing what you started. How does one lose well? How does one win well? These were all topics of discussion in the teachable moments of life.

I remember walking around the track at Providence Day School after a workout with him, just cooling down. I don't remember the context, but I remember his words: "Jennifer, the mark of a Christian is gratitude. A Christian is so grateful for the gift of grace shown to him by Jesus that they cannot help but live in gratitude. An ungrateful person is a self-centered person."

We watched movies, and then he would have us break down the world-life view presented in the movie. We would be asked to dissect the "general truth" that existed in the movie plot and the flawed thinking that was present. He taught us how to think critically and strategically with a biblical worldview. Every single teaching moment, from the Catechism and the Greek alphabet, taught to us after dinner on the kitchen table, to the dialogues we had up until the day he died, shaped how Ikie, Abby, and I live our lives.

Vocational Calling

The fourth area in which Dad was intentional was in his view on work, specifically his work as a pastor and our family's role in his vocational calling. "The saying is trustworthy: If anyone aspires to the office of overseer, he desires a noble task" (1 Tim. 3:1); Dad believed in the "noble task" of being an overseer. But he also believed in the importance of the calling that came to the family: "He must manage his own household well, with all dignity keeping his children submissive, for if someone does not know how to manage his own household, how will he care for God's church?" (1 Tim. 3:4-5). The pastor's family is faced with so many challenges around family and the ministry.

Before I share with you how our parents raised "preacher's kids," I also have to say that we were far from perfect (except Abby, of course). All joking aside, Abby, the youngest of the three of us, has lived a life where she did not "rebel" against God, Dad, or Mom, and the Lord has indeed blessed her commitment to obedience. Ikie and I both had our share of walking away from the Lord. Ikie has shared much of his story in the book *Surviving the Fish Bowl: Letters to Pastors' Kids* compiled by Catherine Stewart. Ike's chapter focused on being The Prodigal Son. In that chapter, he briefly mentioned my period of rebellion, and I won't go into it here, but suffice it to say as an adult after college, I, too, steered away from all that I knew and made sinful choices that broke the hearts of my parents. Praise God, He restored both Ikie and me and turned our respective "ashes" into beautiful gardens glorifying Him.

With that being said, let me explain further how intentional Dad was around the family and ministry. Dad's calling as a pastor was a calling our entire family shared. We believed in this shared calling because of two modeled behaviors: The first is a credit to our mother. Mother never considered the church as her competition. She believed a pastor's wife was to do everything in her power to free up her husband to minister freely. The idea of her saying or even thinking anything along the lines of "I just wish he wouldn't work so much" is foreign to us, to Dad, and to Mom. She wanted to keep the path clear of any distractions or disturbances that would slow him down in preaching, teaching, leading, mentoring, discipling, and counseling. Remember, I shared earlier that her priority was Christ, not Daddy. So, they were in one accord that together, they would serve Christ and the church of Christ. Her mindset trickled down to become our mindset, and so we were fully committed. Whatever we could do to help, we did it.

The second modeled behavior was that Dad brought us "into" his work. He took us with him to hospital visits, Bible studies, meetings, preaching engagements—anything that he could appropriately bring us along for, he did. We wanted to be the one he picked to go with him. The time in the car was precious; the things we learned listening to him in his ministry activity and the perspective we had around the importance of shepherding being given to the body of Christ were invaluable. He did not minister and work in a silo of himself and himself alone. He incorporated us into so many aspects that we never experienced any sort of "us versus them" thought process. What he also modeled to us through those actions was his work ethic. Dad was indefatigable in ministry—he just never stopped. His battery life and bandwidth up until the day he died at seventy-five years old were seemingly never-ending, and Mother ran right with him. She kept pace and stride with him from day one until his last.

Intentional Words

The fifth way Dad showed intentionality was through words. If you knew Harry Reeder personally, this would not be a new revelation to you. My writing partner, Bruce Stallings, has been on the other end of Dad's verbal processing personality for twenty-three years. However, in this paragraph, when I refer to words, I am referring to his verbal encouragement. He never withheld praise, encouragement, advice, counsel, or affirmation. He was the greatest promotor of his family, yet he was not blindly positive.

In those same words, he found ways to positively challenge us to grow. He never accepted the "status quo."

Now one may read this and think, "It sounds like he was encouraging, but the family was never good enough." That is simply not the case. Somehow, he had an uncanny ability to lift you up without condition, and push and stretch you to reach for growth. That is a fascinating tightrope to walk, and he knew how to do it. I am fifty-two years old, and to this day, some of my favorite words to hear were, "Jennifer, you did an excellent job doing (insert whatever task)." When he died, I can speak for my siblings and my mother when I say, he left us with our cups overflowing with memories of his vocalized love and support. There are no regrets.

Use of Time

The sixth and final way Dad showed his intentionality was in the use of time. Our family is a simple family. For us, entertainment was being together. Family time was not around elaborate or planned excursions, experiences, and trips, although we certainly took trips and had great adventures together. In the day-to-day rhythm of life, Dad modeled a lifestyle of time spent together in the everyday moments. He intentionally communicated with all of us on the phone, by text, or in person.

One of the biggest surprises in my parents' lives was that by 2014, all three of their children were in Birmingham, Alabama. We all live within fifteen minutes of each other. I understand that not every adult family gets to experience this, but in our case, we took full advantage of this fact. We were in and out of their home constantly, day in and day out, just spending time. Their grandchildren behave the same way. They come in and out almost daily to see and visit with their grandparents. This all happens now because we were taught this as young children and teenagers. Family is a gift from the Lord, and we are to cherish what we have been given.

A Forever Legacy

The legacy that Dad has left our family is that we are to have a lifestyle of worship. If you'll remember that little time around the track when Dad said, "Jennifer, the hallmark of the Christian life is gratitude." Well, he also loved to tell us that "an attitude of gratitude leads to a lifestyle of worship." If your heart is full of gratitude, then what else can you do but let that gratitude pour out into worship to the One to whom you are grateful? As Hebrews, puts it, "Therefore, since we are receiving a kingdom that cannot be shaken, let us be thankful, and so worship God acceptably with reverence and awe" (12:28).

Dad believed in three specific forms of worship that are to be followed in our lives. First, we must have personal worship. We are to have daily time in the Word and prayer, spending quiet space with our Savior. Dad believed in starting the day in the Word and prayer and ending the day in the Word and prayer. One of our favorite things to see, no matter who was there, was Dad and Mom, standing in the kitchen and hugging and praying for each other, their kids, and their families every morning.

Second, we are to have family worship. It is not an exaggeration to say that from the time we can remember, our family had worship together every night. We were given a curfew as teenagers, in large part so that we could be home to worship together. Every single night we prayed together and read Scripture. These worship sessions eventually took on a rhythm of sitting on our parent's beds. We would all end up in their room on the bed listening to Dad or one of us read a passage, listen to him exposit briefly a lesson from it, and pray together. As we became teenagers and into college, if our friends were spending the night with us or if we brought home friends from college, we just dragged them into Mom and Dad's bedroom for family worship. Mom and Dad would be in bed, sitting up, and we'd read and pray and even sometimes sing. My sister Abby and I both ran cross country and track in college, and both of us brought home our teams when we competed in Charlotte. In our years of competition, the Liberty

University women's cross-country team and the Appalachian State women's cross-country team all experienced Reeder Family worship as we always do it. Sometimes even trying to figure out how to fit as many runners on the bed as possible!

The third form of worship is corporate worship. Sunday church was not a choice for us. It was the standard. We began each week with the Lord's Day and the ordinary means of grace with the body of Christ. We were taught to bring the morning and evening sacrifices of praise to our God on His Day. Daddy always said he was saved out of a drug problem; he was drug to church his whole life. I think it is fair to say the same for Ikie, Abby, and myself. Worship was part of every single day of our existence. This rhythm of life—personal worship, family worship and corporate worship, resting on the Sabbath—was drummed into our routine to the point that it still is our routine in our own families. Bruce can attest to the truth of this statement—every Sunday morning, the five of us (Dad, Mom, Ikie, Abby, and I) would end up being the last to leave the church building as we would stand there talking to each other. A few hours later, we'd be back for Sunday night church, and the same thing would happen. We would stand in the parking lot by Dad and Mom's car and talk long after everyone except Bruce and Sonya were gone. A random observer would think we never got to see each other! What we found as a family was that our commitment to the corporate worship of our most Holy God came with a side benefit—it provided yet another space where our family drew near to each other.

Dad left a legacy of creating a rich oral tradition. It has already been pointed out that our family shares a verbose trait and enjoys a good conversation. Dad taught us to love telling "the stories." The stories are, of course, the funny memories of events and things that happened that you tell over and over, and they get funnier every time. What happens when you create oral tradition with an intentional biblical worldview is that you weave in and through it the stories of grace. The stories are not always funny stories: they can be stories of how the Lord miraculously intervened, or how He had to work with us in our sin and brokenness, but you tell those stories so the lessons learned are never lost on the next generation.

Dad's most favorite place to tell the stories was at the table. He and Mother set a pattern and habit that we ate together while growing up as much as was possible, given the scheduling demands that showed up in junior high and high school. He taught us to linger at the table, to cherish the time together and to recount the ways God has proven Himself faithful over the years, and to laugh a lot throughout the sharing.

Conclusion

How do I close a chapter talking about what it was like to be the daughter of Harry Reeder? To be honest, I'd rather not close the chapter. I'd rather keep talking about it and writing about it. As Bruce said at Dad's funeral, "I don't know where to start talking about Harry Reeder, and I don't know where to end talking about Harry Reeder. So I'm just going to keep talking about Harry Reeder until Jesus takes me home." A big part of me feels that way as I bring this to a close. Bruce and I and many others will continue to talk about Harry Reeder—not because Harry Reeder was a great man, but because Harry Reeder served a great Savior and when we share Dad's stories and life, we get to share the Gospel. As I think back to the countless sermons I have listened to Dad preach, Bruce and I both agree we have to close this chapter, in the same way, Dad would close a sermon: with a life takeaway. We will leave you with five principles.

> 1. Make a personal commitment to the stewardship of the sovereignly appointed familial gifts and relationships. Steward these gifts from God with intentional focus and actions and with consistency and excellence.
>
> 2. Prioritize relationships correctly. Christ is THE priority. The relationship between the husband and the wife must be prioritized above the children, and the children revolve into the family.

3. For pastors' families, do not pit the family against the church. Bring the family into the ministry and let your ministry be a hallmark of your family.

4. Nurture, lead, and grow your family with intentionality and dependence on the power of the Holy Spirit. This power is rejuvenated in prayer and daily personal worship, family worship, and corporate worship.

5. Pass down the legacy of faith—faith in Christ is the greatest generational wealth one can create, possess, and pass down.

I am so thankful to be the daughter of Harry Reeder. My sister and brother say the same. Our mother shared a life overflowing with the joy of the Lord in and through their marriage. Bruce is thankful to have spent over two decades sitting in a front-row seat alongside Harry Reeder to learn from his example and teaching. We pray the Lord uses our words and thoughts to encourage you in your marriage and parenting for the glory of God.

Contributors

Derrick E. Brite (Reformed Theological Seminary, Atlanta, MDiv) is the pastor of First Presbyterian Church in Aliceville, Alabama. He is a professor of Systematic Theology at Birmingham Theological Seminary and is currently pursuing a PhD in Systematic Theology at Puritan Reformed Theological Seminary

Brian H. Cosby (PhD) is senior minister of Wayside Presbyterian Church (PCA) and adjunct professor of historical theology at Reformed Theological Seminary in Atlanta and at Ligonier's Reformation Bible College in Florida. He is a general council member of the Gospel Reformation Network and the author of over a dozen books.

Kevin DeYoung (PhD) is the senior pastor at Christ Covenant Church (PCA) in Matthews, North Carolina and associate professor of systematic theology at Reformed Theological Seminary (Charlotte). He is the author of more than twenty books and a popular columnist, blogger, and podcaster. Kevin's work can be found on clearlyreformed.org. Kevin and his wife, Trisha, have nine children.

Howard A. Eyrich (B.S., Bob Jones University; B.D., Faith Theological Seminary; Th.M., Dallas Theological Seminary; M.A., Liberty University; D.Min., Western Conservative Baptist Seminary; Post-doctoral Studies in Gerontology, University of Georgia) has sustained a collegial relationship with Harry Reeder since Harry's seminary days, and has worked under his leadership as President of Birmingham Theological Seminary and as Director of the Counseling Ministry for nearly twenty years at Briarwood Presbyterian Church.

George Grant (BA, MDiv, PhD, DHum, DPhil) is the Pastor Emeritus of Parish Presbyterian Church and the Founder of Franklin Classical School, the Comenius School, New College Franklin, King's Meadow Study Center, and the Chalmers Fund. The author of dozens of books, he regularly contributes to World Radio's *The World and Everything in It,* and the church history podcast, *Resistance and Reformation.*

Fred Greco (University of Buffalo, BA; University of Chicago, MA; Michigan Law, JD; Reformed Theological Seminary, MDiv) is the Senior Pastor of Christ Church in Katy, TX. He was elected as the Moderator of the 50th PCA General Assembly in Memphis (2023) and serves on the PCA's Standing Judicial Commission. Fred also teaches Practical Theology courses at Reformed Theological Seminary and Birmingham Theological Seminary.

John E. Haines (BA, Colorado Christian University; MM, University of Rochester, Eastman School of Music; M.Div, St. Timothy's Theological College and Seminary; MBTh, Th.D. St. Andrew's Theological College and Seminary) is Professor of Applied Theology (Worship Ministry), Birmingham Theological Seminary; adjunct professor of Systematic Theology, St. Timothy's Theological College and Seminary; and the Pastor of Worship at Briarwood Presbyterian Church

Jason Helopoulos (Eastern Illionis University, BA; Dallas Theological Seminary, ThM) is senior pastor of University Reformed Church in East Lansing, Michigan. He is the author of several books, including *Let the Children Worship* and *A Neglected Grace: Family Worship in the Christian Home.*

CONTRIBUTORS

Niel Nielson (Wheaton College, BA; Vanderbilt University, MA, PhD) currently serves as senior advisor to the Pelita Harapan Educational Foundation in Indonesia. Prior service includes financial markets, pastoral ministry, and the presidency of Covenant College (2002-2012). He and his wife Kathleen are members of Christ Presbyterian Church (PCA) in Wheaton, IL, where their son Jon serves as senior pastor.

Rob Pacienza (Samford University, BA; Knox Seminary, MDiv; Westminster Theological Seminary, DMin) Dr. Pacienza is from Fort Lauderdale, Florida, and is the Senior Pastor of Coral Ridge Presbyterian Church, founded by Dr. D. James Kennedy. He also serves as a Senior Fellow in the Center for the American Dream at AFPI. Dr. Pacienza grew up under the ministry of Dr. Kennedy and was mentored by him throughout high school and college. In addition, Dr. Pacienza attended Briarwood Presbyterian Church, under Dr. Reeder, while a student at Samford University.

Jon D. Payne has served as senior minister of Christ Church Presbyterian in Charleston, South Carolina since 2013. In addition, he serves as executive coordinator of the Gospel Reformation Network and series co-editor of the *Lectio Continua Expository Commentary on the New Testament*.

Harry "Ike" L. Reeder, IV (Covenant College, BA; University of Alaska Anchorage, MA; Reformed Theological Seminary, MA (in process)) is the son of Dr. Harry L. Reeder III. Ike is the current President of Birmingham Theological Seminary and a member of Briarwood Presbyterian Church.

Bruce Stallings: (BA, Samford) is the Executive Pastor of Briarwood Presbyterian Church and served alongside Dr. Harry L. Reeder, III for 23 years.

Neil C. Stewart (Queen's, University of Belfast, MD; Reformed Theological Seminary, MDiv) grew up in Northern Ireland during the troubles. After practicing medicine at the Royal Belfast Hospital for Sick Children and being elected a member of the Royal College of Pediatrics and Child Health in 1997, he discerned a call to ministry and moved with his family to the United States. Dr. Stewart is currently the senior pastor of First Presbyterian Church in Columbia, SC.

Jennifer Toomer-Hay (Liberty University, BS) is the daughter of Dr. Harry L Reeder III. Jennifer is the CEO of Keller Williams Vestavia in Birmingham, AL, and a member of Briarwood Presbyterian Church.

Sandy Willson (PhD) is Interim President of The Gospel Coalition and Pastor Emeritus at Second Presbyterian Church, Memphis, Tennessee. Sandy and his wife, Allison, have five children, three daughters-in-law, two sons-in-law, and fourteen grandchildren.

Resources by Harry L. Reeder III

From Embers to a Flame: How God Can Revitalize Your Church, P&R Publishing (2008).

3D Leadership: Defining, Developing and Deploying Christian Leaders Who Can Change the World, Christian Focus Publications (2018).

Harry Reeder's Blog, *InPerspective: Topics and Issues of Life in Biblical Perspective*: https://harryreeder.wordpress.com/

Harry Reeder Podcasts, *Today InPerspective, Fresh Bread* (A five-minute daily devotional), *Ask the Pastor*: https://briarwood.org/in-perspective/

Harry Reeder Collected Sermon Series: https://briarwood.org/resources/sermon-audio/sermon-audio-series-titles/

Christian Focus Publications

Our mission statement –

STAYING FAITHFUL
In dependence upon God we seek to impact the world through literature faithful to His infallible Word, the Bible. Our aim is to ensure that the Lord Jesus Christ is presented as the only hope to obtain forgiveness of sin, live a useful life and look forward to heaven with Him.

Our Books are published in four imprints:

CHRISTIAN FOCUS
popular works including biographies, commentaries, basic doctrine and Christian living.

CHRISTIAN HERITAGE
books representing some of the best material from the rich heritage of the church.

MENTOR
books written at a level suitable for Bible College and seminary students, pastors, and other serious readers. The imprint includes commentaries, doctrinal studies, examination of current issues and church history.

CF4•K
children's books for quality Bible teaching and for all age groups: Sunday school curriculum, puzzle and activity books; personal and family devotional titles, biographies and inspirational stories – because you are never too young to know Jesus!

Christian Focus Publications Ltd,
Geanies House, Fearn, Ross-shire,
IV20 1TW, Scotland, United Kingdom.
www.christianfocus.com